Creating A Life of Art in Italy

The Magic of the Journey - Is the Inner Journey - Book One

A. N. Stuart

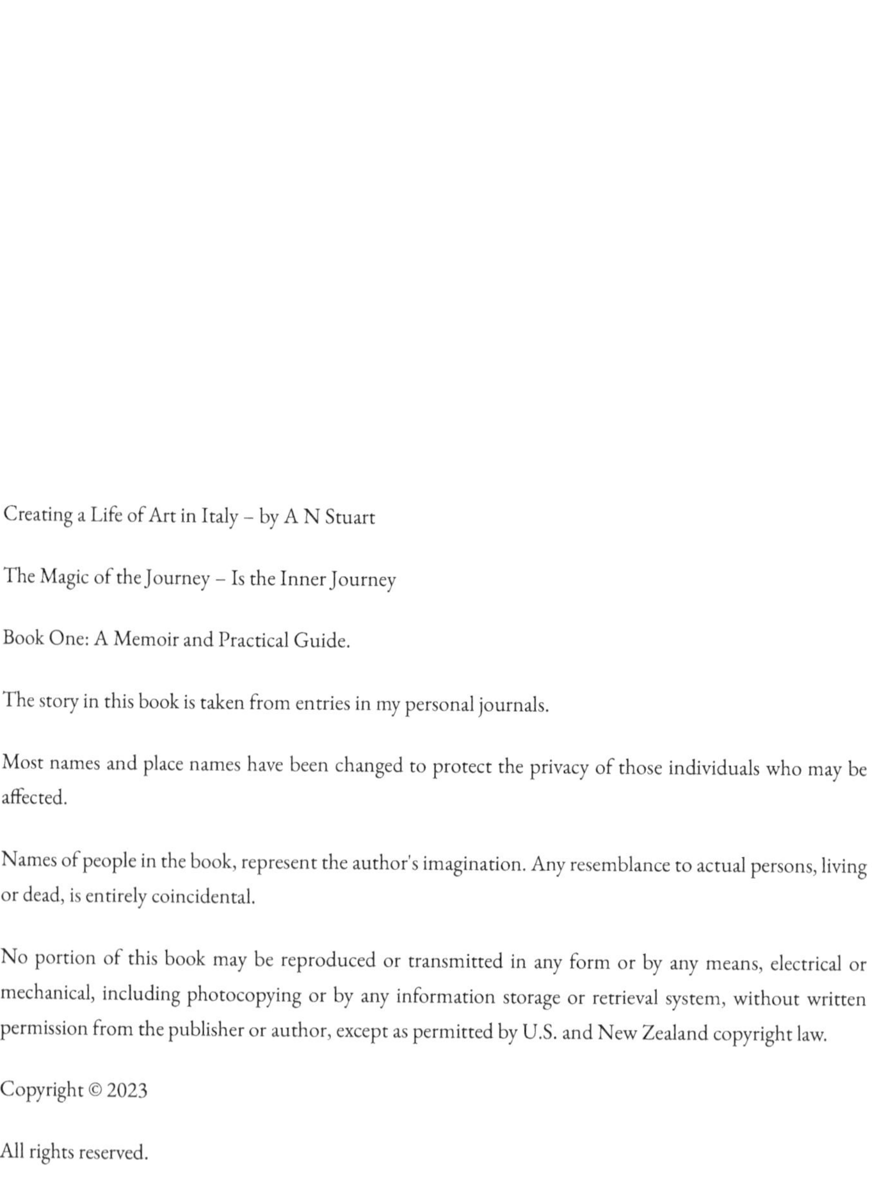

Creating a Life of Art in Italy – by A N Stuart

The Magic of the Journey – Is the Inner Journey

Book One: A Memoir and Practical Guide.

The story in this book is taken from entries in my personal journals.

Most names and place names have been changed to protect the privacy of those individuals who may be affected.

Names of people in the book, represent the author's imagination. Any resemblance to actual persons, living or dead, is entirely coincidental.

No portion of this book may be reproduced or transmitted in any form or by any means, electrical or mechanical, including photocopying or by any information storage or retrieval system, without written permission from the publisher or author, except as permitted by U.S. and New Zealand copyright law.

Copyright © 2023

All rights reserved.

Reviews and Comments

For two years I published weekly episodes of my story on Substack.com. Here are some reviews and comments left by my readers. The series is no longer available on Substack in favour of this, my published book.

Hi Eva

I am thoroughly enjoying your adventures, you write with such authenticity I find myself smiling with each episode. I so admire your courage to take that leap of faith without fear and live your dream. I am a late-blooming artist too and at 63 I am just finding my mojo. My husband died a few weeks ago after a long illness and your stories remind me that life is still filled with possibility.

Thank you Eva.

Julie

Julie, that is such a tear-jerker. I am sorry to hear about your husband. Thank you so much for your kind words. I hope we get to meet down the track. You have an amazing attitude and I wish all the best for you.

Ciao Eva xxx

∞

Hi Eva,

I love your stories ... I am living vicariously through you. A villa in a small village in Spain or Italy has been a long time vision of mine!! Also, being an artist as I have had an amazing emergence artistically in the past couple of years.

Bev

∞

Hi Eva,

Just wanted to tell you that my mother-in-law and her family came from Introdacqua so many years ago. They had a house there until the 60's and then sold it to a friend. My husband has passed away but he would so much have enjoyed your stories. Thanks so much for bringing memories back. - D

Thank you D,

∞

Eva, Thanks for sharing, I'm enjoying reading about your journey!

Helga

∞

Hi Eva,

So pleased I came across your journey. I am thoroughly enjoying your day to day life, making friends, doing an amazing job on your "Italian home", the good the bad and the ugly. You do have quite a talent for expressing yourself and creating such fabulous artworks whether they be with fabric or paint. As a 'sort of' artist myself you have certainly given me a push to create more, and really, take more time out for myself.

Sally

Eva, could you please adopt me . Your life sounds wonderful! I am a little bit envious , loving your story,

Leonie.

Hi Leonie, I'm grinning from ear to ear. I was so pleased to hear this, as I wonder if others are enjoying it. Please remember this was quite a few years ago now. I must confess as I write these episodes each week, it's great to be reliving it all again.

Ciao Eva

For Brugan – what a journey we're on –
Love you always, Anvil.

Contents

Chapter 1 - Follow Your Own Path

I SAID IT - NOW I MUST LIVE IT!

"Twenty years from now you will be more disappointed by the things that you didn't do than by the ones you did do. So, throw off the bowlines, sail away from safe harbour, catch the trade winds in your sails. Explore, Dream, Discover". Mark Twain

In that first winter alone in Italy, I found myself in an unexpected battle with loneliness. Yes! The dreaded "L" word that no one mentions for fear of being judged weird, or there's something wrong with you! "Loneliness" I wasn't prepared for this and each day it wrapped around me like a heavy cloak that I couldn't shake off. The bone-chilling winter only made it worse, as the absence of Bruce, my husband of twenty years and whose laughter once filled the house and my life with a quiet, funny repartee, now left me lost in an unfamiliar solitude.

My TV spoke a foreign language, (Italian) the newspapers were indecipherable, and the warmth of daily conversation had vanished. To escape, I would head to the local bar, but it often led to nights spent in a haze or drowning in wine, a path I knew wouldn't end well.

So I forced myself to stay home, and it was in the quiet of those nights I learned about myself. From the outside I appeared unchanged, but inside, my mind was in turmoil. I knew I had to confront this isolation and learn to be content in my own company. Slowly, day by day, I inched towards this newfound independence, as I started with small steps. I formed new habits, in my diet, in my daily activities and in the studio, even when inspiration wasn't there. I resisted the urge to escape to the Piazza and the bar - instead, I actually found solace in the simple act of cleaning the house and learned it was therapy in itself.

Eventually, I found a rhythm and established a daily routine that brought a sense of order to my life here in Italy, and as the days unfolded, this routine became a steady source of contentment and happiness.

Loneliness or being on my own:

At first, I hated It!

Then I learned to live with It!

Then I learned to love It!

Loneliness shouldn't be mistaken for being lonely. For me, it was one of the toughest yet most valuable lessons I've successfully overcome.

But here I am, getting ahead of myself as usual. Let's go back to how this, my Italian campaign, began.

It started innocently enough, an ordinary day in my home interior and gift store, which was in the heart of a well-heeled part of town. A place I'd opened just a few months before and now realise the enormity of my mistake. But I'll delve into that later. I received an unusual email. The email was from the Florence Biennale Committee, in Italy, inviting me to exhibit my artwork at their esteemed December 2007 art exhibition. Skeptically, I deleted it, dismissing it as a scam.

Instead, I found myself preoccupied with the thought of how quickly I could rid myself of this suffocating business venture.

In the past, I'd had a variety of businesses that granted me freedom during the day, but owning a retail store was altogether different. Soon after the grand opening, I discovered I was shackled to this shop, unable to even take a moment for myself before the tinkling bell above the door heralded another *just browsing'* customer. They'd peruse my shabby-chic offerings, proclaiming the sight of my beautiful wares - *"is good for my soul"*. Yet, such sentiments did little to pay the rent, causing annoyance beneath my polite smile. Dear God, how I longed to escape this silly mistake!

Six weeks passed, and another peculiar email from the Florence committee landed in my inbox. This time, I did some research and after a bit of Googling and digging around, everything seemed to check out. Well, I thought to myself, I'm at a crossroads and wondering where to next – so why not Italy – right? I've always done things in an unconventional order. So, why should my aspiration to become an artist be any different?

There I was at fifty seven and still harbouring this long-held desire to be an artist. I'd been dabbling with art for a while, even daring to share a few of my collages on this newfangled thing called the Internet. But what were the odds of someone of actual importance stumbling upon them? I assumed they were close to nil. Yet, that's what had happened, leading to this unexpected invitation.

Meanwhile, I'd been taking weekly art lessons from a reputable artist, and I mentioned the invitation at my next lesson. She looked at me in disbelief, then after it sank in, she turned and said *'It should've been me!'* And she was right. It should've been her that received the invite. I mean, she was somebody in the art world. The art lessons weren't much fun after that, so I stopped going.

Alright, so the Florence Biennale might not carry the same prestige as its cousin, the Venice Biennale, but it's still a significant event. That year, they invited eight artists from New Zealand and a whopping eight hundred and forty artists from various corners of the world. Despite the cost associated with securing a stand, this wasn't an opportunity to be dismissed lightly.

Here lay the dilemma: Was I prepared for such a momentous opportunity? For some years now, a longing had lived deep within me, an elusive yet persistent presence. Have you, dear reader, ever sensed it yourself? Despite our outward contentment, an insistent undercurrent tugs at us, questioning, searching. What lies beyond? Is this all there is?

Rarely do we venture into that contemplative space, and it's not solely about travel; it goes much deeper. While it had lingered in my thoughts for most of my life, true unrest surfaced in my mid-fifties. The crux of the matter: should I act now or bide my time until retirement? Most of us know someone whose life was suddenly disrupted by illness, such as my favourite Aunty, who was struck down in her prime by cancer or someone in an unforeseen accident. Would I come to regret ignoring this newfound opportunity? Was this the time to take a leap of faith and not only pursue this art opportunity, but to take it further and actually go and live in Italy?

I delved deep into contemplation, evaluating our current situation and our plans, and after weighing every aspect the timing at this present point in time, felt right.

So here we are, a few months down the track, I've sold the business and I'm winging my way to Italy!

Friday 1st June 2007

The night before my flight, I found myself wide awake at four in the morning, my mind racing through checklists to ensure I had everything I needed. It was one of those early morning episodes where exaggerated worries and nonsense seem to take centre stage. Honestly, what was there to fret about? Yes, it was my first trip to Europe, and yes, I was embarking on it solo. But after hours of discussions with Bruce, we both agreed that this was my time to do something like this. He, with his recent high-pressure job in the construction industry, wasn't ready for such an adventure.

So, in short, I'm off to Italy, on my own. It's now June, and the exhibition isn't until the beginning of December, but I decided to go to Italy early on a whim. I had a couple of months up my sleeve and the excuse was to check out accommodation in Florence before the exhibition. But really, I just wanted to get on a plane and go to Italy.

It was a stroke of luck or fate, I'd met Gwen just a few weeks before. She had built a business around connecting people from New Zealand with a trustworthy real estate agent in Abruzzo and I was sort of playing with the idea of maybe buying a house. She invited me to stay at her home that she and her husband, Jim, had bought in Corfinio the year before, even offering to pick me up in Rome when I arrived, with the unspoken hope that I might make that decision.

On arriving at Fiumicino Airport the first thing that struck me was the absence of extensive security checks. It was a straightforward passage through customs, and as I navigated my way through the bustling crowds of people and clouds of cigarette smoke, once outside the heat enveloped me as if I'd opened an oven door.

Gwen eventually arrived, running about three hours late because of heavy traffic. It was a scary wait, as I had yet to learn about buying a sim card for my phone, so communication wasn't the best. Anyway, she duly arrived, and with her was Lucia, her American-Italian friend. During the two and half hour drive east towards the Adriatic Sea, the car was filled with lively chat, but my attention drifted to the breathtaking, rugged mountainous landscape and the ancient villages that clung to the lofty peaks, seeming to defy gravity.

Monday 5th June 2007

Gwen's house was in need of renovating and work is due to start when Jim arrives next month. The lounge, where I was sleeping on the sofa bed, opened onto a balcony accessed through quaint French doors. From there, the views across the valley to the high mountain ranges in the distance were soft, with a slight haze rising. It was breathtaking.

Corfinio, is a medieval village perched on a plateau in the Valle Peligna. It is approximately fifteen kilometres from the ancient city of Sulmona. My first impressions were of weathered stone buildings, their plaster peeling in places and old terracotta roof tiles, some showing signs of wear from the harsh winters. The muted colours of the village blended seamlessly with the landscape, where poppies and cypress trees stretched into the distance. Everything I'd read about the misty hues of this region held true: pale blues, delicate pinks, and terracotta shades painted the surroundings in an earthy palette.

Another New Zealander, Hine, who was also staying in the house, was looking to buy in this area. Today, Hine, Gwen, and I went for a walk around the small village, stopping at a little corner grocery store, an alimentari. There, we bought a handful of essentials - cheese, crackers, and a bottle of wine - the true necessities, if you ask me.

In the quiet central Piazza, retired men were chatting in small groups, some meandering while others were playing cards. In this straight-out-of-movie scene there was a large, run-down stately house with a sign reading *Vendesi – 'For Sale'* – in the window. The lady from the store, whose son, an architect, owned the house, said she could arrange for him to show us around later that day if we wanted. Yes, please, we said. Gwen was busy with her computer set up, so Hine and I went to view the large house. She shouted a last-minute instruction as we were leaving: *'Don't ask about the price!'*

On entry, I fell in love with it. It was like the house in the movie *'Chocolat'*, with beautiful blue and white tiles in the foyer and a large curved staircase leading to the next floor. It would make a fabulous B&B. We continued up through the many rooms on various levels. The guy showing us around spoke good English and just as we were leaving, I cringed as Hine asked about the price. He mumbled something, but I was outside by this time and didn't hear his answer. We reported back to Gwen about how much we liked it, but she assured us there were many buildings like this in the area and we shouldn't be too hasty.

"Did you ask about the price?" Gwen asked. Hine sort of murmured an *'Mmmm, yes...'* in response. Gwen didn't reply.

I became lost in my thoughts: Could I really call this place on the other side of the world my home? Everything felt so different, a stark contrast to the landscapes back in New Zealand. These villages, built long before Captain Cook even set foot on our shores, had an air of history and timelessness that captured my imagination.

But the task for today, apart from checking out the house in the Piazza, was trying to get Gwen's computer connected to the outside world. And, it was no easy feat.

Wednesday 6th June 2007

What a night! Around two in the morning, Gwen's frustration finally boiled over. It had been building up, and Hine's question about the house price set her off, even though Gwen had specifically asked her not to ask. Doors slammed, and the noise stirred up the village dogs. Poor Hine bore the brunt of Gwen's anger and she had no choice, the next morning she packed her bags and left. I tried to reason with Gwen, but she was having none of it. The atmosphere at house was now quite tense, and I realised I had to tread carefully.

We spent the next few days re-organising her house and going on short trips. Gwen hadn't bought a car yet, so Lucia took us around to show me some of the nearby ancient villages. Lucia, with her three grown sons, had returned to Italy to live in her family home after many years in America. She wanted to show me her house and her village, Criessa. I knew as soon as we started driving up the steep road into the town, that I had no intention of looking at houses in this area, even though it turned out to be very beautiful with fantastic views, it was just too precarious for me. We hadn't yet reached her house when I said to both of them, "Look, I'm not very keen on living this far from Sulmona, so I don't want to look at any houses here."

Well, that went down like a lead balloon! Apparently, they had quite a few houses sorted for me to view and had seen me as a soft touch. Things became frosty with them for a while but didn't last too long. Lucia's house was up a steep road and perched on the side of a hill with amazing views across the valley. One of her sons was renovating the bathroom, so it was all a bit jumbled. Her mother was living in a small apartment downstairs.

Thursday 7th June 2007

Lucia arrived early to take Gwen to Pescara to buy a car that one of Lucia's sons had organised. I opted out, needing time to myself and to wander around the trails close by.

Friday 8th June 2007

Yesterday was glorious. It gave me time to think and to take in the surrounding countryside with the rugged mountains giving way to expanses of farmland and crops. Gwen and Lucia arrived back late afternoon with Gwen driving her small red car, which would be great for her to whizz around in. We went out for pizza at a traditional family restaurant to celebrate.

Our first trip in her car was to Sulmona, where finally, I met the English-speaking real estate agent Giorgio, with whom Gwen works. He was charming and good-looking, to boot! Think Telly Savalas. We hopped into his black beamer – what else! – and off we went to view some houses. I'd made a fairly long list of what I was looking for in a house.

To begin with, I wanted to live in a village not out in the country, as I wanted to feel like I belonged to a community. A liveable house, not a ruin. I didn't have the time nor the inclination for a large project. I wouldn't like to live on a steep slope or have to drive up a mountain, and it must have a sunny garden, a place for my workroom and maybe a small art gallery that opened onto the street. And finally, near Sulmona would be ideal. We went to see the only house that ticked most of my boxes. It was over 200 years old and in the village of Introdacqua. Though the village was in the hills, the house itself was on a flat part of the town, a short walk from the main Piazza. Some areas in the village were very steep, especially up by the ancient tower.

The first glimpse of the house wasn't the most welcoming. It was in need of some serious TLC. Large brown and gold plaster sheets were peeling off the exterior up to the third floor. The front door, typical of old houses, opened directly onto the street and was sticking. Giorgio pushed it open, revealing a small entryway with stairs leading up or a door on the right to what was once a wine cellar, now filled with clutter. Two ground floor rooms, one with street access, had small beds, bikes, and a door to a tiny garden. Upstairs, a spacious room held a dining table, chairs, and a retro kitchen cabinet, leading into a small kitchen. By modern standards, it was basic: a sink, a gas stove, and a few cupboards. Nearby, a small room housed a toilet, laundry tub, and washing machine.

From the kitchen, you stepped onto a decent-sized terrace with stairs leading to the garden. Inside, the lounge was simple, with a sofa, a couple of chairs, an open fireplace, and French doors opening onto a Juliet balcony that overlooked the cobblestone street—a feature I liked.

Upstairs, the third floor had two spacious bedrooms and a main bathroom. The dark green tiles and terracotta fixtures made the bathroom feel a bit cramped, and a small bath with a shower sat in the corner. The main bedroom, with its dark brown wallpaper, felt a little gloomy, though it had French doors leading to another Juliet balcony.

The second bedroom was less appealing, with water stains from a roof leak and a musty smell. It had a double and single bed, plus French doors that led to a large, sunny terrace with a clothesline and a covered roof. The view was impressive—medieval towers to the right, vegetable gardens, orchards, and ancient stone houses beyond. Below was a small, overgrown garden with a fig tree and weeds, but it was sunny and full of potential. Despite the grime, the house had charm: marble stairs, coved ceilings, Juliet balconies, and French doors. It had solid bones and just needed some care.

Giorgio showed me another couple of houses that were out of my price range, and that was it. When he dropped us back at the office in Sulmona, I told him I'd think about it.

That afternoon, Gwen and I went to Scanno village for a drive in her new car. The two lakes on the way were stunning, so we stopped for a photoshoot. On arriving at the village, I felt sure I'd stepped into the last century. There were men outside the shop playing cards and as we took in the sights of the town we passed some older women who still wore the black traditional mourning dress. Tourist shops were filled with gold filigree jewellery, which this region is famous for, and it's also the home of the most beautiful and intricate lace.

After an hour or so when we returned to where the car should've been, it wasn't where we left it! Apparently, the hand brake had failed and it had rolled about sixty yards or so before it was stopped by the curb. A young lad with broken English came over and explained what had happened. Well, we got the giggles, as we wondered what the card playing, old fella's had made of this spectacle and we considered ourselves very lucky the car hadn't rolled all the way down the hill knocking them and their card tables into the gelato shop!

Chapter 2 - An Exciting Time, Buying a house in Italy

I GET THE KEYS TO MY HOUSE.

"A great fire burns within me, but no one stops to warm themselves at it, and passers-by only see a wisp of smoke". Vincent Van Gogh

Saturday 9th June 2007

After sleeping on the idea, I decided the house would work for me, even though it was the only house I'd seen in my price range. Gwen and I were going to have another look after we'd been to the Saturday market in Sulmona.

Sulmona is a drop-dead gorgeous city and although it is very appealing, I didn't want to live there. But to live close by would be perfect, so Introdacqua was ideally located. Sulmona was one of the most important cities of the Paeligni. The Paeligni were a tribe that occupied Abruzzo. It is known for being the home of the poet Ovid, of whom there is a bronze statue on the town's main corso.

We had another look at the house and I was happy to confirm it was structurally sound. Bruce is a builder, and we'd renovated around eight houses in the past, so I was confident that with some creative effort, it would come up a treat. The coved ceilings gave height and strength and they looked fabulous. On the surface, the house looked worse than it was. The front façade and the water damage in the spare room from a major leak in the roof were relatively easy to fix. It needed a new kitchen, bathroom, and a paint job throughout. None of which would be surmountable and the village was a delight, being only about a six or seven-minute drive down the easy grade to Sulmona.

I was excited! There was much to like about the house and as I was now of an age where possessions meant little and making the 'right' impression on others meant nothing at all - then why not do this?

Sunday 10th June 2007

Gwen and I went to Popoli to look at more houses. We looked at two, but I wasn't sure about this location. The girl we met there who showed us the houses was friendly and spoke good English. She asked me about my name, Ava. From day two of my arrival, I'd realised my real name, Averil, wasn't going to cut it. It was difficult to pronounce in Italian, as every letter is pronounced separately and differently. To make life easier for myself and others I began calling myself Ava while I was in Italy. She pointed out to me that Ava was the name of a very popular laundry powder in Italy and that it was pronounced 'Ar v ar'. "Oh," I said "then what should I call myself?' She suggested I call myself "Eva", which is pronounced similar to Ava, though the 'A' is soft – not 'Eeeva', more 'Aeva'. So, I started calling myself Eva. In a weird twist of events, it seems I had come full circle, as Mum had planned to call me Eva, after her best friend. It felt right to be called that now, even though it is pronounced differently. Aeva!

The houses we viewed in Popoli, though cheaper, didn't show as much promise as the house in Introdacqua.

After Popoli, the cherry festival being held in Raiano was in full swing. Everything was bright and colourful, especially the women's traditional costumes. There were musicians, dancers, cherry pies and desserts, cherry gelato, row upon row of cherries everywhere. We had a marvellous time and stayed until late into the night.

Back at home, I rang Bruce. We discussed the house. "Yes, I'm sure I'll be happy there," I told him. "Maybe I could rent the spare room for a bit of pocket money. The old wine cellar on street level will make a fabulous work studio and small art gallery, as it opens out onto the street. It's close to the main Piazza in the village. It has a garden. Though it hasn't been weeded for years, it gets the sun all day. The house has two large sunny balconies. Yes, it will take a bit of work."

Tuesday 12th June 2007

We went and had another look at the Introdacqua house. I liked it, although it was quite pricey, as the New Zealand Dollar is only half that of the Euro. I was led to believe I'd be able to buy a decent house in the area for around €70,000, but the market was buoyant.

The village had everything I needed: an alimentari, a post office, a bank, a little bar, two restaurants and the commune, (every village has a commune. This is where you pay house and land tax, file for residency and all matters pertaining to your house etc.) all within walking distance. It's going to be a lovely place to live.

I'll talk to Giorgio in a couple of days about money and the steps needed to take to purchase a property in Italy.

Thursday 14th June 2007

Well, I did it! I put an offer in for the house. Not quite what they were asking! Naturally, Gwen wanted me to pay what they were asking, so we'll see what happens.

Saturday 16th June 2007

Giorgio summoned us. The owner of the house, Gino, wasn't happy with the offer, but he had reluctantly accepted it.

Yay, it looks like we're buying a house in Italy!

I rang Bruce, laughing and crying all in the same breath and told him the good news. Later, he sent me a reassuring text "Hey, that's great news. You're doing the right thing. There's nothing to be afraid of. We're lucky we can do this. We're doing it!" he said. "It passes the rocking chair test, so it'll be OK". We have this thing we call the 'rocking chair test'. The idea is, that we don't want to look back on our lives, when we're in our rocking chairs, and say "I wonder what would've happened if we'd bought that house in Italy". We used this same test when we decided to leave the city years ago and build a large barn-house and live in the country. I longed for him to be with me at this moment. I would give him a big fat hug.

Wednesday 20th June 2007

These past few days have been a whirlwind of preparations here in Italy, as Giorgio helps me with opening a bank account. It was a surprisingly straight-forward process. Next, we headed to the Government office to obtain a Codice Fiscale (My tax number), which, much to my surprise, turned out to be quite an easy task as well. The Government office was on the other side of town and over the big bridge, and Giorgio, it seems, likes to parade his new clients through the streets of Sulmona. We could've driven to the office, but no, I had to walk in the midday heat with new shoes, which were pinching. As we walked the walk that day, there was an undeniable sense of him being "the man." You know, you could hear it in the way people greeted him. "Ciao Gio" "Buongiorno Giorgio". It was evident that he was held in high regard around town.

We agreed on settlement day to be four months away, at the end of October. I was booked to go back to New Zealand in six weeks' time, then I'd have three months to pack up my belongings in New Zealand and head back to Italy.

Friday 22nd June 2007

A lucky break! After I handed over the €1000 holding deposit to Giorgio, he gave me the keys to the house! I was going to be able to stay in the house for the duration of my time here in Italy. This certainly does not happen in New Zealand! It comes fully furnished with everything, including crockery, cutlery, and linens. I just needed to bring my clothes and buy some food. Gino's mother had died some years prior (in hospital) and the house was pretty much as she'd left it. Gwen has agreed to drive me over on Monday.

Serendipity has been playing a big role in my life these past few weeks.

Chapter 3 - High Drama When Scorpions Invade

Moving into my house.

"I am seeking, I am striving, I am in it with all my heart." Vincent Van Gogh

The next couple of weeks are a bit of a blur, dates and times have eluded me!

On Sunday night, we went with Lucia to the artichoke festival held in a local village. Artichokes: they took me back to another place and time. When I was much younger, with my baby in tow, having escaped from my violent, first husband, I found myself working on an isolated country estate as a carer for an elderly lady. The enormous kitchen was straight from Downton Abbey. The old matriarch was small and withered and had a strong, determined will. She taught me how to cook artichokes in béchamel sauce. With her thin bony hands, she showed me the importance of combining the flour into the butter slowly; of cooking the flour at each stage; then slowly stirring in the milk until the required consistency is achieved before adding the sauce to the steamed artichoke hearts.

It was a lesson I never forgot, and I was forever grateful to her for teaching me how to make a proper béchamel sauce. This memory crops up whenever I see an artichoke.

The festival opened my eyes to the many ways you can prepare them. There were artichoke pies, pickled artichokes, artichoke lasagnas, spreads, and many other delectable delicacies, all the while Italian music was rollicking and happy in the background. We sat out in the Piazza eating our food alfresco with the townsfolk. I felt like I'd come home. It was a surreal situation, sitting among the medieval buildings, singing and dancing, with wine flowing freely!

Yesterday, Gwen drove me to my new house. I'm looking forward to starting this new chapter of my Italian adventure and to finally be free of her mood swings. I was eager to meet my neighbours and immerse myself in the life of this quaint, medieval village. On the way, we made a quick stop to buy some groceries. Then she dropped me off and just like that, she was gone. It had been a tense time for me this past week or so, since that night! But, I was grateful for the time I had spent with her.

Finally, I was on my own. I rolled up my sleeves and cleaned the house from top to toe, which took most of two days to complete. The house had been in a derelict state for some time. As I cleaned I discovered some treasures in the house, like vintage Italian linen. I made up the bed with crisp, white cotton sheets and heavily hand-embroidered pillow shams, which were in the well-stocked linen cupboard. The large 1970s cabinet in the dining room, held good quality dinner sets and other crockery, with drawers filled with cutlery and cooking utensils.

Over the past year, the nephew of the owner had been using the house as party central and last night I heard voices on the lower stairs and from my bed, I yelled out "Who goes there?" They got such a fright – I heard them race back down the stairs, slamming the door behind them! The nephew obviously hadn't realised I was now in residence.

Giorgio organised for Michele to replace the locks on the back and front doors. It was a pleasure to meet Michele, he was to become our maintenance man for all things related to the house.

Last night I made myself a meal of pasta with mushroom sauce and then had a few too many wines. The scene from the balcony at the back of the house is idyllic. My neighbours introduced themselves, Fiona and her Mama Maria. They were sitting in their garden chatting. Fiona, speaks fairly good English. The air is warm and as I survey my new surroundings. The castle tower, a ruin, is the dominating feature of the skyline. It sits high above the village. At night it's lit up and stands like a sentinel, guarding all below. Close your eyes and you can imagine the castle long ago in action. There are slits in the side of the walls for soldiers to fire their bows and arrows through. They would've been guarding the water. The rulers in this walled-in secure village were kings of the hill in this region. They had access to all the water, which provided the vast plains of the valley below. Introdacqua: the name of the village means it was built 'in the water,' because of the abundance in this region. The village is listed in the top one hundred most beautiful villages in Italy. This is no mean feat, as there are over eight thousand small villages in Italy.

View from my balcony.

There was much for me to explore here and most days I would walk around the village, up a very steep street to the tower around the tower and back down the other side. The rooftops of the village are visible from the top. It took awhile for me to find my rooftop, and then I smiled happily when I spotted it out of the many. Every Thursday morning there's a local market in the Piazza near the Commune. It sells fruit, vegetables, fish, and cheese of every variety and I've become quite partial to Gorgonzola cheese, washed down with a Montepulciano red vino. Also at the little market were a couple of clothing stalls and kitchenware stalls.

Everyone was friendly and I imagined they'd heard about this woman from New Zealand, who had bought Maria's house from her son Gino. After a few days within the village, their nods and hushed greetings of "Ciao Eva" held a special resonance for me.

I'm still not used to the shops closing at one o'clock each day. They reopen again from four o'clock until eight in the evening. I liked the idea that most people were at home for lunch and the stats say 95% of Italians are sitting down to eat either pasta or pizza around 1.30 each day. There are very few takeaway places.

The bus service each day down to Sulmona, a trip of about ten minutes is first rate. So today away I went. They don't muck around on the downhill slope and often I had to close my eyes, amazed at how they managed to miss other vehicles and cyclists! Italian drivers appear to be reckless and I was continually fascinated by their dodgem car antics. It seemed like organised chaos! They spend most of their time dodging everything, driving either on the centre line or on the wrong side of the centre line. Admittedly, they're competent in the art of dodging other vehicles, walkers and cyclists, but it made me feel apprehensive about getting a car of my own. From the bus, I snapped some photos of the glorious fields of poppies and wildflowers.

View from the bus.

Gwen rang. She had trouble the other night. Scorpions had invaded her house and she wanted to come and stay with me until the bug exterminator had been. It was possible she'd be with me for a week, just when I was getting a routine going. Oh, well, what could I say? She came yesterday!

Part of the agreement for me to live in the house over these six weeks, the owner Gino, who lives in Rome, was permitted to bring his children and stay in the house on some weekends. They're due to arrive tomorrow. I prepared their beds downstairs in the wine cellar and they'll dine at his sister's house.

Gwen arrived, bag and baggage. I made up the spare bedroom for her. We went to Sulmona markets on Saturday and I bought some specialities from the region. Delicious porchetta (pork) cooked on a spit, filled with herbs. They slice off large chunks of pork and stuff it in a bun. I also brought home a rotisserie-cooked chicken for lunch. The chicken was delicious, this is due to the way they prepare and cook it. The rotisserie is fired by wood, so the flavours are retained and the texture is melt-in-your-mouth.

Chickens cooking in the large wood-fired rotisserie at the market.

Later that afternoon, we strolled to the Piazza to listen to a jazz band playing and for €6.00 had a meal and were entertained. Roberto, a local, introduced himself when he overheard our English voices. He was born here and then moved to America. He returned to his family home a few years ago after a divorce. A romance blossomed between him and his childhood sweetheart he went to school with. Since returning he's in the process of restoring his late father's small farm and vineyard.

This morning, I'd secretly asked Gino if I could come to Rome with him in the evening. I'll stay in a hotel for a few days and see the sights. When Gwen heard I was heading to Rome, she was ropable, shouting at me 'I was counting on you to help me get my house ready for the exterminator today!' So, to keep the peace, I agreed. I'd be back in time to head to Rome with Gino and the children.

After lunch, we went over to her house to cover the furniture with sheets. I was apprehensive about going in, knowing it was full of scorpions. In New Zealand, we don't have many nasty things like that. Not like Australia, where they have all sorts of creatures that are out to get you! The walls of the house were pitted with the slain remnants of scorpions that Gwen had squished with her shoes. I was a bit jumpy while we were there and as I was out in the backyard busy putting pot plants out of range of the exterminator's spray, I heard this blood-curdling scream coming from the upstairs bedroom. I raced up the stairs to find Gwen trapped under the wardrobe! She was lying face-down on the bed with the wardrobe on top of her. I quickly pulled the wardrobe off of her – it was light enough that I could do this alone. I checked to see that she was alright. She said she was OK. Fortunately, she wasn't injured.

We looked at each other and collapsed into uncontrolled laughter, tears streaming down our faces. It was the funniest thing I'd seen for a long time! She'd been emptying the clothes from the drawers in the bottom of the wardrobe, it unbalanced as she had her back to it and toppled over pinning her to the bed! It was almost like it went in for the attack covering her completely – she was sprawled across the bed with her arms sticking out each side. She could see the funny side, considering how she'd been telling me just days earlier that the house was trying to kill her. She'd been booted across the kitchen by a faulty electrical power plug; she fell down the stairs the year prior and broke her ankle; she broke her wrist on another occasion; her washing machine gave her an electric shock and had stopped working; and now this. She could add the wardrobe episode to the list. She can be a bit of a hoot at times.

We finished sorting the house. All the furniture was covered and ready for the exterminators. When we arrived back at my place, I suggested maybe Lucia could come over and be with her if she felt she needed someone. She said she'd ring her.

I packed and left her in charge of my house.

It was wonderful to be in Rome with the entire city to explore over the next couple of days. On arrival the previous evening, Gino had driven me around the city, showing me various tourist spots like the Colosseum, St Angelo's Castle, and St Peter's Square, before he dropped me off at a hotel near the Vatican. The next morning, I enjoyed a hearty colazione and from where I sat in the breakfast room, there was a good view of the Dome of St. Peter's Basilica. I planned to do a tour of the ancient ruins of Rome.

It was incredibly hot, as our little tour group trudged around the Roman Forum. The rectangular space is surrounded by the ruins of several important ancient government buildings, at the centre of the city of Rome.

It was, for centuries, the centre of Roman public life: the site of triumphal processions and elections, the venue for public speeches, criminal trials, gladiatorial matches and the nucleus of commercial affairs. This was the heart of ancient Rome. It is in the small valley between the Palatine and Capitoline Hills. The Forum today is a sprawling ruin of architectural fragments and intermittent archaeological excavations. These included the ancient former royal residence, the Regia, and the Temple of Vesta, as well as the surrounding complex of the Vestal Virgins, all of which were rebuilt after the rise of Imperial Rome. Wikipedia

Even though I was hot and tired from the day's excursions, I agreed to meet with some people from the UK whom I'd met on the tour for dinner. They'd chosen the most delightful old traditional family restaurant. It was decked out in the classic red-and-white-checked tablecloths with candles. We shared a large platter of antipasto, including much prosciutto, which is a salt-cured, dry-aged Italian ham. Slices of melon accompanied this. For my next course, I had homemade ravioli. The filling of ravioli varies according to the area where they are prepared, and in Rome, they made the filling with ricotta cheese, spinach, nutmeg and black pepper. All of this was accompanied by a traditional Chianti.

Afterwards, we visited Trevi Fountain. It was lit up and stunningly beautiful. Hordes of tourists, even at this late hour, were vying for a spot close to the fountain. I did the classic routine of throwing a coin over my shoulder with my back to the fountain and made a wish as it landed in the water. Wednesday was spent looking around the shops and I was elated to find a couple of fabric shops where I added to the fabric stash I keep for my work as a textile artist.

I decided not to visit the Vatican or the Colosseum on this trip, preferring to wait until Bruce was here so we could visit them together.

Thursday: Because of the heatwave, I opted to have a day on the double-decker tourist bus. It was an easy option for exploring the outer regions of the city.

I could wax lyrical about my visit to Rome, but it was just too hot to enjoy. Maybe I'll appreciate it more on my next trip.

Saturday 30th June 2007

I arrived back home Thursday night. Gwen was still here, she reluctantly picked me up from the station and then went back to her home yesterday.

I cleaned the house, so I could relax and enjoy the rest of my time here. The evenings continued to be bliss. Neighbours out in their gardens, no high fences here. I noticed around town, people were out in the street laughing and chatting, hands demonstrating the importance of what they were saying! You'll see this as you travel around Italy, chairs and bench seats outside their homes. They're specifically placed there for soaking up the last rays of evening sunlight and of course for chatting to all who wander past. Though the constant sound of dogs barking was darned annoying! But the people here seemed oblivious to it.

Sunday 1st July 2007

Roberto came Saturday and whizzed over the backyard with a weed-eater. The yard, full of weeds and high grass, hadn't been touched for at least ten years,

€30.00 was a great investment to make it more inviting. The fig tree and plum tree were now going to thrive.

My small garden, now tidied.

On Saturday night, I seriously considered not going through with the house sale! I know it sounds absurd, but the treatment from Gwen and even Lucia, their moods are all over the place and at times it gets to me and upsets me. So, why did I stay then?

I've had time to think about what I was hoping to achieve from living here in Italy. What was the outcome I was aiming for? Why was I compelled to do this? One thing was certain: I wouldn't get an opportunity like this again. I wanted to give it the best shot possible. Fiona, my neighbour, spoke good English and had actually said she hoped I would consider her my sister. Though this idea was deeply moving for me, it was not a reason to come and live in Introdacqua entirely. She often said how my being there had changed her life. The one obvious reason for this was prior to my living here in the house, it had been used as party central and had been noisy for her and the nearby neighbours!

Fiona, an only child, told me how her father had died when she was a baby and over the years her mother had become quite needy. Fi owned a small newspaper agency in the main Piazza in the village and worked from 9.30am until lunchtime. After lunch, she spent her time tending the house and garden.

Apart from Fi, there were other things to consider: I was applying to the British Embassy for an ancestry visa, which would give me a five-year window of opportunity to work in the UK for three or four months each year. I'd be able to work in the home care industry and earn British Pounds, to help with the day-to-day cost of living in Italy. I had experience working with the elderly – way back when I was younger, I had been a caregiver in an old people's home for a while and in more recent years, had owned and operated my own elderly care facility in New Zealand.

The other idea I had for earning money, apart from a small income I received from an investment in New Zealand, was that we could renovate a few houses here in Italy and sell them. The location of the village was especially good, only two hours east of Rome. But, there was no urgency and we could think about that later.

Chapter 4 - It Happened - The Magic of Italy

ROME - HERE I COME

"I am always doing what I cannot do yet, in order to learn how to do it". Vincent Van Gogh

Introdacqua - view from my favourite walk.

Monday 2nd July 2007

What a difference a day makes, as the song goes. Unlike yesterday, all thoughts of abandoning ship have disappeared!

On Sunday I read for most of the day, something I hadn't managed to do for a long time. There was a bike here, it came with the house, so I pumped the tyres and went for a ride, remembering to ride on the other side of the road at all times, since in New Zealand, we drive and ride on the opposite side. It was fun, but a hard slog on the return home. I think I'll opt for walking.

A buzzer rings in the house each morning. It buzzed now and again when I was in bed writing in my journal. Quite spooky! It's ridiculous! Did I have a ghost in the house?

I opened a new account at another bank. This bank was more user-friendly than the other, which was incredibly slow. You almost needed to pack a lunch, as you had to queue for ages. They had promised me a Bancomat card to use at the machine, but I was still waiting! This new bank had more women tellers for a start. The banks here tend to be dominated by older males – old farts, I call them. Francesca was going to be in charge of my account at this bank and she was a breath of fresh air. Her English was quite good, always a bonus, and already she had issued me with a Bancomat card. Progress!

Damn! I missed the one o'clock bus back to Introdacqua, so I had to wait three hours until the next one. Even though it was scorching hot, I walked around Sulmona and took photos. There was a photo to be captured around every corner. Delicious, narrow cobblestone streets, variously coloured doors and villas, geraniums and petunias dripping from cute balconies along with washing on lines suspended from most houses, with clothes and underwear of all shapes and sizes. I smiled to myself as I viewed them. In New Zealand, we wouldn't dare let our undies hang out in public for all and sundry to see! The streets were deserted. I was the only one around. and after an hour or so, I settled into a local bar and filled in the rest of the time drinking a few Proseccos, bubbly wine similar to our

Lindauer in New Zealand. I got pretty merry, and when I arrived home, I crashed. I forgot to text Bruce for his birthday! Hm, I don't think he'll be happy with me.

Wednesday 4th July 2007

Bruce's birthday. It was the day prior, New Zealand time. I felt bad about not being there for him. He was going out to celebrate with his family. I went for a very long walk up the mountain taking photos, and dedicated the walk and the day to him. Happy birthday, my love. The views were to die for and I took some great shots of the village to send him. The walk took me well over two hours.

Views down to Sulmona.

Thursday 5th July 2007

This morning, I woke up unhappy with everything! Dogs barking. Chilly mornings. If it's this cold now, it must surely be freezing in the winter! The situation with Gwen, my gift from Bruce, which I still hadn't received yet. Jim was bringing me a gift. I don't know, maybe I'm just homesick! I seem to be up one day and down the next. What is that all about?

I went for an extra long walk. First, I walked briskly up the mountain. It was a good pick-me-up. Feeling better when I came back down I decided to keep walking - continuing on the road toward Sulmona, then turned left onto a side road which took me past the cemetery. This type of crypt-like cemetery is new to me. So I stopped to study it for a while. There were large crypts with magnificent Romanesque pillars at the entrance. The smaller crypts seemed to be plain, but still beautiful. Further towards the back there were, what seemed like walls and layers of burial chambers. These were colourful with the names, photos and flowers resting in vases.

Moving on, I reached the top of the road. And Boom! The wide sweeping views were stunning as you looked towards the unusual shape of Gran Sasso, the highest mountain in Abruzzo. It alone was spectacular. The mountain range is rugged and dramatic with Sulmona nestled below.

I met Marco on the way down and he stopped to chat – his English is good. He invited me out with his family, his wife, Maria, and their two children for dinner in Sulmona. Their son and daughter were in a band and were playing at the restaurant that night. It just so happened I had no other engagements tonight (tongue in cheek) yes, I'd love to. As I entered my street, I ran into my neighbour Fiona and her Mama, Maria. They invited me in to show me their lovely house. We had a cup of coffee and I was introduced to the two loves of Fiona's life, her two cats. They showed me around and explained how they had renovated the old house back in the 1990s. It was a massive undertaking. All the tiles were gouged out with jackhammers and new tiles were laid throughout. They'd added another toilet upstairs, a new kitchen, dining room, lounge and new double glazed, aluminium windows with outside shutters. Once the tour was over Mama gave me some homemade biscuits to take home.

That afternoon, another pleasant surprise was in store. I went through the gate at the bottom of my garden to speak with Delio. He and his wife Maria are a lovely older couple who live in a large house at the back of my house. He speaks some

English, as he was a prisoner of war in Australia in WWII. He was captured in Africa and shipped out to Australia and kept in a POW camp for a few years. Remember, Italy was ruled by a fascist leader and friend of Hitler, Mussolini – Italy was on the wrong side of the war for the first few years. It was during this time that Giuseppe learned to speak English, and he retained it all these years later.

They have a large plot of land where they worked most days growing a variety of fruit and vegetables. Every week, the water was sent down from a spring high above in the hills, to the community below for crop irrigation. It was truly delightful. It spilled down through the purpose-built channels into the gardens. If I wanted, I could pay a small fee to the commune, and could also have the water come into my garden by opening a small channel. When the gardens had their fill of water, Delio let it flood onto their lawn at the back yard of their house. All this crystal clear water – particularly lovely on a parched hot day like this one. So, there I was in their yard, shoes off, paddling around to cool down. Fresh, cool, clear water gushing down the channels each Thursday.

Marco and Maria picked me up and we went to a traditional Italian restaurant and the meal was delicious. Martina, their daughter, sang with the band and their son, Simone, played the keyboard. Both are talented. Martina's voice is strong, sounding like Eva Cassidy. Simone, only 17, reminds me of Bruce, who I'm sure would've been just like him at that age. Bruce plays the keyboard and piano beautifully. It was a fabulous evening, being outside in the warm evening air, talking and listening to good music.

Again, I think what a difference a day makes. I had asked for a sign that it was right for me to stay and to live in this village and today I had plenty of signs.

Ahh, I found out why the buzzer rings each morning! There's a switch on the wall behind my headboard and when I lean back now and then as I'm writing my journal entries, it rings! It's probably used if you're ill, for getting attention from someone downstairs. I was just pleased to confirm it was not Gino's mama who came back to haunt me!

I had a new resolve. I'm not going to let Gwen or barking dogs spoil my exciting life in Italy. Or ghosts, for that matter. I've decided to go to Florence next week on the train. I want to check out places to stay when I attend the Biennale exhibition in December. I also went and paid the main deposit on the house and I was happy to do it, although I hadn't been happy about it a few days before – did that mean I was fickle? Who knew, only time would tell.

Sunday 8th July 2007

Over the course of a few days this week, the magic of Italy has happened for me. Being with Michele, Marco's family, Fiona and Maria and coming into contact with other 'real Italiano' people was life-changing. Living in this particular village with the old architecture, the proximity to Rome and the ancient city of Sulmona, the refrains of "Ciao, Eva!", the matriarchs of the village who come and sit on the benches, not far from my window to chat and laugh every evening until late, even until after midnight sometimes. The countryside, the people, the food, the air. And no wind!

Magic, that's what it was! That's why people want to live in Italy. It is real, and it's not just a dream.

Friday was the turning point I'd needed. If I hadn't ventured out for my walk, I would have missed these random moments that put me in a better headspace. That's the secret, to get out and be social. Not all the time, but at least a few times a week.

On Saturday, I went to the beach at Pescara on the train and it's what I'd later call having alone fun! Yes, I've discovered you can have tremendous fun on your own. It's a concept that's quite new to me and I'm revelling in the freedom it brings. I packed my togs and towel. An early start saw me on the bus to the railway station. I caught the regional train to Pescara. The train runs through steep, rugged mountains, and gives way to breathtaking scenery, before emerging into a downhill run to the coastal city of Pescara.

From the station, I walked down the main corso, to where the shores of the Adriatic Sea stretched out before me. In order to actually get onto the beach, I had to go into one of the beach-side restaurants to pay – yep, you pay to be on the beach here! This concept was all very new to me, as in New Zealand you just go to the beach. I'd never had to pay before! For around €20, you get an umbrella and a couple of sunbeds. They were all set up in colourful rows, miles and miles, row upon row of them. They belonged to different eating outlets and acted as one-stop shops. You can lay in the sun, go for a swim and leave all your stuff under your umbrella, you can buy your lunch, go to the toilet, get changed and not worry about your things being stolen.

If you didn't want to pay, there were some public beaches, though they don't have any facilities and are pretty basic. There are moves for this system to change and for the communes of beach-side cities and towns to provide toilets and changing sheds on the public beaches.

I spent the day reading, swimming, eating and people watching. Wow, the Italian gals are stunners! I observed the Italian families and noted how well behaved the children were and how happy they all seemed in general. On the way back to the Stazione, I did a spot of shopping in the stunning shops of Pescara, adding a pair of shorts and T-shirt to my wardrobe. It's what I'd call a delicious day!

Back to Sulmona on the train. I do love to travel that way.

Chapter 5 - Off to Explore Florence

Travelling by train

"Color is my daylong obsession, joy, and torment" Claude Monet

Sunday 8th July 2007

It's been a while since I'd been this excited – even more excited than when I came to Italy for the first time! "Florence in Tuscany," I whispered to myself, "I'm going to Firenze, in Toscana! On the train!"

"On the bloody train!" I shouted in excitement – to my empty house!

These days, you see so many young people travelling everywhere, and it makes you wonder – do they get excited about visiting a new place or city, or is it just another day on the road for them? For me, travelling later in life comes with its own set of perks. I've been daydreaming and reading about faraway places like this for years, so it's a huge deal when I finally get here. I mused on these ideas as I washed and sorted clothes for my trip. It's funny how age can bring a different perspective to our travels, isn't it?

Monday 9th July 2007

Another early start saw me on the 9.50am bus to Sulmona, then onto the 10.15am bus to Termini Station in Rome, where I caught the train to Florence, arriving around five o'clock.

Let's talk about travelling by train – can anything compare to the pleasure of a train journey? And not the everyday commuter train for work, mind you. I'm referring to those scenic train journeys, where landscapes unfold before you. Italy elevates train travel to a new echelon like the exhilaration of identifying the Tuscan countryside, a distinct contrast to the rugged Abruzzo mountains I'd left behind. Transitioning through the rolling hills of Tuscany, the sight of cypress-lined driveways leading to charming Italian estates, expanses of vineyards and olive groves stretching for miles under the gentle, hazed sunlight of this renowned region – it all felt surreal, and look over there, is that Cortona, perched over on that distant hill? Other familiar-sounding names on signposts whiz by: Orvieto and Assisi to name a couple. In an elated state, when I arrived at Santa Maria Novella station, I made my way to the hotel I'd booked online.

After a shower and freshening up, I headed off to explore the city, strolling the narrow cobblestone streets along with throngs of hot, sweaty tourists. I stopped for a gelato while taking in the sights. Then, amid the lively chaos, I spotted it – the Duomo. It emerged like a beacon of beauty. The carved details of its exterior marble were nothing short of exquisite. The sight was a moment of unexpected splendour that left me breathless. Naturally, I'd seen photos of Florence's most famous landmark in books and on screens, but to witness it up close was something else. It was a reminder that travel has the ability to surprise us, to reveal beauty where we least expect it. As someone hailing from New Zealand, where history is measured in a couple of centuries, not thousands, it was a humbling experience.

As dusk closed in, I settled into a little bar opposite to study the Duomo at length and a conversation developed with an Aussie couple seated close by. Maddie and John, as it turned out, were a fun couple. He was a real Aussie bloke, and he'd done a pretty decent job of planning their whole trip, without Maddie's knowledge, then presenting her with this surprise holiday to Italy for her birthday! We shared a pasta meal, a result of these unexpected and friendly encounters fostered by Italy's warm weather and outdoor café culture.

Wednesday 11th July 2007

Yesterday, Tuesday, I rose early to beat the queues for the Duomo's entrance. As I entered this architectural marvel, I wasn't prepared for the scale of the interior, it was vast and imposing. The first thing to catch my eye was the mesmerizing frescoed dome, but the grand interior is further heightened by the stunning stained glass windows that filtered sunlight into a riot of colours. The day I was there entry to the top gallery was closed. The rest of the day I spent on the double-decker tourist bus, stopping off at various points along the way, such as the Galleria dell'Accademia to see Michelangelo's 'David' and his other sculptures, many were lunging from the huge marble slabs. Were they half-finished or was this what he intended? I'd say the latter, as they were very dramatic! The bus also took us to the outskirts of Florence and up to the hilltop village of Fiesole, stopping at Piazzale Michelangelo, an observation point overlooking the city.

Back in the city, I meandered the streets arriving at the Ponte Vecchio and was in awe of the exquisite jewellery that adorned the shop windows. Each piece was a masterpiece in its own right. Diamonds and sapphires sparkled in the sunlight. Gold necklaces with intricate filigree work. Crossing the bridge, I enjoyed a view of Pitti Palace. I'm leaving this and other famous landmarks until December when Bruce will be here. So much to see. I had a coffee at Piazza Della Liberta.

I found Fortezza da Basso. This is where the Florence Biennale Exhibition was going to be held in December. The fortress was huge. I walked around the perimeter to get my bearings. I couldn't believe I was going to be exhibiting here in a few months. Not even in my wildest imagination did I ever think I would be here, experiencing all of this, leaving a lot for me to think about while I enjoyed an evening meal of pasta – I love pasta, as you may have guessed! It was fairly late by the time I enjoyed a hot soak in the bath and turned in.

Florence is beautiful and immensely popular with tourists, so with this amount of people around, it surprised me that there was such a lack of basic facilities. It can be a bit difficult, at times to locate a decent public toilet. When I needed a loo stop, I found the best bet was to buy a coffee at a cafe, which gives you access to their facilities, such as their toilet. The tourist buses are a great way to get an overall perspective of interesting sights, but unfortunately, they add another layer of grime to the city, as they spew out large amounts of diesel fumes in such narrow streets and confined spaces. It's exhausting being a tourist in the heat at times and the buses do allow you to take the weight off your feet!

Thursday 12th July 2007

I spent the afternoon checking accommodation for my upcoming ten-day stay here. The B&B I had thought looked quite good on the internet turned out to be quite run down. The search was now on to find something within my budget that was OK and close to where the exhibition was going to be held at the fortress.

During my search, I ran into a woman from New Zealand, Elizabeth, and her English friend Anne, who were travelling together. We went for a cool drink and chatted. They took me to see their apartment. It was OK, but I was hoping to find something nicer. I decided to keep looking. Later, we met up for dinner. We got on well and had some interesting conversations. It was great to be in the company of well-travelled gals. At some point, Anne mentioned how she often had trouble finding a toilet in Florence. And we all agreed that a few more public toilets would be helpful and much appreciated by their tourists. Later, as we were paying for the meal and out of earshot, Anne whispered to me, almost in tears, that Elizabeth was becoming very bossy and she couldn't wait for the trip to end. It had been a nightmare for her, it would seem.

Traveller beware, I say. I realised how lucky I was to be travelling alone and that I didn't have to worry about being with someone who tends to be erratic. After walking with me to my hotel, they had a quick look at my room and we said our farewells.

The girls had told me about the Eurostar, the fast train. I discovered I'd travelled to Florence from Rome on the regional train. I didn't know about the fast train. No wonder it took ages to get here! Talk about taking the slow boat to China. It didn't matter though, I had loved it anyway.

First thing in the morning, I went over to the station and changed my ticket to the Eurostar. It didn't leave until two o'clock, so I checked out another couple of accommodation options and then I found the ancient and famous Profumo-Far-maceutica di Santa Maria Novella. I'd read about this fascinating place and had it on my list as a must-visit. It didn't disappoint.

From the entrance, you can feel that it's a special place with its four hundred years of history and you can buy a piece of this history! Of course, the prices are on the high side, but the quality deserves the price tag. They have been crafting beautiful fragrances, remedies and herbal products since 1221. It was like stepping back in time to a bygone era. All the perfumes, lotions and potions are brought to you in the gorgeous old bottles and jars from decades past. The ambience and furnishings are delectable. I loved it, and I made a note to myself to visit each time I'm in Florence. It was a delight for the senses and good for the soul.

A Paul Cezanne exhibition was on in Florence and I berated myself for not allowing more time to view it. Instead, I had a brief look, then dashed back to the hotel to pick up my things, then into McDonald's for a quick Caesar salad for €5.40 – probably the best deal in town and they have the best loos!

I caught the super-fast Eurostar back to Rome.

Travelling on the Eurostar from Florence, was in stark contrast to the regional train! It was splendid, luxurious even. We sped through the Tuscan countryside lickety-split at 200 kilometres an hour. Now, this is the way to travel!

From Rome, I caught the rumpty, graffiti-plastered Regional train to Sulmona. But I don't care, it's one of those incredible train rides that takes you through rugged mountains with ancient villages dotted in the most unlikely places. Just when you think the scenery couldn't become more captivating, you emerge from the final tunnel into the Valle Peligna, and there lies Sulmona in all its magnificent splendour. Truly breathtaking.

I arrived in Sulmona and then hopped on the bus from the Stazione to reach my doorstep in Introdacqua. It took five hours. It's amazing how convenient public transport is in Italy. You can travel around the country so effortlessly, and the prices are quite reasonable.

Chapter 6 - It's a Great Wee Village - Introdacqua

THERE'S A LOT GOING ON.

"Don't be an art critic. Paint. There lies salvation" Paul Cezanne

Friday 13th July 2007

A lazy day today, getting over my trip and catching up on chores. The washing machine is out to get me. I received a shock last week, so now I put everything in and out using a wooden spoon for fear of getting another electric shock and being thrown across the room.

Text Bruce...no reply.

It's now a daily occurrence to chat with my neighbours. Lucia rang and cancelled our lunch date for tomorrow, as she has a renovation going on.

Saturday 14th July 2007

Text Bruce. No reply.

Today is market day in Sulmona. I bought my vegetables and a delicious chicken for lunch. While I was there I ran into Mary and her eight year old son, Len at the market. I'd met them a few days before my trip to Florence. Mary has bought a ruin up by the tower in Introdacqua. She's had a run of bad luck with the motor scooter she bought for €800.00, only to discover the law prevents her from taking Len as a pillion passenger because he's too young! So, now she has to try and get her money back. Not an easy task. We agreed to meet tonight in the Piazza.

When I arrived home, Fiona came over for a chat and I'm thankful she speaks good English, as she's organising for an electrician to come and fix my washing machine. Then Antonella spoke to us from her balcony. Her house is next to Fiona's and her English is quite good also. Most people have a handle on our language in this village, as it was taught at school. Later, I met Mary and Len in the Square where a jazz band was playing and all you can eat pizza for €5. It was a wonderful warm evening. Mary is the resident social butterfly and seems to know everyone in the village. She introduced me to Jean, an American woman, who teaches English at the high school and is married to an Italian and Lena, was born here and works in a solicitor's office. Like most people here, both work in Sulmona.

It's a pleasure to meet local people and they're curious as to why I have ended up here. "Why here?" they ask "In this village!" They don't understand why I would possibly want to buy a house here! I told them I was a textile/mixed media artist and I planned to open a workplace studio, with a small art gallery. If anyone is interested, I'll teach them to make quilts - and it will take place in the old wine cellar at my house. They just gave me a blank look and didn't have a clue what I was talking about. The idea of a married woman coming here for an adventure and leaving a perfectly good husband to boot was, to them, inexplicable! I did explain that Bruce would be here for a few months each year.

I still haven't heard from Bruce. He hasn't replied to my four text messages! Finally, I got a reply from him, yes, he was OK, though he hadn't received my other texts. Italian telecom is not always reliable!

So, all is well in my world again.

Sunday 15th July 2007

Such a beautiful morning, birds singing, sun on my back, (I know, sounds corny, but it was) I sat outside and wrote in my journal. Mary and Len dropped in. We went for a walk up the hill to see the ruin she'd bought last year. She's renting a house for this summer and plans are drawn up for the intended renovation to start next year. It was dank, dark, and at present unliveable.

I must say - this project wouldn't suit me. It had all the hallmarks of being a money pit! It's in my category of *life is too short* basket. The price she's been given for the renovation was quite staggering! It makes my house look like a palace. But then, Mary is young and has the time to give to such a long-term challenge. On the way back down we went by her friend's house. Their renovations were well underway, she called from the street and they popped their heads over the balcony and invited us to have a look through. Tim and Shirley are from America and this is their intended holiday home. It's had major surgery to get it to where it is though still requires substantial work to become habitable. The work is being carried out by a construction company in Sulmona and they do know how to charge us English! The view from the house down the valley to Sulmona is stunning. We met later for dinner at the local restaurant 'La Trota'. They passed my house on the way to the restaurant and thought it had good possibilities. Though, I knew what they were thinking...no view! The view is not that important to me at this stage. I think in the winter the people who live by the Tower will have an awful time with the snow and ice, so I'm happy to be living on the flat part of town. Mind you, unlike me, they won't be sticking around for winter!

Roberto was also dining. I asked if he knew of someone who could give me a price for installing a new gas boiler and he said he would organise a plumber to come and give me a quote.

Giorgio was right about living in Introdacqua. It's a great wee village with plenty of interesting people coming and going. The crime rate is virtually nil, so I'm feeling quite safe. At the back of my house is a large wall surrounding the perimeter of the gardens. The gates through to the gardens are all locked, so there's not much chance of anyone entering through the back.

Only a week to go before I go back to New Zealand

Tuesday 17th July 2007

Monday unfolded as one of those uneventful but soothing days. I had a rendezvous with Annie, who I'd met at Giorgio's office. She's from Ireland and has bought a house in Sulmona. We sat in a quaint cafe, sipping coffee and sharing stories. As the conversation flowed, Annie painted a picture of Sulmona's hot summers. The city is nestled in a basin and there was no respite from the heat. In contrast, Introdacqua, enjoyed the relief of a gentle mountain breeze that helped keep the village cooler, making it a retreat for some of the residents here.

Later, as I was sitting on the back terrace, Antonella called to me to come and see her house (the house next to Fiona) she showed me through and although it's a little narrower than mine, she and her husband, Walter have painted it and furnished it beautifully. They have two teenage boys. We had a coffee and chatted. Her English is limited, but it's surprising how we can understand each other. She wanted to learn all about New Zealand.

Such a hot day. The only place that remains cool is my old cantina. Michele kindly offered to drive Mary, Len and I to the outdoor pool in Sulmona and he picked us up later. It's best to go after two o'clock as it's half price and you get a sun bed and umbrella for €5.

Wednesday 18th July 2007

Today I decided to check out L'Aquila. I took the bus and arrived there at around twelve noon, only to remember that the shops were going to shut at one o'clock. So, I quickly looked at a few stores, then it was all over! I was on my own in a deserted city. Honestly, it was a mass evacuation at one o'clock!

I stumbled on a fantastic spot for lunch in a park, then later I meandered around the awe-inspiring ancient fortress, snapping photos of diverse monuments and the small forest nearby. However, the scorching heat left me utterly drained, so I caught an earlier train back home, departing at four o'clock. Home at 5.30pm. Tony came in the evening to give me a price to change the diesel boiler to a gas boiler. €5700 That's twice as much as Giorgio indicated it would cost!

Thursday 19th July 2007

Today I'm sorting the linen in the house. There is a beautiful array of vintage linens, sheets, bed covers, tablecloths, doilies, etc. Just lovely. Some of the sheets are very heavy, pure linen, incredible. This is gold to a fabricaholic, such as myself. Later that afternoon Fiona and I went for a stroll - arm and arm, something I'm not accustomed to. It's a common practice here and I found it comforting. She wanted to show me her store in the Piazza. She has a little store in the main street, selling newspapers and other bits and bobs. Even though it's small and dark, it's the main hub of the village. A place where people meet to chat in the street outside. She's only open from 9.30am to one o'clock, then Mama has her lunch on the table when she gets home. A routine that works well for them both.

Friday 20th July 2007

Late yesterday it was exciting to register the sale contract with Giorgio. It meant going to the same austere place as he'd taken me to get my Codice Fiscale (My Italian tax number).

Sunday 22nd July 2007

Last night I went with my new friends Michele, Sergio, Mary and Len, up to the top of the mountain to a restaurant overlooking the Sulmona lights flickering in the distance. Dining alfresco amongst tall pine trees, we were entertained again with Simone and Martina's band. For the first time, I tried the delicacy of this region, arrosticini, small pieces of succulent lamb kebabs, sprinkled with herbs and cooked over a specially made BBQ, served in tin foil to keep them warm, they're delicious. I had ten, then another ten! What?? I was hungry!

*Arrosticini, served in lots of ten, wrapped in foil
to keep warm.*

From there we went down to Cantone village - for the huge porchetta (pork) festival.

Well, they were having a ball. The large concreted area was full of people, men and women, line dancing in bulk. I'd never seen so many people all dancing in unison at one place at one time. I make a mental note...learn line dancing before you get back here in October. I loved the idea that everyone was having a great time, all outside in the open air. Young and old together, with young children still up at such a late hour.

Monday 23rd July 2007

Another plumber came today to give me a quote for the new boiler – €3700, which is better than the last one. I'll make a decision on what to do when I get back in October.

I've said my goodbyes to Fiona and her Mama, Antonella and her family, Mario, and a few others. Roberto has kindly offered to drive me to Sulmona station at five o'clock in the morning.

Chapter 7 - Back in New Zealand

WORKING ON ART PIECES

*"I have such a desire to do everything, my
head is bursting with it". Claude Monet*

Tuesday 24th July 2007

Up and showered early. Roberto will be here soon. My luggage is always
heavy. Each item weighs nothing, but as soon as you pack it, it weighs a couple
of pounds well, not really, it's the one thing about travel that I struggle with the
most.

Roberto saw me onto the train at Sulmona and the trip to Rome allowed me to
pause and reflect on the past couple of months. The warmth of new friendships
made in such a short time. The serendipitous moments, Gwen and her battles,
the speed of buying the house, the delights of living in Introdacqua, the magic of
being in the moment. The sadness of leaving, the excitement of returning. Much
to ponder.

On arriving at Termini station in Rome, I panicked and boarded the wrong
train. Turns out there are two trains that run to Fiumicino airport. Instead of

catching the Leonardo Express - I've managed to now be on the regular suburban service, by mistake. It was slow and stopped at every station on the way to the airport. There were no places for bags and suitcases and not wanting to leave them, I sat on my case. I broke the handle used for pulling it. Then, when I was on the escalator, it broke some more. Somehow, I ended up with this ungainly piece of steel sticking out the end of the suitcase. When I arrived at the check-in, the girl on the counter wasn't very happy with my protruding spike! She sent me to another counter. It was the check-in for 'odd things'. At this other counter, they didn't care about the weight. I was lucky, as my luggage was so heavy, I'm sure I would've been up for overweight fees. I reckon I saved a few hundred dollars.

Thursday 26th July 2007

Home again. Bruce looks great. He's dressed in snazzy new clothes, has pulled out all the stops for my welcome home and has booked a night at a top hotel. We indulged in a lovely fruit platter on arrival. This is the longest time we've been apart. I discovered he's also been on a self-exploratory journey. Taking singing lessons, buying new clothes and cycling more.

That evening unfolded with a candlelit dinner full of romance. I've fallen for this new guy, and it seems he's equally smitten with me. He expresses himself openly, even calling me his 'soul mate,' a kind of conversation we haven't had in years. Before my departure for Italy, things between us were ordinary, just okay. But now, everything has changed; it's like we're swept up in a new love affair. We've come to understand how much we truly mean to each other, and we're fully immersed in the present moment. Our conversations are endless, our eyes stay locked, and we can't seem to stop touching. We held each other close, not wanting to release the embrace.

All is well in our world.

The next day, after a hearty New Zealand breakfast, we went shopping. For the first time in our married life, Bruce took me shopping! You know.... proper shopping. Not the normal 'man shopping', where they look for the nearest seat in the corner and a bodybuilding magazine to bury their head in. No, he was fully engaged and interested in what I was choosing. Giving an opinion even. The end of winter sales are on, so we bought some super new clothes. Boots, jeans and a coat.

A superb day.

Sunday 29th July 2007

Today we drove out to a beach-side village, Sumner. Bruce is looking to buy a longboard for surfing. We had a delicious lunch and I'm basking in this new closeness, this togetherness. It goes to show how wrapped up we were in our busy, busy lives before my departure to Italy.

Jean, our lovely, long-time family friend who also used to work for us, had a stroke while I was away. We popped into the hospital to visit her. She's looking good. Her words are a bit slurry. But we were told that with care, she would improve. Such a treasure.

We had tea with Bruce's parents. They were genuinely interested in my trip to Italy, though they couldn't understand it!

They both turn eighty in September and we're starting to think about a combined birthday celebration. It'll be a great occasion, as both are social and outgoing. They sing with a large group who visit and entertain at Nursing Homes around the city. Jean is also a member of the singing group. On many occasions at our fast food outlet, while making her famous sandwiches, she would burst into song with her beautiful, smooth soprano voice. What a treat for our lunchtime customers!

Thursday 9th August 2007

This past week I've been involved in the process of applying for a British Ancestry Visa. It is a mission. This five year visa is only open to the grandchildren of British immigrants. Bruce's Grandfather came to New Zealand with his brother in 1908 to work on the Otira Tunnel. It is the rail tunnel that runs for five miles under and through the Southern Alps of the South Island. It connects the West Coast of the Island to the East Coast. Back in the day, it was known as the job from hell. Otira is in the middle of nowhere and though it is surrounded by beautiful and dramatic scenery, the weather is atrocious. Fog, rain, snow, more rain, rain and snow. It was a very hard life for him in a strange country. He worked and lived on his own for a few years before he could afford to bring his wife and family out to New Zealand.

They were tough in those days. Anyway, because he was a UK citizen and came out to New Zealand to work and live, we are eligible to apply for this visa. Having an Ancestry Visa will allow both Bruce and I to live and work in England for five years. Bruce isn't interested in working in England, but I am. I thought with my background in nursing the elderly, I would easily get a position caring for elderly people in their homes. I've spoken to quite a few women who do this on a regular basis and it means I could pop over to England from Italy and do three-month stints. The pay is excellent, plus your meals and accommodation are included. Well, that's the plan. I've been actively applying for positions at various Home Care agencies and have started the process of applying to the British Embassy here in Wellington for this Visa.

I have papers, paraphernalia and certificates spread all over the lounge floor... birth certificates, marriage license, driver's licenses, passports, medical records of my latest health, and a police record check, (all good, I might add) CVs, references and I'm waiting for several people to get back to me with other documents.

We're in the process of organising Bruce's parents' eightieth birthday celebrations. Designing and sending the one hundred and forty invitations out to friends and family. Plus viewing various venues.

Tuesday 14th August 2007

Finally, after a huge effort and many documents, I posted the application for the UK Ancestry visa. I hope I did everything right. I await to see if we get the precious visas. Now, I can get on and finish my art pieces. The three art pieces I'm working on for the exhibition are starting to take shape. Each art piece is a different technique and will be a representation of what I want to teach in Italy. I live in a state of euphoria, as I plan in my mind how the studio/workroom and small art gallery in Introdacqua will come together.

Friday 24th August 2007

This is hard for me to write. I've made so many mistakes. Stuffed up in many ways relating to buying the house in Italy. Most of it centres around the bloody New Zealand exchange rate. The currency exchange rates have gone through the roof and are all against me. So far I've lost $NZ10,000...AHHH. It is painful watching the rates. I'm not sure I bargained enough with Giorgio! It is hard to concentrate on my art.

Every day melds into the next. I continue to live in my head. So, much going on in there! My mind is playing tricks with me! I mean, for Christ's sake, who do I think I am? An artist!! At times, the Biennale is the devil in disguise. I now have a love/hate relationship with it.

Unbeknownst to Bruce, I'm grappling with these inner, mental conflicts. He's engrossed in his new building project and management role, and I won't worry him with my anxieties.

The art project I'm working on does offer some respite from my busy mind. The work titled *'Africano Dorato'* (African Gold) is taking shape. I've been experimenting with new techniques involving image transfers onto fabric, quite invigorating. The theme revolves around Africa, as I'm captivated by its colours and essence. The artwork is being created on a sizable painted canvas, adorned with collaged photo transparencies and African fabric, then enriched with the addition of gold leaf. I've incorporated various wild animals into the composition, though they remain concealed and not immediately apparent at first glance. Remembering, I haven't had experience in making art, only some brief moments in time and so I'm winging it. It's a daring venture, and it's like stepping into the unknown, as I don't have a roadmap, but I expect it's about embracing the unknown, and just letting my inner voice guide me.

Sunday 2nd September 2007

Last night we welcomed one hundred and forty family and friends into the large hall to celebrate the combined eightieth birthday of Bruce's parents. Dubbed *'the big party'*, as they are both very well known and outgoing. Because they've been involved with music, there was plenty on offer and Bruce was brilliant with his performance of songs from *'Phantom of the Opera'*. He was dressed for the part, including the long black cape, hat and mask.

Since he's been having singing lessons, it shows in his new-found professionalism. I heard his uncle say - "Who's singing?" "It's Bruce," I said. They were pretty impressed. Pop sang his famous *'Chimney Sweep'* song to lots of laughter. Bruce's Mum and her group *'The High Flyers'* sang songs from their repertoire. What a wonderful sight they were in their colourful, sparkly costumes. I was the chief photographer and organiser of supper. A memorable night.

I've booked tickets to the *'World of Wearable Art'* Show in Wellington for 29th September. This is the fifth WOW show we've been to. Being held in Wellington will allow us to go to Te Papa, the National Museum of New Zealand.

Wednesday 19th September 2007

In between working on my art pieces for the exhibition, I've been sorting, packing and throwing things out in preparation for shipping my art stuff to Italy. I can ship more than I thought. 6.4 cubic metres. Weight is not a problem when shipped by sea. It's calculated by overall mass. My art supplies have been jammed into three large trunks, plus I have other large cartons and a few bits of furniture. All up the cost was $2,300, so not bad. Steve arrived to pick it up yesterday. All my possessions in the shipment have left. So, now let's dedicate some time to getting my artwork finished.

Bruce's singing teacher has bought my car. Time is marching on and I have much to do before I head back to Introdacqua. Each day is filled with working on my art and working in the garden.

Monday 1st Oct 2007

We flew to Wellington on Saturday morning to attend this evening's live performance of the *'World of Wearable Arts'* show. True to form, this was an amazing show, as were the other shows we've been to in the past. We're fortunate to have this wonderful event in New Zealand every year. Each year I think about entering, but life gets in the way. Either, we're head down bum up in a new business venture, or a home renovation, or building a huge barn home in the country and now, here I am heading off to Italy. So, it looks like I won't be entering for the next few years.

Wellington's weather lived up to its name and the gale-force winds made the windows in the apartment whistle. So we didn't get much sleep. We battled the wind and rain for two days walking through the art district taking in the wonderful art galleries, and then onto Tinakori Road, which is a favourite - with character houses, quaint shops and art galleries. Then it was off to Te Papa, where we ran into Bruce's nephew Matt. Te Papa is our national museum. A superb display of all things New Zealand. Bruce is cultured out! But, this weekend was just what we needed to refresh.

Sunday 7th October 2007

The World Cup Rugby matches are being held in the evenings in Europe and the UK, which allows us to watch the All Blacks play, (the New Zealand National rugby team). The matches are live in the mornings, New Zealand time. Though I'm not a huge rugby fan, it's been a great form of entertainment most mornings. But, we've had a major upset in the All Blacks camp. They've LOST to France in the quarter-finals of the World Cup Series. New Zealand, 18. France, 20.

Crikey, they haven't even made it into the finals, as was expected! Normally, I wouldn't be concerned, but this World Cup was different. They were touted to win...big time! The whole country was behind them, even folks like me. This defeat has left me with an empty feeling in the pit of my stomach. How fabulous it would've been, had they won or at the very least made it into the finals! The one thing that stood out for me - they didn't have a sense of urgency in their game plan. Right from the start, they didn't appear to play with passion! It's embarrassing to be booted out in the quarter-finals and sent home. All they had to do in the last ten minutes was to kick the ball for an easy drop goal. I mean how difficult could it be?

I can now see how people get carried away with their sport!

After the rugby, we drove out to the countryside for a picnic. Beyond the city's urban hustle and bustle, the area surrounding Christchurch is, to put it plainly, a sight to behold. The Canterbury Plains, with the majestic backdrop of the Southern Alps, and the rolling hills, a vibrant green that seems to stretch on forever, gives you a sense of space and freedom. From the air, the Plains are like a patchwork quilt of farms where life unfolds at its own unhurried pace. This landscape is a reminder that sometimes all you need is the beauty of nature to fill your heart and calm your soul. It's a place where you can find the simple joys in life, where the beauty lies in the everyday moments of being surrounded by the charm of New Zealand's countryside. We finished our laid-back, contemplative day by visiting a country art gallery. Perfect.

I've finished my three art pieces:

'Poppies in Peeled Paint'

'Africano Dorato'

'Raw Colour'

During the week we cooked a BBQ for our family and friends. It was a going away evening for me. Sad, as I won't be seeing them all for a few years. Of course, the match was discussed at length.

Friday 12th October 2007

Our Ancestry visas have arrived from the British Embassy. But, I don't like the look of mine. It says I can only go into the UK if I'm accompanied by my husband, who is the visa holder, and I'm only the wife. Since it's me who wants to go to the UK to work, I was hoping to come and go as I please. This is worse, because without the visa I can, as of right and being a New Zealand citizen, I can come and go into the UK when I want to. Though, I'm not able to work without the visa! So it's a catch-22. If I complain, they could cancel it. So, I'll wait to worry. I've informed my friend who works in a travel agency about the situation and she's agreed, when the time comes, to write up a dummy itinerary for Bruce, should I need it.

Saturday 26th October 2007

Saying goodbye to my life here is hard. It gets harder, not easier. Doubts buzzing around in my head, again! What on earth am I thinking? Walking away from a perfectly fine marriage to go live in a foreign country! How is this even going to pan out? We haven't charted any course for the future; we're navigating this on a day-to-day basis. I can understand why Bruce doesn't want to travel right now; he's just not at that stage, unlike me. His new job is all-consuming and he's dealing with extra pressures and time constraints that accompany the building industry. To be honest, I am relieved he has this new position, as he'll be so busy he won't miss me as much and now we've established our new relationship, everything is clearer. This arrangement grants us the freedom to pursue our individual paths without guilt or unnecessary worry about each other. He's booked to come on December 6th to spend the remaining five days with me in Florence then stay for around two months to have Christmas and New Year at our house in Introdacqua.

Chapter 8 - Return to Italy

BUYING THE HOUSE

"People must first of all learn to look at nature, and only then may they see and understand what we are trying to do" Claude Monet

Monday 29th October

Due to my naivety and my oversized art case – which Bruce made for my art, we had an awful time at the airport before leaving. And although it's a superb case for protecting my art pieces, it's too big! I thought it would've gone in that unusual place at the airport where surfboards and odd things go!

No! it has to be sent unaccompanied! Plus, one of my suitcases was overweight, so I'm also sending it unaccompanied. What a fiasco. Finally, everything was sorted, we had last kisses, hugs and crying. I was off. I didn't cry for long, you need to concentrate when catching overseas flights. Forms to fill in, bags to put through the x-ray machine, etc. From New Zealand, aboard Emirates, it's three hours to Sydney, wait three hours for a connecting flight to Dubai, then Sydney to Dubai is fourteen hours. Wait three or four hours in Dubai, and then onto Rome, six hours.

Arriving at Fiumicino Airport as I've said before, it's easy to go through customs, and you're out the door. I struggled with my bags, as my large suitcase and a small cabin bag weighed well over the limit and I had to pretend I wasn't struggling when I put the twelve-kilo bag up into the overhead compartment, trying to make out it was the regulation seven kilos. My large handbag is crammed full, as is my computer bag also filled to the brim, with more than just my laptop. As I make my way to the airport train station, I'm loaded down like a packhorse and after twenty-four hours on the plane, I look and feel like shit. As I stepped onto the escalator, to my surprise my bloody alarm clock, in my suitcase started to go off. The Italian guy behind me jokingly yelled, "ha una bomba" "She has a bomb"! Christ! Why doesn't he shut up!

When I reached the top of the escalator there were three or four Carabinieri with machine guns. No, I am not joking. They walk around the airport armed to the hilt with AK47s, as a security measure. Well, I thought, this is it, they're just going to shoot me. I floundered in the bag to shut the damned thing off. It worked out OK - and I'm lucky they're Italian (well, I know that now, but not at the time) they just laughed and went on by.

I threw a scornful look at the man behind me.

Boarding the Leonardo Express train was an act in itself, as the carriage was about two feet off the platform. You have to virtually throw your bags up. You'd think being an airport express train, it would be more user friendly! It takes about forty-five minutes, even on the express, to get to Termini, the main station in Rome. Once there, buy your ticket for the Metro to Tiburtina, €1. It's only a ten minute trip. I struggled as I heaved myself and my bags up the stairs and escalators from the metro into the brilliant daylight of Tiburtina station. I think a heart attack was staved off by the kind person who helped me. I stop now for a breather as I read the partenza board to find what time and what platform the train leaves for Sulmona. It's quite a long walk, up and down more stairs before arriving on the platform to catch the regional train to Sulmona. I can finally relax for my favourite two-hour train journey. Oh, what a pleasure this is. From there, I go by taxi to Introdacqua.

Finally home, I rummaged in my bag and produced the key to unlock the front door to the house that would be mine in a few days.

Tuesday 30th October 2007

While I was away in New Zealand, Gino, the owner of the house, had taken more possessions than what we had agreed to before I left three months ago. I rang Giorgio. He came to see what the problem was. I told him how I felt I'd been given a raw deal. There were other things I wasn't happy with. So, after much discussion and a performance on the scale Scarlett O'Hara would be proud of, it was agreed that Gino return the chattels in question and pay for a new gas boiler and two new radiators to be installed down in the old wine cellar. I still smile with the memory of Gino and his friend running down the street with a queen-size mattress on their heads.

Wednesday 31st October 2007

Today Gino, Giorgio and I met at the Notario's office and signed all the papers to finalise the house deal. I was astounded by the sheer volume of papers I had to sign - I handed over the balance of the money.

We celebrated with Proseccos and pizza.

Today, I'm shopping with Sara, who works at Giorgio's office. She's helping me buy a new washing machine, a toaster and a vacuum cleaner. The toaster and vacuum cleaner were easy. I prefer a top-loading washing machine, but I'll have to settle for a front-loader. Sara also helped me fill in the forms for telecom. Not only will it be great to have a landline, but it is necessary for an Internet connection. I do have my mobile phone and that's all the communication I have with Bruce, just texting. If I want to email him I'll need to go into Sulmona on the bus to the Internet cafe. (remember them). So, it's pretty important to get the Internet on ASAP.

The village only has dial-up at present. Still, it's better than nothing.

Saturday 3rd November 2007

After unpacking, sorting and a few days to get used to being on my own, I'm feeling miserable. I'm cold, lonely and it gets dark early. I only have a little fan heater to keep me warm.

Let the makeover begin. Fiona took me into Sulmona in her little Fiat 500. No, not a Bambini, similar but squarer, though just as small. I bought some white paint, brushes and rollers as I'm eager to get started on the walls and ceilings of the spare room, by stripping all the dingy, water-stained wallpaper off. I love the coved ceilings in the house, which, I'm told, are stronger and safer. They look beautiful.

The plumbers are due next week to replace the old boiler (no, not me!) with a new gas one. How wonderful it will be to live in a house that is heated from top to bottom. Every room will be warm. Not like in New Zealand. We're a bit weird, we heat the main living area, but the hallway and bedrooms freeze. So you run quickly, get ready for bed and jump in. No, I don't know why we do this. Electricity is expensive is the main reason. Things are changing, with houses now being required to be properly insulated.

Tuesday 6th November 2007

I've received notification that my art case and the other unaccompanied bag have arrived at Fiumicino airport. Great, as I've been worried about my artwork.

The guest room is complete, though I'll admit it's not my finest work. However, the overall result is quite lovely. I've kept everything in shades of white, and the bed is adorned with the beautiful vintage linens that came with the house.

It appears the women in this village aren't accustomed to undertaking renovations like I am. They find it rather peculiar that I'm renovating the house, painting the bedroom and not waiting until B comes here. Giorgio found a builder to temporarily patch the roof until Bruce can get to it.

I'll start painting my room next after I've been to Fiumicino Airport to pick up my suitcase and large art case, which has my three pieces of art for the exhibition in December.

When you buy a house here, you can then apply for residency. And for that, you need a Permesso di Soggiorno. I'm starting the procedure by applying at the Polizia (Police) Station in Sulmona. I think the document is also important for buying a second-hand car. The Italian Government is desperate to sell new cars here and they'll allow you to buy a brand new car without the document, though I don't want to invest in a new car.

As I don't have a TV yet, I catch up on some reading. Presently it's *'The Colour of Heaven'* by James Runcie. Mary and Len are due to arrive back from the States soon, which I must say I am looking forward to. We'll be socialising. I haven't had a chance to go out. Much too busy with the renovation.

Chapter 9 - The Search For The Art Crate

COMING TO TERMS WITH THINGS.

"When you go out to paint, try to forget what objects you have before you, a tree, a house, a field, or whatever. Merely think, here is a little square of blue, here an oblong of pink, here a streak of yellow". Claude Monet

Tuesday 6th November 2007

It's becoming increasingly difficult with no phone, fax or Internet - which all rely on a landline. So, I make notes to myself:

Artwork to be picked up from Fiumicino. I'll go tomorrow. It's obvious, I can't do anything by cell phone. The language is a big problem and the signal here in the hills is not brilliant.

Ask Roberto about a courier to transport the artwork to Florence when the time comes.

Buy paint for the other bedroom, then lug it back on the bus. Maybe Lucia will help.

Life here presents its fair share of challenges and surprises. It's a place that keeps you on your toes, and it demands careful planning and a sharp financial eye. Our New Zealand dollar is ever at odds with us when we leave our shores. Regardless of our destination, it has a knack for dwindling faster than expected. Australia offers some respite at times. But here in Italy, we lose a sizable chunk when converting to the Euro. Yet, it's important for me to remember that this journey is not just about the money. It's about experiences, about savouring every moment, regardless of the financial ebbs and flows. So, we adapt, we make do, and we continue to embrace this adventure with open hearts and open wallets.

One of my other concerns is how to keep myself occupied during these long winter evenings without my artwork, handwork, TV, radio or newspaper. I didn't think of this sort of stuff when I was sitting in the comfort of my other life. Only now it dawns on me that I should've been more prepared. This will be remedied when my shipment arrives from New Zealand.

During the day there's plenty to occupy my busy mind. Like trying new ways to prepare meals. The supermarkets have a range of different types of food. Row upon row of pasta. I didn't know there were so many varieties, colours and shapes of pasta. Penne, Ravioli, Linguine, Rigatoni, Farfalle, Fusilli, Cannelloni to name a few.

Then there are my daily walks, no matter what the weather. Trying to learn the language. It's not easy, this Italian language. The constant head chatter seems to have gone up a notch or two since my arrival here! Yes, we know Italy is difficult.

They do things differently here. Just suck it up and get on with it!

Wednesday 7th November 2007

Yesterday evening, I struggled with my aloneness and the constant barrage of whirling thoughts. So on the spur of the moment, I caught the 5.20pm bus to Sulmona. It was a bit worrying, as it went a different route. I had this horrifying thought that maybe this bus doesn't go to Sulmona at all, and I'll end up goodness knows where in the middle of the night! Nevertheless, it was a beautiful scenic drive, as we wound our way around the hills, passing through tiny ancient villages, bathed in street lights that cast a golden, eerie glow on the medieval buildings. It was unexpected and magical. Then, relief after forty minutes as we pulled into Sulmona. Great value for €1. I came home on the return bus at 7.30pm, giving me enough time in Sulmona to have a Prosecco while I watched the passeggiata.

Passeggiata, a definition: around six o'clock, an evening ritual is about to begin, the Italian tradition of passeggiata is a gentle stroll (slow! think slow!) through the main streets of the old town, usually in the pedestrian zones in the Centro Storico, the historic centre. In this case along the Corso with all the other residents of Sulmona city. Sulmona is famous for having one of the most popular Passeggiata.

I love it! I love it! This new life.

Today Lucia and I are going to the Sulmona market. The markets are a treat, with a multitude of colourful stalls of fresh fruit and vegetables - all grown locally.

The food trucks and trailers, where there's always a hub of activity, each one has tantalising aromas that waft in the air. These mobile kitchens, powered by wood fires, crackled and sizzled the rotisserie chickens and pork - slowly turning on their spits, creating absolutely irresistible flavours.

Fruit and vegetable display at the Sulmona market.

And then there are trucks overflowing with cheeses, salamis, prosciutto, and not forgetting the other trucks and vans full of fresh fish. The market is filled with everything from trinkets to handy household items. Further along, there were rows and rows of stylish yet affordable clothes. In the midst of all the hustle, we found a seat at a café, the perfect spot for viewing families strolling by. Mothers, arms full of fresh food, paused to chat with friends and neighbours. With the sun shining brightly, it was a day of little things that make you smile.

All too soon we had to leave. Lucia has arranged for me to sign the gas contract, but when we reached the office, it wasn't possible for some unexplained reason. I now have to come back at another time. Next, it was to the mobile phone shop, where I met Alex, who was to become a very good friend to me over the years. His English is excellent. He explained to me the different services that are available in our village, regarding the phone and Internet. Apart from Telecom, there isn't a very good signal in the hills, so I will have to wait for them to hook up my landline. It looks like it will be another month. That isn't too bad now, as the owner of the local bar is allowing me to use his Internet. Yesterday, I was able to check my emails, so things are progressing.

We also went and bought a TV and some more paint to finish my bedroom. Lucia's son Alberto, joined us and we went for a long lunch at a traditional family restaurant. After such a hectic morning, it was fun to relax and have some laughter. Lucia has such a great sense of humour. We cleared the air about many things, including Gwen and how things had deteriorated between them. This will benefit our friendship. What is even more fantastic, she has insisted on taking me to Fiumicino Airport tomorrow to pick up my artwork. Because of the size of the art case, we'll have to strap it to the top of her car roof to transport it home. A bit scary! Her car is fairly small.

As frustrating as everything is to organise in this country, I feel energised and alive. I'm looking forward to the day I can set up my studio, work on my art and have my little art gallery.

The Search For The Art Crate

Friday 9th November 2007

The day from hell yesterday, started pleasantly enough with Lucia picking me up on a clear sunny day at eight o'clock.

When we arrived at Fiumicino Airport almost three hours later, our first port of call was Cargo City. This is a huge area away from the main airport. There was a security check, which meant we had to leave our passports with the armed security guards and proceed through a body X-ray. We were sent to look in the huge warehouse-type buildings. They were so huge, you could drive a truck down the aisles. We asked all available personnel where my art crate could possibly be.

We searched high and low in the areas we were allowed, to no avail. We were there for over an hour.

From there we went to terminal C. They wouldn't allow Lucia into the lost and found baggage area at Air Italia and yes, success of sorts, my black suitcase was there, but not the art crate! The significance of not finding my artwork has just hit me. I lost my composure at that moment and wept. I wept for the amount of time I'd spent on my art pieces, the time Bruce had spent on making this neat art crate, with wheels, to ship my art pieces. For the amount of money it has cost me to be at the Florence Biennale, the people who are behind and giving me such wonderful support in this project. Now the whole mission is in jeopardy. If I don't find my art, there won't be any Florence exhibition for me! After a while, I regained my composure and asked the officials if Lucia would be allowed in the back to help me look.

Backwards and forwards we went from room to huge room. The art crate wasn't anywhere to be found!

There was one last option. Alitalia Cargo. Another huge building. We headed over there.

An overworked, impatient woman looked at my waybill, she checked her computer for the number, but it wasn't on her computer. She sent us to another area of lost bags. We were astounded by the amount of lost baggage in these rooms.

About six rooms full of suitcases and bags of all shapes and sizes. The shelves soared above our heads and groaned under the weight of thousands of bags. I couldn't help feeling sad for all the people who'd lost their belongings and the anguish they must've gone through. Some of the bags and cases were beautiful and expensive.

Well, here they are folks! I can tell you, they're stacked to the gunnels in this huge Alitalia Cargo building waiting to be claimed. I suppose people don't even know they're here. Again, we went from room to room, pushing bags out of the way to get through, but no luck. Our crate was not here.

So, back we went to the impatient woman. She happened to be leaving the building when Lucia called her back and demanded to speak to her supervisor. Lucia has had experience with airlines, having worked for a major airline company in the USA for many years. The woman begrudgingly went back into the office. She went away to find her boss. By this time it's getting close to five o'clock. We were worried they were going to close everything down and go home.

Then, blow me down, twenty minutes later she came back with the documentation for my art crate! We looked at each other with our mouths open! We could so easily have left this area and gone home, being none the wiser that the crate was in this building. So, with renewed vigour and documents in hand, we went to the customs office down the hall where this little man said we wouldn't be able to take the art, wait for it, *as it might be stolen artworks from abroad!*" He went on and on.

Then, by some miracle, a woman in the same office took us away from that little man and up a few levels to another office where we met Gino. He proceeded to read up on the laws between Italy and New Zealand. He made two very long phone calls, based on the fact that Italy and New Zealand had signed reciprocal agreements at the end of WWII, really? Finally, he said yes, everything was in order and we could collect the crate from downstairs. He shook my hand and said, "Welcome to Italy".

So, back downstairs to where the Grumpy woman and horrid little man were. When he saw us, he started on again about how we could not take the crate. Lucia stood firm "We don't need you, we have authority from Gino".

Then over to Grumpy, she had tallied up my bill! And wanted €8.31, which I gladly paid. Now, we can go down to the dock and load the crate. Yay o' Yay...progress!

Out at the loading dock, we have Mr Bloody Important, the security guard and two other ugly, no-teeth, fat guys lounging around. We handed the documents to the guy on the forklift. He went away. He came back and checked the computer.

No luck! Back down the rows, he went, then back to the computer. Then away again down the rows. We weren't allowed into the huge warehouse.

Wait, lo and behold - here he comes out the door, rolling the crate with him.

Bloody hell, do you believe this? Here it is, all intact, with a few bruises, even a large footprint on it! Then Mr Security thought he'd put in his two pennies worth in, so he checked, then re-checked the documentation. Another harrowing ten minutes! He gave the OK and the two fat uglies helped us load it into the car. It was a very snug fit in the boot with the back seats folded down. We couldn't put the boot down, but with some bungees, we managed to secure the back door though partly open.

But, to top the awful day off, one fat ugly was helping me, as we were trying to wrangle the crate into the car. And each time as he passed me, he would touch my tits and bum! I yelled to Lucia, "Hey, he's touching me!" "yes," she said, "I know, he's telling the other guy in Italian"!

Honestly, get me outta here!!

With that, we were off.

By now, it was nearly six o'clock and pitch black. Out into the peak hour of Roman traffic. We crawled through the outskirts of Rome, through the black countryside, lights twinkling from villages high in the mountains, back towards home.

What can I say about this girl, Lucia, what a great person to have by my side. I could never have accomplished what we did without her tenacity, kindness and impeccable Italian. I will be forever grateful for her help.

Chapter 10 - Applying For The Permesso di Soggiorno

BUREAUCRACY GONE MAD!

"It is good to love many things, for therein lies the true strength, and whosoever loves much performs much, and can accomplish much, and what is done in love is well done." Vincent Van Gogh

Saturday 10th November 2007

After Thursday's marathon trip, yesterday was calm and uneventful. I'm feeling cosy, knowing that my art is safe and in my care. I spent the day whistling and singing while I cleaned the kitchen cupboards and the large cupboard that will work as a pantry. Exhausting, but satisfying. I find cleaning to be therapeutic.

Throughout the day, I mulled over the help I had received from Lucia and how immensely grateful I was to her. She's warm, jovial and candidly shared with me how returning to her family home in Italy had been life-changing for her. The move, she said, has shaped her into the new person she is now. She opened up about how this return brought her a newfound calmness, and how she effortlessly reintegrated into the Italian way of life. Lucia's American years had been marred by an unhappy marriage, followed by divorce, and the challenges of raising her three boys on her own. Her health started to wane, leading to the loss of her job, which is why she made a pivotal decision to return to Italy to care for her ailing mother. With all her grown boys now working and living with her, she attests that this choice has proven to be one of her best moves.

Next week, I've noted what I need to concentrate on.

Phone

Gas

Printer/fax

Set up my website

Arrange quotes from DHL, and FedEx to courier my art to Florence.

But, today I'm off to the market and this evening Lucia and I going to Pescara. She's looking for a new kitchen. Should be fun.

The villagers here are open and friendly. They often stop to introduce themselves when I'm out on one of my walks, and gesture towards their homes. They say they're happy to have me here in their village (I think that's what they're trying to convey!).

My parcel from New Zealand is still not here. My shipment of all my goods that are coming by ship will not be here for another month or so.

Tomorrow is La Fiesta del Ringraziamento. From what I can gather, it's a sort of Thanksgiving/harvest day, where artisans and craftspeople from all over the region come to Introdacqua with their crafts and special regional food. It is held in the main Piazza and the surrounding narrow streets.

Tuesday 13th November 2007

Sunday dawned sunny for La Fiesta, but it was bone-chilling cold! Mixing with the locals on this much heralded big day out was wonderful and I was surprised by the number of people I knew already, mainly due to Mary, as she's been coming here for a few years and knows everyone.

The Fiesta itself was teeming with artisans showcasing their crafts - basket weavers, leatherworkers, stone sculptors, and a multitude of oil painting artists. Several women were also engaged in the meticulous craft of lace-making, a fading art. Fascinating to watch.

There was plenty of local and regional food on offer. I bought a variety of cheeses, salami and a big loaf of fresh bread. Food, food, food, pizzas, soups, loaves of bread and of course a constant supply of arrosticini. The aroma's are intoxicating. For lunch, I indulged in pasta with tomato sauce and a porchetta bun, basically, pork spit roast flavoured with herbs, sliced, then put in a bun. Roberto was busy with queues of people waiting for his BBQ-style sausages in a bun.

All in all a great day. Lucia and Alberto came over later. It turns out he's a tiler and is going to give me a price to lay new tiles in my art gallery.

Mary and Michele came to my house after the Fiesta for a nightcap of Ratafia. A cherry liquor. Very good.

I told them how much the day had inspired me and that I hoped to have my studio up and running for next year's Ringraziamento. I wondered if the local women would be interested in my traditional American-style quilt making.

Wednesday 14th November 2007

Good news. I had word today that my shipment by sea will arrive in Milan tomorrow!

Still wondering about telecom and my phone. Yesterday was taken up with sorting out the gas documents. It took hours.

Everything is a mission.

In the evening, I went to Sulmona to fax documents to the shipping company. I also had to get a gas document to the plumber who is installing the new boiler. Luckily, he's a friend of Giorgio's and came into the office while I was there.

In between time, I'm painting my bedroom. It's coming on and looking good. Again it is all white, which suits this style of house. Getting rid of dark dreary wallpaper has given my spirits a boost.

Thursday 15th November 2007

It was Mike's (my son) birthday yesterday. I sent him a message and he sent me a text back saying how proud he was of me for doing what I was doing and the Florence Biennale and all.

I finished painting the bedroom. Mary came with a bottle of Montepulciano red wine, which I've become quite partial to. We had a little party with music. At least I have my CDs. However, I am paying for it this morning.

Roberto has sorted out a courier to take my art to Florence.

Friday 16th November 2007

The only way Bruce and I can communicate at the moment is by texting. Unless when I go into Sulmona I email him.

He texted me. He sounds quite stressed. I think he is working too hard. His new job is full-on. But, on the bright side, he's looking forward to coming over in three weeks.

Today is wet here and looks like it may snow. I have repacked the art crate with the three pieces of art that I'll be displaying at the exhibition. "Poppies 'n Peeled

Paint", "Africano Dorato" and "Raw Colour" The courier is coming by this afternoon to pick it up, as it needs to be in Florence by early next week.

Even though it's cold out, this little fan heater does keep the room warm. It's started to snow and it's going to be wonderful when I can switch the gas heating on with radiators in each room. You know, as much as the weather has packed it in and still so much to organise, gas, phone, computer, etc. I'm genuinely in high spirits. I contemplate whether I would've coped with these tricky circumstances, had I postponed my adventure until retirement. New Zealand retirement age is sixty five years and you need to have all your wits about you if you move to Italy. Everything is complicated.

I ran into Ana, another Italian/American, who lives in the village permanently, with her Italian husband. She's offered to help me with my Permesso di Soggiorno and residency card. That was a fluke and such good luck meeting her.

Sunday 18th November 2007

The courier came to pick up my art crate with my art pieces tucked inside, on Friday afternoon. So good news, they're on their way to Florence.

Friday night Mary and I were invited to Sergio's family get together at the local restaurant, La Trota. It was a wonderful family night. Children playing quietly, not screaming around. Good old-fashioned Italian music, with Sergio's son playing the sax...adorable, sighed Mary. We did have a wonderful night. Saturday I went to the market. The snow didn't come to much and has all melted. I had to pop in to see Giorgio, he has papers for the gas to be signed... thirty-two pages! Don't ask me!

I came home and spent the afternoon in bed. I can't stop sleeping!

Mary and I were invited to Marco's apartment in Sulmona. Fabrizio took us. Marco, in another lifetime, had been quite a famous entertainer/singer. He cooked us a superb Italian dinner and gave us the leftovers to take home. He's very kind and generous and gave us some warm lambs wool leggings.

Today I'm cleaning the old wine cantina, on the ground floor, in preparation for my New Zealand shipment coming from Milan.

Wednesday 21st November 2007

It's been a hectic couple of days, sorting out the Permesso di Soggiorno with Ana. A long and arduous task. She's been so helpful. This document permits you to stay in Italy for longer than three months. (I think).

On Monday we went to an office in a run-down ex-palace building in Sulmona and the procedure went like this:

All pages, even the blank pages of my passport had to be photocopied, including my Codice Fiscale and my house sale agreement. Then it was off to another place, a Tabacchi, a tobacco shop, to buy a stamp, €14.32 to be precise. It's quite crucial, this stamp! Off to the Post Office to have everything processed and paid for. All the documents were sent to Rome and I'll be contacted in due course.

The total cost for everything so far is around €80.00.

The first step is completed. Now, to get the Residency card. Collect all the receipts and go and see Tomasino at the commune. He filled out more forms, stamped many things, and photocopied the passport (again). It's been a colossal amount of documentation.

All these documents now go to the Mayor for him to sign. After all necessary steps are concluded, I will get an ID Resident card from the Mayor's office. Which is different from a Permesso di Soggiorno.

Sara rang the shipping company in Milan and they said my cargo would arrive in three days. Well, that's promising news.

Word came today from the recruitment people about working with aged care in the UK. My police check is all OK and it looks like I've been approved to work over there in England.

Last night I cooked a kiwi meal for Mary, Len, Michele and Fabrizio. A roast of lamb with roast vegetables. We started with Bruschetta we cooked over the open fire. Bruschetta is an antipasto (starter dish) consisting of toasted bread rubbed with garlic and topped with tomatoes, olive oil, salt and pepper. They all seemed to enjoy the evening, though they were surprised to have the main meal served together as one large meal, rather than having, say, the vegetables served separately.

Saturday 24th November 2007

The shipment didn't arrive as promised yesterday. But one good thing did happen. I became a Resident of Introdacqua. An official document and all.

The last couple of evenings have been delicious. Reading by the open fire. Listening to CDs. I bought a little radio and CD player a while ago.

John Denver, Sarah Brightman, Russell Watson, Chris Rea, Supertramp, Dusty Springfield and others. I'm reading Christine Fernyhough 'Road to Castle Hill'. It's OK. I like the layout of the book.

Sunday 25th Nov 2007

As I sit here in bed, (I write my journal in bed in the mornings, before I get up) I'm watching the florist across the road. She's immersed in titivating the outside of her shop with an array of Christmas decorations. A medley of twinkling lights, colourful ornaments and wreaths transform the façade into a festive storefront. This lovely transformation has given the feeling and spirit of Christmas. It reminds me that this will be my first Christmas here in the Northern

Hemisphere. I'm looking forward to it eagerly, as Bruce will be here to share it. This time next week is the opening of the Florence Biennale.

Yesterday, I went for a walk up by the Tower. I diverted to where Giorgio had shown me a house he was going to renovate. As you push through the tangled weeds and bushes, the thick undergrowth opens up to this charming ruin.

It sort of reminded me of Scarlett in *'Gone With the Wind'* when she returned to the ruins of '*Tara*'. This ruin is nowhere near the scale or opulence of Tara, but lovely in its way, with blue peeling stucco, two iron balconies, and shutters in disrepair. French doors falling away. It had old fireplaces and some lovely old watermarked embossed wallpaper. The tiles on the roof had almost fallen into the house. I named it *'Tara'* and go there now and then to take photos with the idea of doing an art piece on it in the future.

Just up past the house is a wonderful view out to the Maiella mountains to Gran Sasso, the tallest peak in the Abruzzo. From here, cast your eye down the valley and in the distance to the terracotta rooftops of Sulmona, spread out before you. The mountains are layered in that Italian hazy light. You can hear the shepherd in the surrounding hills calling to his sheep and goats. Yes, there is a resident shepherd up here. We don't have shepherds and open grazing in New Zealand. The sight of the shepherd on these hilly roads and meadows is a sight I'll always cherish. The sound of the animals with their bells is delightful.

Local shepherd.

Another wonderful sight at this time of year is the locals harvesting olives. Once the olives are picked, they're transported to the olive press in our village, not far from my house. I go there with my five-litre jar and get it filled with freshly pressed olive oil.

Yes, I remind myself, I was in Italy. I've been so bogged down with bureaucracy and Mary lately, that I haven't had time to stop and consider where I was. I make a note to myself, to go out walking more often.

As I meandered home, I came across some locals harvesting olives. I stopped to enquire if I could help. Yes, I was made most welcome.

The harvesting of olives is a simple procedure. Large nets are laid on the ground. The trees are shaken or raked, so the plump green olives fall onto the netting. The nets are scooped up and the olives are tipped into large drums. It turned out the olive trees belonged to Agent Giorgio's sister, Rina, a lovely lady. They gave me afternoon tea with plenty of Italian goodies and orange juice.

I stayed and helped for most of the afternoon, before making my way home.

Chapter 11 - The Florence Biennale

A MISSING HUSBAND AT THE AIRPORT!

"Life beats down and crushes the soul - and art reminds you that you have one". Stella Adler

Monday 26th November 2007

Saturday I met Lucia at the Sulmona market and I discovered a stall with vintage Italian linens. Such good quality, very clean and reasonable prices. Lucia bought a large crocheted tablecloth in mint condition. I bought some bits and bobs of finely crocheted doilies. These are beautiful and I intend to give them another life through my artwork. On the way home we stopped at the electrical store where she helped me buy a printer. After lunch, I walked up to Tara, then dropped in on my new friends to lend a hand with the olive harvest again.

I've had a sore throat for a day or two. Spent the evening in front of the fire reading.

Sunday was St Cecilia Day. The Patron Saint of Music. Introdacqua has two brass bands and they marched and played throughout the village in the morning.

It was a wonderful sight and happy sounds. In the evening there was a procession, with the beautiful statue of St Cecilia raised on the shoulders of the men of the town. The procession went right by my house. Fiona and I watched from the balcony.

I haven't been feeling very well, so I've spent most of the day in bed resting. I need to be well for next week's trip to Florence.

The TV is going OK. Of course, everything is in Italian. It seems they dub the English-speaking movies with Italiano. Somehow John Wayne doesn't quite sound the same, in Italian!

Things I'd like to happen this week.

The gas is on.

Telephone landline to be hooked up. Honestly, why is it taking so long?

My shipment is to arrive from Milan.

My other parcel of clothes from New Zealand is to arrive.

Buy a post box to be put on my outside wall.

Then I'm off up to the Biennale for the opening next week.

Tuesday 27th November 2007

No action on any of the above. Still, have this darned sore throat. I'm not sleeping that well. It looks like the shipment is going to be a problem now, as the Dogana, which is the Italian Customs, wants me to pay duty! I don't understand why, as everything in the shipment is used household items.

Wednesday 28th November 2007

Last night was an interesting experience. Antonella took me to her specialist doctor. No, it wasn't my sore throat, as that has cleared up. I wanted to have a spot on my left boob checked out as it's changed colour and is itchy.

Wow, for a doctor's surgery, the building is palatial. The waiting room, a huge space, is done out in the most gorgeous marble and devoid of furniture, except for a row of chairs following the wall around the room. People sitting waiting were speaking in hushed whispers that echoed eerily. We waited and waited for over two hours. Then the doctor appeared and ushered us into his almost as large surgery. No privacy issues here. He examined me with Antonella still in the room and no nurse. He shone a special light on my mole and deemed it not serious. Prescribed some cream for me to apply. €50.00 thanks. He didn't take any notes, not even my name.

Yesterday I popped into Sulmona and asked Giorgio to ring the shipping company to find out why I have to pay duty when everything is my personal furniture and it's not new. He said he'd look into it.

Later at the Internet cafe, I met Robyn an Aussie who has lived with her husband in Sulmona and Pescocostanzo for forty years. Over a cup of coffee, we shared our stories and laughter as kindred spirits. Relating her story to me, how, as a young girl she was backpacking around Italy and fell in love, married and is still here. Robyn had a wealth of knowledge with regards to the region, and what she doesn't know isn't worth knowing. As we chatted about her experiences and insights, she opened up a new-found understanding for me about my new home. A reminder that even in the heart of a foreign land, friends can enrich our lives with new perspectives. And so with a sense of achievement, we said our goodbyes and a promise to get together again soon. I ran to catch my bus, grateful for a new friend that had brightened my day.

Friday 30th November 2007

Drama. I'm unable to travel to Florence today, as there's a transport strike on. So I'm going to miss the opening night of the exhibition! Opening night is a day earlier than open to the public.

I'll now go tomorrow.

Florence Biennale 2007

Sunday 2nd December 2007

Again, with my large heavy suitcase, as I'm away for over two weeks and will be attending the exhibition each day, so a girl has to have clothes, but I still haven't mastered the art of travelling lite. A taxi drove me to the apartment office to check in and pick up the key. Alex told me I still had to pay for Friday night, even though it was a transport strike and not my fault...creep! With the door key in hand, I trundled off to find my apartment. The key didn't fit. I rang and told him. He rang the cleaner and twenty minutes later she arrived on her scooter with the key. Crikey, that didn't fit either. Give me a break! I rang him again. He decided to come himself (twenty minutes later). He's decided to shift me to another apartment and I have to return at six o'clock to get the key.

Finally, I can go to the Biennale.

Exhausted and emotionally drained, I reached the Fortress (Fortessa) by four o'clock. The sense of relief and joy was so overwhelming that I couldn't help the tears that welled up. Reaching this point had been a lengthy ride, especially considering the challenges, like searching for my art at Fiumicino Airport. Standing before the entrance of the Fortessa, I paused, allowing the weight of the obstacles I'd overcome to sink in and to really appreciate the significance of this moment.

A girl, who looked like my sister was sitting on a bench outside the large gates. How I wished it was. I could have done with some family support at that moment, not to mention the fun we could have in Florence together. I sighed, not to be. I stayed there for a while before venturing down to the entrance.

As I stepped into the expansive Fortress it was like entering a bustling world of its own. Everywhere I looked, there was a hive of activity. The air inside was warm and there was a palpable sense of excitement. At the reception desk, I was greeted with a welcome bag and the enormous 2007 catalogue with my beautiful certificate inside. The attendants pointed me in the direction of my stand. Such a large exhibition of 840 artists worldwide and little ol' me! It took a while to find my stand. My art was displayed how I'd asked. I was very proud of myself. And there in the catalogue was my 'Poppies in Peeled Paint'.

Artist Nancy, from the States, whom I met as I arrived, was my neighbour next to my stand. I stayed at the exhibition for two hours and then had to dash back to check into my apartment. The new apartment is OK, though the people upstairs are noisy. It's big and has everything, even hair in the bath. I cleaned the bath and treated myself to a long hot soak. There is no soap nor dishwashing liquid. Florence hosts can be so mean!

Monday 3rd December 2007

Bruce rang this morning and while we were talking, I made the decision to go down to Fiumicino Airport on the Eurostar to meet him on Thursday.

Today on arrival at the exhibition, I set up my stand, carefully arranging my cards, displaying my album showcasing previous works, and laying out brochures. However, as I chatted with fellow artists, a common complaint was echoed - the lack of visitors to the exhibition. It was hard to ignore as the majority of those present throughout the day were artists themselves. It was a disappointing reality, especially considering the significant financial and emotional investments we'd made to be part of this event. Despite this shared frustration, there were bright spots in the day. I had the opportunity to connect with the New Zealand contingent and other artists from around the world. Additionally, a woman from an art gallery in the U.S. expressed genuine interest in my work. It was a glimmer of promise amid the challenges, a reminder that sometimes, it only takes one connection to change the course of one's journey.

After the end of the day, seven of us met for dinner. It was fun to finally let our hair down. We all drank too much, talked too much, laughed and laughed!

Tuesday 4th December 2007

Today, I'm looking for somewhere else to stay and I've found a better place. It's lovely and closer to the Fortress. It features a fresco on the ceiling and a expansive view out over Florence's tiled rooftops to the hills beyond. And it has an electric kettle with tea and coffee. That's not a normal thing to find in hotels in Italy. I won't talk about the effort of picking up my bags and lugging them over to the new place in the rain and it is so cold.

Once again, all is well in my world. I am happy. Honestly, living here and attending the Biennale is one constant change of fortune. The smallest thing that goes right, makes you ecstatic.

After a day of interacting with other artists and visitors, a new group of us went out for dinner to celebrate my neighbour, Nancy's birthday. I met Sue and her husband Peter from Canada. They're here to give support to Peter's artist brother. Peter will get on well with Bruce, as they have a shared love of rugby, as does the French artist Jon Paul.

I haven't had so much fun in ages.

I'm booked to go on a day trip to Siena tomorrow. I'd wait for Bruce to arrive and do the trip with him, but I have to admit, hanging around at the exhibition all day is quite tiresome.

Wednesday 5th December 2007

Today, I'm on a picturesque trip, winding through the rolling hills of the Tuscan countryside. It was a scene straight out of a travel magazine. But the real gem of the day was Siena. The city was well kept and free from any unsightly dog poo. What was even more surprising is, I didn't feel the sudden urge to grab a broom and start sweeping the streets myself.

We joined a walking tour around the city with the most gorgeous Italian lady. She was around my age and had a delicious sense of style. She brought the city to life with her commentary on the history, particularly the Palio di Siena, which Siena is most famous for. It's a horse race held twice each year, on 2nd July and 16th August, in the Piazza. From there, it was back on the bus to a country winery estate for lunch. Apart from the quintessential Italian lunch, we were privileged to have this lovely older gentleman playing the piano accordion, giving us some authentic Italian songs. I'll admit, I couldn't seem to wipe this silly grin off my face the whole time. What a day it was.

Tomorrow, I am travelling down to Rome on the Eurostar to meet Bruce at Fiumicino Airport.

Friday 7th December 2007

I left Florence early so I could stop in Rome and shop for a couple of hours before catching the express out to Fiumicino. What a breeze to travel with no baggage. All I have is a handbag and now, another large bag which has two feather Goose Down coats, which I bought for half price in a shop not far from Termini station. Having a quality Goose Down coat here is essential, as the winters are so cold. I couldn't believe my luck seeing these lovely coats on sale.

At the airport I waited and waited, checked the timetable, yes his plane had been delayed, but it's now been one and a half hours since his plane touched down and still, there was no sign of Bruce! I went to the Emirates counter and told them I was missing a husband. They sent me upstairs. I told the receptionist that my husband hadn't arrived on the flight he was supposed to. She looked at her computer and said, "Yes, he was on the plane. It was diverted to Milan. He got off, then we had to take his bags off before we flew onto Fiumicino" "What!!" I exclaimed, "That's silly! He wouldn't do that!" "Yes, he did". Distraught, I went back downstairs and lo and behold there he was coming through the automatic doors. I wiped my tears and we threw ourselves together. (Yep, just like the movies) What happened? Yes, they had diverted to Milan, but it was two women who had left the plane and didn't return. It was their bags that were taken off the plane. However, by mistake, they took Bruce's bags off too. They lost his luggage! He's been out the back all this time filling in forms.

It was so cold and all his clothes were in his bags, of course. But, luckily I had plenty of warm coats. He put my one on. He'd left New Zealand in the summer and arrived here in Italy in the middle of winter, now he's without warm clothes. We caught the train to Rome. Wrong train. Instead of Termini, by mistake, we were on the slow suburban train to Tiburtina.

Tiburtina station was being renovated. It was dark, and dingy, with graffiti everywhere. What a sight! Here was Bruce, dressed in my old coat! It was trimmed all around with fur and the sleeves came halfway up his arms. We both started laughing. It was clearly too small and he looked so funny. Not quite the first impression of Italy for him, that I'd imagined.

We hopped on the next train heading back to Termini Station via the Metro, where we caught the Eurostar for our trip to Florence. It was wonderful to be together again, and we had a lot to catch up on.

Chapter 12 - Besotted with Florence and Venice

BRUCE'S FIRST LOOK AT THE HOUSE!

"Art is unquestionably one of the purest and highest elements in human happiness. It trains the mind through the eye, and the eye through the mind. As the sun colours flowers, so does art colour life" John Lubbock

Friday 7th Dec 2007

Well rested and after a hearty breakfast we headed off to find a coat shop. There was one near our hotel, where Bruce bought a reasonably priced padded winter jacket and a few toiletries at another shop. These will keep him going until his luggage is back. It was late morning by the time we arrived at the exhibition. I introduced him to my new friends. He was pretty impressed with the way my artwork was displayed and the rest of the day was spent viewing the exhibition artwork and meeting other artists in the massive Fortress.

That evening a group of us went for dinner. Bruce ordered a steak. and when it came to the table, he looked at it forlornly. That was it, a steak on his plate, nothing else. Where were the vegetables? "Is this all I get for €16? I thought I was going to get a meal". He was not happy and complained to the waitress. She explained to us the vegetables had to be ordered separately! Whoops, I'm sorry.

We're in Italy, remember?

Thankfully, his bags turned up on the second night. They were dropped off at the hotel and were in the foyer when we returned from dinner.

Each day we dedicated a few hours in the morning to the exhibition, then made the most of our time in Florence by exploring the sights and indulging in some shopping. As we wandered the cobbled streets of Florence, we couldn't help but be enchanted by the city's Christmas decorations. They adorned every corner, turning the heart of this Italian gem into a scene from a winter fairy tale. It was a magical time for us, as first-timers to a Northern Christmas we revelled in the festive lights and the cosy glow that enveloped the city. Florence had a way of making it a Christmas we would always cherish as an unforgettable memory. Out of the blue, Bruce has developed an interest in shopping. First for new boots and then clothes – quite the unexpected turn! I'm thoroughly enjoying this new side of him, a result of being influenced by the style of Italian menswear and clothing stores we've encountered so far. Honestly, I can relate, as I find myself experiencing something similar.

It's worth noting, that for more than two decades, we've been engrossed in a multitude of all-consuming projects, and business ventures, in between renovating houses. At the end of this time, we were utterly drained. But now, a shift has occurred and we're basking in this newfound lightness and freedom, which has breathed new life into both of us, providing a fresh start with a renewed sense of vitality.

Mon 10th Dec 2007

It's our last day today. A relaxing day pottering around town and the exhibition, taking in a last-minute tour of Palazzo Pitti. We learn about the Medici family, who bought it in 1549. It became the chief residence of the ruling families of the Grand Duchy of Tuscany. Palazzo Pitti developed into a great treasure house as later generations amassed paintings, jewellery and luxurious possessions and was used as a power base by Napoleon. Later served as the principal royal palace of the newly united Italy. The palace and its contents were donated to the Italian people by King Victor Emmanuel III in 1919.

Afterwards, we headed back to the hotel to get dolled up for the grand dinner event of the night. It marked our last night here. We sat with Sue, Peter and others we had become close to over the last ten days. Tonight's event drew a crowd of 1300 attendees, including their partners and I must say, it was a seamless affair. The food was simply exceptional and we were treated to the absolute pinnacle of Italian cuisine. Here are a few examples:

Risotto alla Milanese, is saffron-infused risotto from Milan and is known for its creamy, luxurious texture and rich, aromatic flavour.

Bistecca alla Fiorentina: In Tuscany, a thick T-bone steak, is seasoned only with olive oil and salt. An example of Italian meat perfection.

Tiramisu: For dessert, a delightful combination of mascarpone cheese, coffee-soaked ladyfingers, and cocoa, is a sweet treat that encapsulates Italian dessert excellence.

Complemented by superb performances of Italian opera singers.

Being part of the Biennale has been an absolute privilege – an experience that's been truly marvellous!

To summarise the event: This event has reaffirmed to me to go with life's flow and it was a reminder of the importance to embrace unexpected opportunities.

When faced with the unforeseen, the key is to say yes and navigate the path as it unfolds. Interestingly, I hadn't really considered myself an artist, even though the desire was there. It would've been easy to have said no to this chance. Perhaps all one truly needs is that spark of desire to set things in motion.

From the time I received the weird email in my inbox nine months ago until now, has been a life-changing experience, and one I would've missed had I deleted it- the email! Which I could easily have done, as I'm not, or should I say I wasn't an experienced or confident artist. Things are about to change in that department.

Wednesday 12th December 2007

Yesterday, we spent the day with Sue and Peter on a day tour into the country for lunch and to sample wine and cheese from the area. We visited a couple of wineries. For lunch, we tasted locally made cheeses with pizza and pasta. Stopping at a few ancient villages to do some shopping and exploring. It was informative and fun.

San Gimignano was delightful. Known as the Town of Fine Towers, it is famous for its unique preservation of about a dozen of its tower houses, which, with its hilltop setting and encircling walls, form "an unforgettable skyline" and the views to the surrounding picturesque countryside are not to be missed. Before catching the bus back to Florence, we had a big fat gelato.

It was around eight o'clock when we arrived back in the city. There were big hugs all around as we said our fond and sad farewells to the Canadians. We enjoyed their fun company and shared many laughs over the past two weeks.

Off to Venice

This morning we set off early aboard the Eurostar, bound for Venice. Despite the damp and chilly weather, the thrill of visiting Venice for the first time is undeniable. And now, here we are – and everyone was absolutely right!

Venice is beautiful. I'm utterly smitten! Inside, I'm practically shouting it – "I love it! I love it! I love it!"

Venice, with its unique canals, stunning architecture, and rich textures, has sparked a whole new side of my creativity I never knew existed. The standouts for me were:

The Canals: They're amazing and create an absolutely captivating scene.

Venetian Palazzos: These historic palazzos showcase intricate stonework, which give a window into the city's history.

Cobbled Streets and Bridges: Worn, smooth cobblestone streets and timeless arched bridges. You are transported back to another era.

Venetian Glass: Vibrant Murano glass, crafted in intricate shapes and colors, is a true work of art.

The Gondolas: Each gondola, with its polished wood and delicate details, is a uniquely Venetian visual treat.

Mosaic Art: Stunning mosaics, from the Basilica di San Marco to smaller church facades.

The textures in Venice, whether underfoot or the aged buildings with their various hues of terracotta plaster, gently peeling from the walls, hold a special charm and quite literally made me giddy with ideas for art the whole time I was there.

And the Grand Canal – what an incredible sight! People, water taxis, barges and boats. Everything is transported on large barges. Food, construction products, fire engine boats, police boats, gondolas weaving in and out.

Grand Canal

The gondoliers look exceptionally handsome in their striped T-shirts, black pants and hats. They rule the waterways.

'Look out for me, because I'm so wonderful and gorgeous and all the ladies love me'.

Well, they're right.

The water around Venice is surprisingly clean and it doesn't stink at all. Honestly, if you were to believe what people tell you about different places in the world, you'd not venture anywhere.

Like many people, I too, hate to see the large cruise ships sailing down the small canal to the port. They simply dwarf San Marco Tower and the Square. They are too big and carry too many people. When they dock, four or five thousand people are expunged onto the tiny island. Sometimes there are two or three ships in port at once. Pouring into Venice every day in summer. This amount of people puts huge demands on facilities. The small alleyways become so crowded you can hardly move. What I can surmise from the locals is the cruise ship tourists have a hearty breakfast before leaving the ship, they get by with a snack for lunch, and then rush back to the ship for a hearty dinner. They buy trinkets and don't add that much value to the economy at all, except for port fees.

Anyway, I hear that the amount and the size of the ships are to be reduced.

After five days of gorgeousness, we're back on the Eurostar - zooming through Tuscan landscapes and heading back to Rome.

Bruce's First Look At The House

Sunday 16th December 2009

A little jaded, we arrived home from Venice late on Friday. Arriving into Introdacqua on the 7.30 bus from Sulmona.

It was dark, cold, drizzling and bleak. Emerging through the darkness were twinkling Christmas lights and decorations on the houses and in the streets. As usual, we were weighed down with bags and suitcases. Bruce hasn't been here and he has yet to see the house. (He went straight to Florence from Fiumicino).

We clambered out of the bus. It was not exactly the best time for viewing, with the plaster stucco peeling off the facade, exposing unsightly gaps. The gloom and drizzle added to the awful exterior. I asked him to look around and see if he could tell which one was our house.

Well, the whole sight looked dreary in the misty rain.

Ever the diplomat, he said, "Ahh, not quite sure." He had, of course, seen photos, but everything looked different in the night light. I pointed it out. "Yes" "Well, the front is easily fixed, we'll be able to strip this old plaster skin off in no time. Come on, show me the rest".

First look at the house.

On entering, it was cold and damp. I cranked the little fan heater into gear, even though the new gas boiler is hooked up and I turned the radiators on, it would take a while to heat the house. We walked through, commenting on each room. Like me, he loved it and could see that with a bit of hard work, and paint, it was going to come up a treat. We then settled down for a cup of tea, but, damn it all, the gas stove wasn't working. I couldn't boil the water or cook anything, for that matter.

I rang the plumber and luckily he was free to come and take a look. Turns out, because we had switched from bottled gas to mains gas supply we need to change this minuscule fitting for each of the burners on the stove and no, he didn't have these fittings. But, he explained, we could buy them from the gas stove supplier in Sulmona.

There you go, no dinner tonight and we were too exhausted to go out, so we settled for wine instead. We forced it down:)

The next morning it was starting to snow. We caught the ten o'clock bus to town. Our objective was to locate the gas fitting shop or else we wouldn't be able to cook anything for days. Next, will they have the parts? It turned out to be a huge mission, as we battled a blizzard!

By the time we arrived in Sulmona, it was starting to snow quite heavily. It was hard going and I only had a vague idea of where the store was and it was further than I expected. Somehow, Gino's friend recognised us and offered to drive us. He was in a hurry to beat the snow, so he couldn't wait while we were in the shop. I'm not sure what we would've done had he not picked us up. Yes, the shop did have the fittings.

At a fast pace, we made our way back to the bus stop. It wasn't easy, as by now it was blizzard conditions! In a hurry, we quickly stopped at a supermarket to grab some food. We scrambled onto the bus in the nick of time. It was touch and go, but the buses were still running even though the snow was coming down thick and fast. Turns out it was the last bus for days!

The gas fittings were good and were easily fitted. Yes, we can cook and the house had warmed up. I cooked soup, we lit the fire, hunkered down and watched a movie, dubbed in Italian.

Chapter 13 - Let the Renovations Begin

STARTING WITH THE OLD BATHROOM

"Do not go where the path may lead, go instead where there is no path and leave a trail" Ralph Waldo Emerson

Tuesday 18th December 2007

It didn't take Bruce long to start renovations. First, let's demolish the outdated bathroom. The terracotta-coloured hand basin and toilet were the first to get the heave-ho! After going into town to buy the tools required for the job, he took to it with gusto. First, by taking out the little bath and removing a corner of the wall, it made the space larger for a shower. However, this fairly easy job turned into a nightmare, which is pretty normal for a renovation.

Bathroom - Before

The rocks in the wall were huge, I mean, they were really big and heavy. We had no idea how we were going to get them down two flights of stairs. Isn't it weird, how when you start something, things fall into place? Such was the serendipity here. Lorenzo and Claudio were two big strapping construction workers from Poland, who were now working in Introdacqua. We'd met them at the bar a few days ago. Their English was OK, so we could converse. They agreed to come and work for us for a few days (paid) and help with manhandling the huge rocks into the wheelbarrow and then manoeuvre them slowly down the two flights of stairs into the garden, where they remain today as part of a garden feature. It took a week to demolish the small corner of the bathroom.

Friday 21st December 2007

Michele has come to the rescue several times assisting us with the buying of building products and he introduced us to the local hardware store, which is on the outskirts of town and it proves difficult for us to get to, but he has offered to take us whenever we want. Such kindness is everywhere we go.

Sulmona:

I've been introducing Bruce to Sulmona, which has been like rediscovering it for the first time myself. Such a beautiful ancient city. Apart from the passeggiata and the well known for the markets every Wednesday and Saturday, it's also worth mentioning, it's the home of the Italian confectionery known as Confetti. These are sugar-coated almonds and are traditionally given to friends and relatives at weddings and other special occasions. Confetti can be eaten or simply used as decoration. The local artisans also colour these candies and craft them into flowers and other creations. There are two main factories in town and several shops that sell these items, the most famous of which is Confetti Mario Pelino.

Sulmona Confetti

Christmas 2007

Our first white Christmas and thanks to the town's decorations and twinkling lights, turned out to be quite magical. It was a low-key event, for the first time in our married life, it was just the two of us. I prepared a classic roast of lamb, complemented by roasted potatoes and vegetables. For dessert, we enjoyed a storc-bought Italian dessert paired with ice cream. While I typically would have made a traditional Christmas Pudding made in a cloth, time and ingredients were in short supply this time around. A Christmas Pudding in a cloth was once my forte; I'd diligently boil the fruit pudding in a calico cloth, then hang it to mature for a couple of months.

Once we finished our meal and drank way too much, the evening unfolded cosily in front of the fire, a calming and stress-free affair.

A pattern is emerging. We renovate during the day and then most evenings we wander down to the bar where Bruce has met a few people who've become friends. Now and then we'll dine at the local family restaurant for a pizza or pasta.

On New Year's Eve, we were invited to a community night at the hall. It was a family event and a lot of fun. Before midnight we played games and did the limbo rock and dances, like the Grand ol' Duke of York (in Italian). Just before the clock struck midnight, everyone was prepared with their Prosecco and cake for the toasts. When the toasts were done, we went outside to see a brilliant fireworks display, which they didn't skimp on. Then, surprisingly, out came the bingo cards and we played bingo and other board games. We danced and danced to Italian music and didn't get home until four in the morning. Nobody got drunk, the teenagers didn't mind being with the olds and the children didn't appear to be getting cranky with the lateness of the hour.

Such well behaved, pleasant children. Is it because they get so much attention and everyone delights in the children here?

A New Kitchen!

Wednesday 9th January 2008

Lucia has been phoning Telecom for me every couple of days. That's right, still no phone. She and Alberto have been over. Alberto is going to tile the bathroom. He took us to Pratola to choose the bathroom tiles and tiles for the art gallery floor. For the new bathroom I've chosen white glossy rectangle tiles and, for contrast inserted in two places are tiles with transparent white roses. Lucia is also having her new kitchen installed and she's giving me her old kitchen. I insisted on paying her, but she wouldn't hear of it, saying she had no way to dispose of things like a large kitchen and saying it would cost her money to dump it, therefore I'd be doing her a favour by taking it away.

Fiona organised a man who had a truck and off we went over to Lucia's village to pick it up. The kitchen and all the bits and pieces related to it, such as the gas stove and a fabulous granite bench, were all stored in an old shed. We carefully loaded it onto the back of the truck and then drove slowly home.

We stored it in our downstairs cantina, where we set it out to see how it looked and if it would fit in the space. It's really nice and I would've chosen something like this, had I shopped for one. I'm not sure why she'd gone to the expense of buying another kitchen when this one was in good condition. The only thing she had against it was the colour and preferred a timber look. So, it's our good fortune.

My old kitchen, you could hardly call it a kitchen. A gas stove, a small sink and bench, a table used for a bench, and a cupboard above for the plates to drain. I'm looking forward to seeing my 'new' kitchen in place.

Old kitchen

We're going to put the new kitchen in the dining room, which is a large empty space between the now kitchen and the lounge. It'll work well as an eat-in dining room and kitchen combined. We won't be starting this stage until the upstairs bathroom is finished.

Meanwhile, we can use the other small bathroom on the middle floor.

I've had a notice about my home-caring job in the UK. I am to start my four day training on 9th February. Another five weeks.

My shipment from Milan still hasn't arrived. Giorgio has been investigating. He's so helpful, he rang a friend in the ministry in Rome to find out why I have to pay duty on my personal goods. Thanks to that phone call, it looks like €350.00 has been waived, but I still have to pay €560! I sent a cheque last week. Yes, I've had another call and it looks like it has been released and will be delivered next week.

Friday 11th January 2008

Today, I booked my ticket to London on Ryanair for €85.00 returning on April 29th.

The Permesso di Soggiorno saga; requires another six photos and two photocopies of everything, for a second time!

I've changed banks again. This time to the bank that Lucia uses, San Paulo. How pleasant they are, shaking my hand when I have completed my banking. That certainly does not happen in my hometown, New Zealand.

The bathroom revamp is coming on and the shower has ended up being a good size. Alberto will start laying the bathroom floor tiles today.

Sunday 13th January 2008

My large shipment from New Zealand finally arrived on Friday. I went through the list and surprise, surprise, everything appears to be here with only a couple of minor damages.

A start has been made on the kitchen. The toilet in the room next to where the new kitchen will be, has been smashed and a hole has been drilled through the two-foot thick wall. It was a very difficult job, as they had to drill through large rocks to accomplish the task. This is to allow the services to be put through to the sink and dishwasher. We will need to replace the toilet with a new one.

Tuesday 15th January 2008

Yesterday, the new kitchen was brought up from the cantina and placed into its new position. I love the granite bench and If you didn't know better you'd think it, the kitchen, had been made specifically for this space, as the pieces fit perfectly into its new home. To complete this, we just need a dishwasher and an expel air fan above the stove.

We have quite a few cupboards left over that don't fit in, so we'll be able to utilise them in the studio.

It's only a couple of weeks before Bruce returns to New Zealand and I depart for London a week or so later.

The parcel of clothes for winter, which I had posted some months ago in New Zealand, finally turned up the other day. It's so cold, I have needed them desperately. The artwork from the Florence exhibition has also arrived back safely.

Though things take a while, stuff does happen.

Still no Permesso.

Thursday 17th January 2008

Our new kitchen is functioning. I've been cleaning and restoring the stove. It works just fine. It's a treat to prepare, cook and eat in pleasant surroundings. We've demolished the old kitchen. Fiona took the old stove and most of the other things we didn't need, for her summer kitchen, of sorts. Each summer she moves all her kitchen, food etc, downstairs to her old cantina where they prepare, cook and dine. She and Mama stay cooler down there.

Friday 25th January 2008

This past week we've been putting the final touches on the two bedrooms. Michele has been such a help. He's done all the new electrical work. The radiators are working well. Every room in the house is cosy and warm. We've had the open fire in the lounge roaring every few nights. Toasty warm.

When we venture out to the local restaurant, it's always an occasion. People come to our table to introduce themselves, or we meet others we already know. It's warm, relaxing and the prices are reasonable. The locals are amazed we're still here during the winter, as most foreigners depart when the winter sets in. It's my favourite season, winter. A chance to have an open fire and cook toast on the hot embers and a joy to don my thick woollen clothes, boots, coats and mittens, cooking soups, slow-cooked casseroles with dumplings and making bread are my favourite pastimes over these cooler months.

In another life, we had an antique, double-oven coal-range. On cold, snowy days, I'd crank it up for the pleasure of sitting in my rocking chair and hand-quilting.

My type of 'hygge' before the term was coined.

Chapter 14 - Home-Caring in England

DOESN'T QUITE GO AS PLANNED!

"Always remember that you are absolutely unique. Just like everyone else". Margaret Mead

Wednesday 30th January 2008

I have taken to my bed. Bruce left for New Zealand yesterday. I travelled on the bus with him to Fiumicino. Then I came home on my own. Parting was awful and again, I question what I was doing? What am I doing and why? Yet, he remains totally positive about this move. We'll see how it pans out.

Meanwhile, I am going to stay here, in bed, until I feel better.

Wednesday 13th February 2008

I cleaned the house from top to toe and then proceeded to clear the art gallery space, putting the rest of my shipment away in preparation for Alberto to tile the floor while I'm away in England. He's asked me for payment upfront, as he's going to visit his girlfriend in South America for a couple of weeks. Begrudgingly, I gave him €800.00. I mean, what could I do? Lucia, his mother, has been so helpful to me. He's promised to have the bathroom shower and the floor in the art gallery tiled and completed by the time I return from my stint in England.

I leave for London next week to start my four day training for home caring in England.

Thursday 14th February 2008

Valentines Day. I had a loving text from Bruce.

I'm in a small town in Essex, UK, at the moment. I arrived in London on Tuesday afternoon.

Lucia drove me to Pescara Airport to catch the flight to Stansted Airport. Her friend Richard was with her. He's going to London on the same flight. We sat next to each other and as it turned out he was an interesting chap. A retired Army Officer from the British army. He sold his English pub and has bought a house with some land across the valley from where I live in. Alberto has been tiling his kitchen and lounge.

Richard is totally obsessed with Ovid, who was a famous poet born in 43BC in Sulmona. For the entire two-and-a-half-hour flight, I was educated about him and I made a mental note to read more about this famous man. Richard's ambition is to restore one of the buildings on his property for a multi-roomed B&B, to give lectures and tutorials to Uni students, all centred around Ovid, his work and his life.

It's wonderful to meet passionate people. He is so enthusiastic and I encouraged him to go for it and I look forward to watching his progress.

On arrival into Stansted, Richard went his way, while I was held up in customs over this darned Ancestry Visa and the fact that I wasn't accompanied by my husband! In anticipation of exactly this situation, I'd asked my friend to write a dummy itinerary, saying that Bruce was arriving on a flight from New Zealand tomorrow. I told him (the customs man) that I had been in Italy and we were travelling separately.

It worked. And after a lengthy discussion, I was allowed through. Frankly, the UK customs often handle us New Zealanders as though we're some sort of threat. We undergo intense scrutiny and are met with a sense of disdain. It frustrates me to consider the sacrifice of countless New Zealand soldiers in both World Wars. I'm certain they'd be appalled by the treatment we're subjected to nowadays. Despite New Zealand's Commonwealth membership and Queen Elizabeth being our head of state, we're treated like outsiders or "aliens." Since then, it has happened time and again.

I caught the bus for Liverpool St Station and from there I boarded a train bound for the little obscure village in Essex where the training was to be held. Once I arrived and settled in, I ventured into the common room/kitchen to make a cup of tea. There I met a group of women of my ilk from a variety of countries. Like me, they too, were on their overseas adventures and also like me, thought home caring was an ideal way to earn money and see the country or the world, for that matter. The group is a diverse collection of women aged over fifty hailing from New Zealand, Australia, South Africa and Poland. They are single, married, divorced and widowed. Some have sold their houses and put their possessions into storage, or are renting out their houses while they're away. Others have sold everything to make a new life. This group of women has shed light on the vast array of experiences and choices older women are embarking upon in the wider world who are looking for a fresh start.

The money you earn home-caring is good, around $1300.00 NZD per week. All your meals and accommodation are included in the position.

Friday 22nd February 2008

After completing the course, the majority of girls were assigned their positions and departed, dispersing to jobs primarily within the Suffolk and Essex regions. However, a few of us, including myself, weren't as fortunate. The roles we were designated wouldn't start for another two weeks.

OMG, I had to stay in this awful place for another two weeks! The weather was appalling. I hadn't bought any handwork with me, thinking I would buy some when I got to a town. There were no craft shops in this small village. They moved me from the hostel to a small cottage. The other girls were able to go and stay with friends in the region until their jobs started, but as I didn't know anyone, I was stuck here, in a house with a girl from Poland, whose English was all but non-existent. Though we did establish a pattern where I could help her with her English. I had read all the books I'd bought with me and there was limited Internet.

Do you know how long twelve days can be in this situation? Well, I can tell you, I think I would have preferred prison. I would cry on the phone with Bruce, lamenting how the unorganised Home Care administrators had wasted, stolen even, twelve days of my life. Seems silly now, (in light of our Covid lockdowns) but at the time, it was extremely frustrating. It never occurred to me that this situation could arise and it wasn't brought to my attention that I could be laid up for days on end. As the weather abated I would venture out into the cold, dreary countryside for walks to try and clear my head. I wrote in my journal. 'This is the worst period of my life'. I have since reconsidered and think if that was the worst thing to happen to me, then I am doing OK!

Finally, I have my assignment: On Sunday I travel by train to start my first position on Monday morning. I feel apprehensive, excited and stimulated - all in one breath - to be gone from my present living conditions.

Monday 25th February 2008

For the purposes of your sanity and mine, I have condensed my time with the Home Care agency and the time I spent in the UK to bullet points!

I was assigned to two caring positions for around three weeks each. Both clients had severe disabilities. In New Zealand, these clients would be required to have specialist care in a facility that was qualified to deal with their extreme conditions.

- My first client was a very large gentleman with major disabilities and an angry persona. His house wasn't up to the task of allowing for multi-hoists and wheelchair access into the rooms. The doorways are only 78cm wide. The procedure for bedtime, for instance, was a succession of around twenty five movements which included the client being hoisted on and off a stair lift and a series of four hoists throughout the house. The bathroom, had barely enough room for one person let alone two hoists. The house was small, damp and two stories. Quite impractical for him and his carer.

- The other client was a lovely lady who had extreme dementia. We were locked in her cold, mouldy house 24/7, as she had a tendency to bolt and there were no fences or locked gates! The house was in a bad state of repair and her previous carer was sloppy. There was barely any food and what was in the fridge, was rotten.

Well, you get the picture! Talking about pictures, her photos around the lounge showed a vibrant, beautiful woman and loving mother in her previous life. To now be reduced to a shell, not aware of her surroundings is heartbreaking and hard on all concerned. It is the worst aspect of Alzheimer's disease. I urge everyone to be aware and to learn how to care for their brain health.

I feel I was assigned to these cases, as I was deemed to be the most qualified, due to having owned an elderly care home in New Zealand. Though the authorities try, sometimes the practical solutions are overlooked and there don't appear to be enough checks and balances in the system. When that happens both parties suffer. I stuck out my tenure with the two clients. I managed to finish my time with my last client without going entirely crazy. I terminated my contract with the carer agency, booked my ticket, left England and went back to Italy.

Tuesday 15th April 2008

I arrived back at my house the other day and have since spoken to the other girls (emails) whom I met on the course. Compared to their caring positions, Yes, I did get two traumatic cases, while they had a jolly old time. One even had the use of a car and would go visit friends of the person they were caring for. I have such unhappy memories of my UK experience, that I cannot go into detail here. I am going to put it all behind me and move on.

Meanwhile, let's talk about Alberto, my tiler.

He'd gone off to South America to visit his girlfriend with my advance of €800 in his pocket, on the understanding that he would complete the list of jobs by the time I returned home. With that in mind, I was full of anticipation upon entering the house.

First, I went into the gallery (the old cantina on the ground floor) looking forward to seeing my lovely new tiled floor. But, no it was the same as when I'd left. No work had been done! The tiles in the bathroom shower had been finished to a very poor quality of work and the grout wasn't the right colour! It all needed to be dug out and redone. The poor quality of work surprised me, as the rest of the bathroom he had completed was of a very high standard. I called him. Oh, he might be able to get over here sometime and sort it all out....he might!!

By this time I'm livid. I knew he was over at Richard's working at his house. I rang Richard and explained to him what had happened, only to be informed that he and Alberto had fallen out. No, nothing to do with me.

Saturday 19th April 2008

I finally tracked Alberto down and he arrived a couple of hours later. I asked him what game was he playing, and his reply was "What game?" "Well, what about our agreement and the €800.00 I gave you prior to going on holiday" "What money?" he said. I showed him the receipt, with his signature. "Oh," he said sheepishly "I forgot you gave me the money" honestly! By this time my patience was wearing thin. Together we viewed the awful job in the bathroom. He gave me some cock 'n bull story, but he did agree to fix up his mess and start the floor in the gallery.

I tell you, I'm finished with him once he fixes everything up.

Coming to Italy to live is not for the faint-hearted. You have to hold on to your dreams, otherwise, you may lose them in the day to day frustrations of dealing with the Italian ways, whether it be tradespeople or the huge amount of bureaucracy.

Today I'm thinking back to the time when I first bought the house in June last year. My dream is to have a working art studio, a small art gallery and to teach art at my home.

It all seems a long way off.

I suppose Alberto went home and told Lucia, his mother, some story. Most probably how I let him down! I don't know. I do know that no matter what I say, she will side with him. She has three grown boys and they can do no wrong. When it comes to work, they are tired. Not like their Mother! Even Alberto, who I now know to be very cunning and only works when he has to. Lucia's house has been in shambles for over a year, while she waits for him to finish tiling the kitchen floor. Meanwhile, she struggles between a multitude of boxes and other household stuff, just to get into her bed each night. The other one is still at home, with no job and no motivation!

Thursday, April 24th 2008

This past week has made a big difference in the list of jobs to be done and completed. We, Lucia and I are still OK. Alberto is back on board. He's fixed the shower floor and has finished tiling the art gallery floor. It looks stunning.

It cost me another €700.00 for the levelling compound. He has a worker with him and apparently, according to Richard, he was the one who did the tiling in the shower and made the mess.

I asked Alberto to find a way to get rid of the unsightly flue for the boiler on the outside of the house and replace it. He got his lad to take it down. It was made of asbestos and quite a mission to dismantle and I feared for his helper. He replaced it with a flue made of stainless steel, set in a different position.

Simone, the technician for the gas boiler, said he didn't think it would affect the boiler system. Well, he was wrong. That night, after I was in the shower for a few minutes, it went cold! With a towel wrapped around me, wet and cold, I ran down two flights of stairs to start the boiler again. This happened the following day, so there had to be something major wrong. I called the plumber to sort the problem out! There was quite a set to between us out in the garden and we had a pretty heated argument. From her bathroom window, Fiona tried to intercept and translate for me. It appears Alberto was wrong in removing the other dangerous flue and the new outlet was not suited to this boiler. I either had to replace the chimney with a new large stainless steel chimney or install a new boiler, which would work with the new exhaust. There was no way around it and I ended up upgrading the boiler. Another €1200.00.

The radiators are not working properly. I called Davide (my new plumber) and it appears the guts of the system need to be upgraded, as it has rusted. So another €1700.00 to put in a whole new system. The radiators themselves were OK, just the system that sends the water around to all the radiators. The thermostat has also decided to pack it in.

At the moment it is one thing after another! I still don't have a landline. Telecom is just not coming to sort it out. This has been an ongoing problem for months now and is driving me to distraction. Thank goodness for mobile phones.

Coming to Italy to live by myself has been a bigger challenge than I thought it would be and quite frankly, it's becoming a financial disaster!

Every day is a drama, though I'm making headway with the language, as I make an effort to learn.

The two bedrooms are now more or less finished with my bedding arriving from New Zealand.

The bedroom before.

After

All in all, though and funnily enough, I'm loving it here. I'm rejuvenated. Every morning, I wake up in this cool mountain air, curious to find what the day has in store. The quiet acknowledgement of passersby, 'Ciao Eva, Buongiorno, come stai oggi?' (Good morning, how are you today) 'Buono, grazie' or 'Bene Bene' I reply - makes you feel anything is possible. The poppies are starting to bloom in the fields. On the way to Sulmona on the bus the other day I spied them. They were glorious. I've been for numerous walks, taking photos.

There are definitely some lonely, tough times here on my own. On those evenings, I'll pour a couple of glasses of wine, turn up the music, and let myself dance and sing—basically throwing a little one-man party

It's Thursday. I'll go over to the small vegetable market here and get a few things and then go down to the new supermarket. Yes, we have a small supermarket here in the village now.

When I come back, I'll paint the outside of the doors to the art gallery. A blue lime wash.

Chapter 15 - I am Totally On My Own

STILL NO TELECOM!

"A man must shape himself to a new mark - when the old one goes to ground". Sir Ernest Shackleton.

Thursday 8th May 2008

I'm a huge admirer and fan of Sir Ernest Shackleton - his amazing journey to Antarctica is one of the world's most incredible survival stories. I'm in need of his quote now (above). This is due to my plan being derailed of becoming a home carer in the UK each year - this is my new plan - to venture forth, full steam ahead and get the house ready to take B&B guests.

Over the past couple of weeks, I've made a start, painted and repaired the front entrance door. The door is made up of two doors. You normally only use one door for entry, the other is permanently closed, unless you have a large object to bring into the house. Restoring the door, which has had years of extreme weather beating against it and hasn't had any repairs, was not an easy project. Each door was heavy and had to be lifted up for me to lift it off its hinges, then laid on the ground out in the street. This was the only place I could work, as I used the electric sander to take off the very worn and degraded varnish. There was a lot of preparation work to do apart from sanding, they needed to be scraped and filled in places.

Anyway, the locals seemed to get a great kick out of seeing this New Zealand woman doing renovating stuff out on the street. I don't think Italian women do home renovations, but I could be wrong and I only say this as they were so surprised, aghast even, that I was doing this type of work.

Well, we Kiwi gals do. I've been doing home renovations ever since I had my first home when I was seventeen years old and it's impossible to count the number of doors and windows I've painted, external and internal walls painted or wallpapered and around eight house renovations.

Fifteen years ago I was a builder's labourer for Bruce when we built our large, barn-style house in the country. My jobs included cutting the 4"x 2" timber for the studs, putting up wall frames, painting internal walls, keeping the site clean and tidy and when it came time, interior decorating. These were all part of being a general hand. And now, here I am renovating again! But, this house here in Italy is absolutely my last renovation - I am done!

Back to my front door: I gave the doors two coats of undercoat and a couple of topcoats, as they were open to the elements. The job took a few days to complete, which gave me ample time to chat with people walking past, or they would say "Brava, Brava" as they went by.

Saturday 10th May 2008

Tackling The Garden:

The weather is starting to become warmer, so now I'm fixated on the garden. It hasn't been tended to for many years and has grown wild. Though it's not huge, I'm thankful for it. I borrowed a fork and shovel from Fiona and got stuck in. To get rid of all the weeds, meant turning the soil over with the fork and pulling out the weeds by the roots, shaking the soil and loading them into large black bags which Roberto then collected for disposal. It was backbreaking work, but immensely satisfying. At the end of each day, I was exhausted though happy with my progress. I could actually see where I'd been. Turning the garden over this way is a great form of exercise. In the evening I work on a plan for the new layout of the garden. I'm enjoying the challenge and it's going to be a beautiful retreat.

The neighbours again were surprised by a woman doing what they would call man's work and asked why I didn't get a man into rotary hoe the ground. Yes, I agree, having the ground turned over with a rotary hoe would make the garden look good for a while, though personally, I think the rotary hoe merely disperses the weeds and makes them worse in the long run. I worked with a sense of urgency, as I needed to get the plants in the ground. I'll plant silverbeet (chard), lettuces and a few herbs. Perhaps spread some wildflowers. I want to create an area for an outdoor table and sun umbrella, with a curved path of stepping stones to the back gate. And of course lots of lavender.

Thursday 15th May 2008

Mary and Len arrived back from the States. It was good to see her again. We had a few wines and caught up on all we'd been doing over the past few months since she left. Talking about drinking wine. I now have strict rules in place, as I can see that it wouldn't take much for it to become a habit. Especially here, where the wine is so good and very reasonably priced. So, now I only drink on days beginning with 'T'. Today and Tomorrow. No, seriously, no more than three evenings per week and then one or two glasses.

Mary's been visiting on Monday, Tuesday, Wednesday and she'll most probably come today. She is very depressed over her finances and has put her house renovation on hold. Yesterday, she came over and basically just sat there in silence.

Last night, Michele invited us all to go to dinner with him. I declined. I was exhausted, as I'm still working in the garden, plus painting the French doors in the bedrooms and the furniture throughout the house. I texted and declined, but he insisted. I relented, had a shower and off we went to the local restaurant. Mary held the floor the whole evening.

Lucia rang this morning, no, Telecom is not coming today.

The garden is finally free from all the weeds. I've raked it over. Now, to lay it out. I've been marking out where the footpath and the gardens will go with spray paint.

I can't believe I was so happy last week and this week I am in the depths of despair. I spoke with Giorgio telling him of my anguish over the Telecom debacle. He has assured me that he will contact them and see what's going on.

For me, I have to focus on the plan and that is to finish the house, so I can devote myself entirely to my art and my guests when they arrive! I've become a bit of a recluse, happier when left to my own devices and to see people at my own pace. I've figured out, that here in this village, it's best to let things happen in their own time.

Mary is heading back to the States tomorrow and tells me she's not sure when or if she'll be back again, due to her financial position.

Buying the car

The time has come for me to think about buying a car. Not easy and I'm not sure where to start. I went to a couple of car dealers, but I haven't found one who speaks English.

Wednesday 21st May 2008

I rang Richard to see if he could help me look for a car and together we went to another dealer, with no luck. He then thought of his friend Gianni, who is helping him with the authorities regarding getting his B&B legal. He rang him and made a time for us to meet. I must say I wasn't impressed with Gianni at first. My first thoughts were that he looked a bit dodgy. His clothes were scruffy and he had an unkempt air about him. But, hey I was desperate to buy a car and he seemed to know where to look. He has a good handle on English as he told me he was born in the USA, and his Italian parents moved back to Sulmona when he was ten years old. I explained the type of car I was looking for and the approximate price. He took us to a, just as dodgy-looking mechanic, whose garage was down a graffiti-lined back alleyway, that I was hesitant about entering. He introduced us to Matteo, a little guy with a pleasant smile and not a stitch of English. He told us to come back in a couple of days.

My brother rang from New Zealand and asked how I was and what was I doing. What do you say? After six or seven months I'm still waiting for Telecom to give me a landline so I can at least have dial-up Internet. I am still waiting for my Permesso di Soggiorno, so I can buy a used car. It's difficult for me to get around (well, to the hardware store) and it's difficult to communicate with my loved ones. But, no, I didn't tell him any of my problems. It was great to hear from him and we had a short chat. Mobile phone. (expensive, back then.)

Sometimes, as I said before, I'm in the depths of despair and then just as quickly I'm in the heights of euphoria over something as simple as the views of the magnificent mountains with fields of poppies in the foreground or the men playing cards in the Piazza or ladies chatting on a street bench, as the heat of the day starts to cool. Then there are the schoolchildren in their school uniforms. They're a picture in their pale blue, in what looks like choir-boy tops, which are about knee length and worn over jeans or trousers. The primary school itself is small by New Zealand standards. Tucked in between houses, it's a three-story building with large windows. The outdoor areas are also small, with a tiny play area. They wouldn't be able to play footy or netball. The place for sport is on the outskirts of the village at the sportiva. I've noticed it's a quiet environment for children. There's no screaming around the playground during their breaks, instead, they tend to sit quietly chatting or playing on the swing and the small slide. Quite a contrast to our schools.

But I digress, again, getting back to my fluctuations between despair and euphoria – is this what real living is about? I think it is. I love the challenges it brings on a daily basis. This new life of mine and yes it is mine. At this present point in time, I'm not reliant on anyone else for me to be happy. If it's going to be, then it's definitely up to me and this is what I'm enjoying the most. I don't understand the TV, so I don't see the news on a daily basis and I'm not reading newspapers. When I want to listen to the radio station it has a good mix of the old tunes of the eighties, so that's OK.

And you'll recall, this is where we came in:

This first winter alone, where I found myself in an unexpected battle with loneliness. That dreaded "L" word that no one admits for fear of being deemed unsociable - "Loneliness"! I wasn't prepared for this and each day it wrapped around me like a heavy cloak that I couldn't shake off. The winter chill from outside seeped into my bones, turning even the simplest moments into aches I'd never known before. The absence of Bruce, whose laughter once filled the rooms of the house and my life with quiet, funny repartee, now left me adrift in an unfamiliar solitude.

This solitude was of my own making and it was unlike anything I'd experienced before. My TV spoke a foreign language, the newspapers were indecipherable, and the warmth of daily conversation had vanished. In a bid to escape, I would head down to the local bar, but it often led to nights spent in a haze or drowning in wine, a path I knew was going to end in disaster.

So I forced myself to stay home and it was in the quiet of those nights I began to learn about myself. From the outside, I appeared unchanged, but inside, my mind was in turmoil. I knew I had to confront this isolation and learn to find a way to be content in my own company. Slowly, day by day, I inched towards this newfound independence. I started to form new habits in my diet, in my daily activities and in the art studio, even when inspiration was elusive. I would resist the urge to escape to the Piazza and the bar - instead, I actually found solace in the simple act of cleaning the house. A form of therapy in itself.

It took some time, but eventually, I established a daily routine that brought a sort of order to my life here. And as the days passed, it evolved into a consistent state of contentment and happiness.

Loneliness!

At first, I hated It!

Then I learned to live with It!

Then I learned to love It!

Loneliness conquered! It is one of the hardest, yet most important lessons a woman can learn.

I am enjoying my enforced isolation and feel a sense of freedom in the thought that I'm beginning to resurrect the real me! For the first time in my life, I can say I am totally on my own. Yes, I have Bruce to confide in, but he can't help me here. He's a world away, physically and emotionally.

Actually, this has been a good exercise for him as well. Telling me our separation of sorts has benefited him in many ways and now has to think for himself, I mean in the more mundane ways, like buying groceries, cooking and fending for himself. Cleaning the house, washing and ironing his clothes. In the past I've done all these things, though he does help, he's never had to do these things for himself and he's become more aware of the smaller things in life and I think that's a good thing myself. Furthermore, we've become closer, even though we've always communicated well, now there's more depth. I'm quite concerned for his welfare on a deeper level and he is for me. I'm concerned that his new job isn't getting him down or that he isn't working too hard and long each week.

He was also telling me that he's actually noticing his day-to-day activities more now and finding himself living in the moment, even feeling more invigorated overall. Plus, getting a grip on managing his time efficiently and using it to reflect, gather his thoughts and reading uplifting personal development books. It's like he's rediscovering himself. I guess it makes sense when you're solely depending on your own decisions and actions. I love the idea that we're on this journey/adventure together in our own individual ways.

It's not just the journey, but the magic of the inner journey. And I'm realising that for the first time in a long time, I feel truly joyful when surrounded by Italian culture.

Chapter 16 – The Value of Solitude

DISCOVERING MAY SARTON

"No matter how hard the past is, you can always begin again" Buddha

> May Sarton (*Author: Journal of a Solitude*) says: the value of solitude is - there's nothing to cushion against attacks from within! And there's nothing to help balance at times of stress and or depression. She explains; the reason for depression are not as interesting as the way one handles it! For her, and I quote, 'She started to water the plants and feed her cats and suddenly joy came back - as she was fulfilling a simple need.

Myself, for example, I clean the house, I knit, make art or do handwork. Walking on the beach or in nature is a sure-fire cure for the blues. These days I can add making pasta and bread to this list. The biggest thing IMO - is to be grateful everyday.

Friday 23rd May 2008

We've had good luck on the car front. Yesterday, Gianni drove me back to the mechanic's garage and we took a Fiat Punto out for a run. It has a diesel engine and has been stripped down and re-bored, or whatever. The only problem for me was, it didn't have air-con and it wasn't automatic. According to Lucia and Gianni, both of these aren't very common in used cars here.

I asked Michele to come and check the car out, as in New Zealand we like to have an opinion from a friend or get it checked by the Automobile Association, so I was surprised when he said, 'No, I don't need to look at it. If the guy (the mechanic) says it's good, then it is!' OK, in that case, I offered the mechanic a hundred less than he wanted. He accepted. The deal was done. Buying the car was the easy part, now for the documentation!

This was the procedure for me, it may be different in other parts of Italy.

Yes, the car had to have a revisione, a warrant of fitness. Done. Next, insurance, third-party insurance is required and is extremely expensive, €800.00 per year. Now go to the auto school to change the ownership documents. Wait, you have to have your Permesso di Soggiorno. Mine still hasn't arrived from Rome. A couple of weeks ago I went to the police station to complete the procedure, which entailed more documents, as well as the previous ones. Some papers did come back. They came with a number which I had to take to the Police station. I was then photographed and fingerprinted, yes, every finger, but still, I wait for the final document to come to enable me to buy the car.

Gianni and I both went to the Police Station - let's just stop there for a moment - I was still thinking he may be a bit dodgy, but when he had no qualms about going to the Police Station with me, I realised he was not like that at all and he also had friends here at the station that greeted him in a friendly manner and where, thanks to him, the Police gave me a temporary Permesso, which allowed me to buy the car. Great, but the car is owned by two brothers and one of them can't make it today and everyone has to be in the room on that day to do all the signatures.

So now it will be tomorrow morning for the signing.

Monday 26th May 2008

Saturday morning, after buying my weekly fruit and veggies from the market, I met with Gianni at the office. The brothers arrived. We signed all the necessary documents and then went to the mechanic's garage. I'm now the proud owner of a blue Fiat Punto, nothing fancy, but a good reliable basic car, which I have dubbed the Tractor. Now, to drive my car home. This is the part I've been silently stressing about for some time. We drive on the left-hand side of the road in New Zealand. Here in Italy, I need to drive on the other side. Gianni agreed to drive me home in the car with Matteo following behind to take him back to town. I thanked them both for all their help and they drove off.

The car was parked in the street across from my house. Not directly outside, but I can see it from my lounge balcony. I was so happy to have my own car, even if I wasn't keen on getting behind the wheel yet. I do have an International driver's license, which will suffice until I can figure out how to get an Italian license.

No more buses and bus timetables for me.

Tuesday 27th May 2008

I'm at the end of my tether with Telecom! So, Fi thought it would be a good idea to talk to the Sindaco, the town Mayor. Lina, who works at the commune and speaks very good English, is happy to translate for me. I told him my story and the problems I've been having getting a landline. He immediately picked up the phone and rang Telecom! Wow, I was impressed. I could tell by the tone of his voice he was telling them in no uncertain terms that they were to give me priority. We'll see what happens now.

I'm still looking at my car parked over on the other side of the street, not yet confident about driving. I haven't seen nor heard from Lucia for a while. Man, she is hot and cold, up and down. Either all over you like a rash or shuns you. Frustrating.

Bruce has texted me. He's coming over in about six weeks for the summer.

Meanwhile, I've been painting various pieces of furniture and other bits and bobs around the house. I still have quite a bit of renovating and painting to do before he gets here.

I've been working on all three sets of French doors, as they're in bad shape and need a lot of preparation. I take each one out onto the balcony and work on it there, as both sides need sanding, filled and then I paint them with an undercoat and two topcoat's in an off-white colour. The transformation from the dark peeling varnish to the lighter colour brightens the room and this type of house suits the new white look. Both bedrooms are almost finished and now the French doors are completed the bedrooms have come to life. The dark brown internal doors still need to be painted white as with the large wardrobe and dresser.

Wednesday 28th May 2008

I received a letter from Telecom! They're coming tomorrow. Yeah, right? I'll believe that when I see them. Mind you, I haven't had a letter before.

Yesterday afternoon, when all the shops were closed and the roads were quiet, I gingerly took the car for a run. I drove to the supermarket in Sulmona very slowly! Some supermarkets stay open in the afternoons. What freedom. This is the first time I've been to a supermarket on my own. Normally, I would go on the bus or with Lucia or in Fiona's little car, which had limited space. This time I didn't have to keep my eye on the bus timetable or worry about the number of products I could carry when walking two blocks to the bus. As a rule, I don't enjoy supermarket shopping, but today I did. I had a great time looking at the different foods on offer. There were only a few other people in the store, so it was very relaxing. I loaded my trolley with all sorts of weird and wonderful concoctions. It was certainly cheaper than the local alimentare in the village.

Friday 30th May 2008

I now have the phone on and an immense weight has been lifted from my shoulders. To have a landline again is pure bliss. Not so much for phoning people, as I have my mobile, but because in this small village in the mountains, we don't have access to broadband Internet. We only have dial-up, hence the need for a landline. The linesman was only here for fifteen minutes. That's all it took and no sooner was it hooked up, than my favourite Uncle from New Zealand rang on my mobile phone. I gave him my new number and we talked for over an hour. What a delight. Then I went onto the Internet immediately to download my emails. To email and to be connected to the outside world, I would normally go by bus to town, or to the bar. After being on the Internet for a few hours, I cleaned my car and headed into town. This time I went to the hardware store a few miles out of town to pick up some renovating supplies. I sang all the way back to the village.

This week my whole life has changed and all was well in my world again.

Sunday 1st June 2008

The phone is getting a real workout. Bruce and I spoke for three hours. He's booked tickets for his trip, deciding to go through LA and visit his sister. When he returns here, he's planning to re-roof the house with a long-run, aluminium look-alike, pressed tile in terracotta colour and to finish landscaping the backyard. So:

- I need to organise the roofing materials.

- look for paving tiles for the outdoor seating area.

He's also going to work on the front of the house and for that, we'll need a cherry picker.

I'm still slogging away in the garden and I've used old roof tiles to form the edges of the vegetable garden. I found a number of very heavy concrete blocks and have used these as paving stones to mark a path down to the gate. First, I dug a hole to place them level with the ground and it's been backbreaking work, but it's visually appealing. I'll start planting soon.

Sunday 8th June 2008

In the midst of renovations, painting doors became more than home improvements, as I tried to shake off lingering doubts regarding Bruce's eight day stay in LA. As I painted, silly thoughts surfaced – was this payback for my time in Italy? Will our relationship last as a long distant marriage? It's incredible how physical space can amplify our thoughts and emotions. Friends had hinted at a rocky road. Maybe it won't go the distance. Excuse the pun.

The day-to-day trials must be overcome - like getting the place sorted, without losing sight of the dream itself, which is to be in the studio to work on art each day. I've come to the conclusion that I'm the sort of person who likes to have my T's crossed and my I's dotted before I can start my artist journey. I want to start with the knowledge that all the chores are out of the way so everything is in order and there are no loose ends or distractions.

Thursday 12th June 2008

The first impressions I had of Gianni and Matteo being a bit shady were wrong and I need to re-evaluate and take all my bad thoughts back. They are beautiful, generous people and have been a tremendous help to me with the car and a few other things that have cropped up. Gianni has become a firm friend, one I can trust and he patiently gives me tips and advice on the hows and whys of Italian ways.

Lucia appears to have abandoned me at the moment, well it could be permanent. I hope not, even though at the moment she's been helping her boys and their never-ending dramas. I'll keep to myself and focus on the projects in hand.

Such a pleasure living in this little village; the comings and goings of everyone when I'm out walking, which is a lot. In the evenings I sit on my top balcony and listen to the sounds of Italy - people chatting in the street - the birdlife here is prolific, chaffinches, thrushes, blackbirds, and even robins. I love hearing the woodpeckers. We don't have them in New Zealand, so they're a novelty. I have a variety of walks around the village. All are special but have distinct features. Via Aldo Moro, is a steep walk into the forested hills above my house. Not only does it give your body a complete workout, but all your senses as well. On a warm day, the air is thick with the scent of pine. It is intoxicating. For the visual senses, you're rewarded with enchanting glimpses of the village below. And for me, it's the rock formations that never fail to delight. My imagination is running wild for future art pieces. On reaching the top, I look out over expansive views that stretch across fields and valleys to the distant terracotta rooftops of Sulmona. I stop on the way down to catch my breath at a place where you can sit on the ground and from this elevated vantage point, you can witness the sounds of daily village life below – the rhythmic tolling of church bells, and the drifts of laughter that floats upward. Words fail to capture the essence of this moment, "magical" is the closest that comes to mind.

Glimpse of the village below.

The view as I reach the top of my walk.

I've also been venturing up to Tara a few times a week and I see they've begun renovating the lovely old house and have cleared the scrub and most of the trees. I hope they don't remove the cherry tree in front.

As I write my journal each morning, in the street below, I hear the soft sounds of the man sweeping the streets and chatting with passers-by. He uses a large straw broom and does this part of the village at the same time each morning. I can see the florist across the street, setting up for the day, adding a variety of beautiful flowers and potted trees out on the step.

Chapter 17 - I am here - I wanted to shout

I'M ALMOST THERE!

"Italy has filled up the void left by false and narrow-hearted friends. I already see people here are without envy, hatred or malice." A line inspired by George Eliot

Sunday 15th June 2008

It's glorious sitting up here on the top balcony, with the sun on my back. I'm in a pondering mood. (It seems I ponder a lot lately.) I've just woken and I'm in that semi-drowsy state, thinking about my previous life. The transition to this slower pace of living has been a revelation for me, one that I couldn't have imagined in my previous, frantic existence. Back then, I was running a Nursing Home and was in a constant race against the clock, living in a state of perpetual urgency – a never-ending cycle of "hurry, hurry, scurry, scurry." This is a phrase I used to use a lot, as I juggled Government audits, report preparations, relentless appointments, and a constant stream of people, residents and staff all vying for my attention. It was as if the clock was always working against me, and there were never enough hours in the day to complete the necessary tasks.

Yet today, all of that feels like a distant memory. In this new chapter, I find it hard to fathom the magnitude of this change which has taken place in the span of just one year. In this tranquil and unhurried existence, I've discovered the beauty of slowing down, savouring life's simple moments and appreciating the unhurried cadence of each day. It doesn't matter what has caused this transformation; I'm more than ready to embrace it with open arms.

I've started to organise my studio, unpacking and stacking my entire range of art supplies. I don't have enough shelves.

Last evening was beautiful. Mama and Fiona were in the garden chatting to the other neighbour, Antonella and I was on my balcony doing handwork, making rosettes for a wall hanging. Fiona was singing quietly. This is what I've been working toward. To be able to spend the day quietly working doing handwork. This is it! I've nearly arrived. Though not quite, I still have a bit to do on the house front. But, finally, I am getting close to where it is I want to be. It's so close I can feel it, touch it, smell it.

I yearn for it so badly.

All my life I've wanted to be somewhere else. I can't explain it. I wanted to see what was out there. I knew, somehow a three week holiday wasn't going to be enough. It had to be more. For now, that constant longing appears to have lost its grip on me. *I am here, I am here!* I wanted to shout it out at the top of my voice. But, that would be silly, wouldn't it? But, damn it, *I'm so close and near to where I want to be*.

It's a realisation that happiness can be found right where you are, in the moment you're living. This journey has taught me that sometimes, the most significant discoveries are those we make within ourselves, and the greatest adventure is one of self-acceptance and contentment. So, I keep it to myself, though inside, I'm bursting with the awareness that I'm closer to where I've always wanted to be. It's a quiet victory, a sense of arrival that fills me with an inner peace that I've been trying to get to for what seems like an eternity.

Wednesday 18th June 2008

Most of my problems have been sorted. Things are working out well and I'm starting to spend more time in my studio working, which is presently an old piece I started a while ago.

Monday 23rd June 2008

The studio is coming along, and I can see that with more work and shelving, it'll be a great place to work. Especially as it's so cool in summer. Michelino came by to install the new lights. I've planted geraniums and petunias and drove to Brico Point (the hardware store) to buy shelving and a few plastic planter troughs for the balconies. My driving is good now. I zap around everywhere. However, it took a few trips into Sulmona to gain the confidence I have now. Progress is being made to get my small art gallery set up. Such a wonderful time I'm having these days. My body clock has come into line with the famous Italian lifestyle. There's no hurry to do anything. All in its own time. I'm even beginning to have my evening meal around eight o'clock, instead of six o'clock, as in New Zealand.

Saturday 28th June 2008

Lucia rang, explaining that she'd been so busy with the bar. We plan a trip to the market in the next week or two.

Today I hung the first pieces of my art in my art gallery.

Lately, in between fixing up the workspace, I've been experimenting with different art techniques, like printing an image onto fabric on my new printer. I had a frustrating couple of hours looking for the mirror image button, but it was called T-Shirts. Dah!

Wednesday 2nd July 2008

While in Sulmona the other day I ran into Robyn she was with her friend Kath, also from Aussie. Then, yesterday afternoon they popped out to visit me. It was good to chat and have a cuppa. Kath is quite loud. They have a look at my art and at what I'm doing in the house and the garden, but I could tell they weren't really interested. It was all, where do you get this, where did you buy that, what's it like here? It's all fluff! They're just filling in time.

Thursday 3rd July 2008

Bruce leaves for LA tomorrow. He's panicking. Thankfully, his brother has been on hand to help him through this time and driving him to the airport tomorrow.

Gianni was in the area visiting a friend, so he dropped in to see how I was getting on with my garden. His father is a good vegetable gardener and he gave me the name of the fertiliser I can use. Mama came out for a chat and through Gianni, I heard the stories about the German soldiers that were in the here in the village during the war and how scared they all were. The soldiers stayed in a place up the road, which is now the local restaurant. There is a natural spring further up the mountain, so they (the Germans) built a swimming pool. Nowadays the restaurant is making use of the pool by fattening up wild trout trapped in there. They are a menu favourite. Hence, the restaurant is called La Trota. (trout).

Friday 5th July 2008

I drove over to Brico to order the roofing material. Bruce and I had looked at the type we wanted when he was here. For me, it was quite a difficult mission with the language etc, and it had to be right. I was going to ask Gi if he would help me with this, but I feel as if I have imposed on him enough. While I was in the office, who should see me sitting there, but Robyn's loud-mouthed Aussie friend, Kath. Shit, she's seen me and wanted to have a yap. She came right into the office where I was discussing the quantities and measurements with the boss. She butted in most rudely to ask me if I knew of anywhere she could store her bloody car when she wasn't in Sulmona. "No," I said, wanting her to bugger off, as I was up to my neck with roof business. She wanted to know what I was doing. I had to be rude and say I was busy ordering the roofing materials for my house. She finally got the message and let me get on.

I ordered the roofing material and paid for it. They're going to deliver it next week, so it'll be all set to go when Bruce arrives.

Wednesday 9th July 2008

Yesterday, another trip to Brico Point, the hardware store. This time to buy more shelving units for the studio. I rush home to set them up and finish getting all my stuff out of the trunks. So exciting. This is the first time I've had all my art supplies in one room, well, it's the first time I've ever had a proper workroom. I must say when everything is out and on the shelves, even I'm impressed. I had no idea I had so many art supplies.

You name it, I have it. A whole range of paint. Acrylics, oils, water paints. Crayons of various grades of oil and pastels. Coloured pencils and pens. A large variety of different grades of papers. (Oh my beautiful, precious paper - will I ever have the nerve to use you) Cupboards and plastic containers full of my fabric stash. Maybe, I've got some sort of art-buying syndrome. I've been buying supplies for years in anticipation of this very day. Always, in the back of my mind, I have known that I'll be doing mixed media art which will incorporate all sorts of materials. That day is almost here.

While talking to Bruce the other night, we decided to put a clear plastic roof over the back terrace. MIchele came to measure it, as he'll make the steel frame for it. Such an enterprising and clever man. A retired engineer and train driver. He also does electrical work and beautiful steelwork, making curved balustrades and gates. His work is on show all around the village and he's in great demand. You never see him playing cards or walking up and down the street chatting, as the retired guys do. No, even though he's retired, he's way too busy.

Thursday 10th July 2008

Yesterday I met with Lucia at the market for a coffee. It was so good to catch up with her. Talking and laughing. We had a super morning at the market and I am adding to my collection of lovely vintage doilies and Italian linen. Then I rush home to wash, starch and carefully iron them.

Sunday 13th July 2008

'Stop the world, I want to get off'! These were my thoughts on waking up this morning! I cannot believe how happy I am. Even in the midst of turmoil, at the end of the day, all is well. What is it? Is it living without those outside influences? No news, no TV, movies, books, women's mags, home and garden mags. I used to love my house and garden magazines and the like, but found, like the latter, they encourage feelings of envy and desire. They make you want things you didn't previously think you wanted.

I have long since distanced myself from them.

Here's a challenge for anyone wanting to change their life or break habits. The challenge is to stay in bed for a day or two to detoxify, not only the body but your mind also. No Internet, TV, newspapers, radio, books, or people. Not even handwork, (these days you can add smartphones to the list - no scrolling!) You can have a notebook and a pen. Now sleep, rest. Eat small amounts of food. Drink plenty of water. It's not easy. The urge to get up or to read or do something is hard to ignore. Basically, see what happens. What are your notes? Always write down your first thoughts of the morning. Rest, rest and more rest! We don't get enough sleep or rest in the Western world.

I've decided, that when Bruce arrives next week, I'm going to concentrate solely on us. No gallivanting around to all the social things. We don't have to be going out all the time. We'll just enjoy being together and in each other's company. I'll help him with the roof and painting the outside of the house.

Well, we'll see how long that lasts!

Chapter 18 - Tragedy - A Broken Ankle

A SURPRISE TRIP TO CORTONA.

*"Art enables us to find ourselves and lose
ourselves at the same time." Thomas Mer-
ton*

Saturday 19th July 2008

Tragedy struck on Wednesday afternoon! After returning from Sulmona.
I'd been cleaning the entrance, hosing an area, anyway, I'd popped back up to the
kitchen and on returning I slipped on the wet steps and fell awkwardly, hitting
my head and twisting my ankle! I passed out and came to in a few minutes, I
think. I called Fiona and luckily she was in her garden and heard my feeble cries for
help. She came through the back garden gate and helped me up into the lounge.
Lying on the couch, I surveyed the situation. It wasn't good. Fi and Mama were
at my side when Michele arrived to take more measurements for the veranda. He
had a chuckle when he saw me laid out with my ankle starting to expand like a

balloon. They wanted me to go to the ER at Sulmona Hospital. I was reluctant, mainly because Bruce was in transit as we spoke. There was no way for me to communicate with him and he was expecting me at the airport. If I went to the hospital they may hold me there overnight. I didn't want that. I was pretty sure if I had a walking stick, I'd be able to hobble, via the bus and train to the airport. And anyway, it may only be a strain. I asked Michele if he had a walking stick or something.

Yes, he did and promptly went away to retrieve it. He arrived back ten minutes later with one crutch-type stick, quite a modern one. Yes, I could manage with that. I rang and told Gianni of my predicament and he agreed to come and pick me up in the morning and take me to the bus. He would have driven me to the airport but was committed to an important job.

By morning my ankle was huge. I had put cold presses on overnight. When Gianni and I arrived at the bus stop, he went to the bar and managed to get a couple of bags of ice, which I placed on my bandaged ankle for the trip to Rome. Well, the bus didn't go to the main station, Termini, so now I had to hobble down to the Metro (underground) at Tiburtina, not easy. Shit, then up the stairs to reach Termini. Once on the Express to the airport, I did the one-legged hobble to the arrival terminal. It wasn't too long before Bruce emerged from the double doors. He was shocked to see the condition of my ankle and helped me gingerly onto the top of the bags on the trolley, then wheeled me to the train. From there onto the next train to Sulmona. Gianni was there to greet us. Bruce hadn't met my now Italian brother, as he has become to me. Bruce thanked him for helping me these past months with the car and telephone.

Gianni drove us home, stayed for a coffee and agreed to meet us at the hospital the next morning.

Tuesday 22nd July 2008

On arriving at the hospital the next day, coincidently, Robyn was also in the waiting room and was able to fast track me through the system. My X-ray revealed not a strained ankle, but definitely a broken bone. A plaster cast was applied to my right ankle. The doctor gave me a jab of calcium to aid the healing process and gave strict instructions for me to have seven days of bed rest. The cast was soft on the sole, which didn't allow any pressure. We set the sofa bed up in the lounge to allow me the complete bed rest required and to save me from going upstairs. Each day for seven days, I had to inject calcium into my stomach. From the time I had my accident, everyone even strangers, were kind, helpful and made sure I was comfortable. I'm grateful to have a lovely group of friends around me in such a short time of being here.

But the work must go on and the cherry picker was booked for Bruce and Gi to pick up to start stripping the plaster from the front of the house and then to re-plaster and paint it, all in the required four days. I'd been working with the colourist at the paint shop, trying to develop the right shade of terracotta that I had in mind. It was hard to get it right and I'm still not sure. But we'll soon find out!

I was frustrated at not being able to help the guys.

Four days later the whole front of the house was completed. The cherry picker was delivered back to Sulmona. It cost €450.00. The paint and plaster a couple of hundred. Even the local contractors must've been impressed with the speed and quality of the work carried out. We couldn't help noticing the way they studied our methods each time they passed. Since then I've seen similar jobs requiring scaffolding, a painfully slow resurfacing, and then painting. Taking a minimum of four weeks. The colour wasn't quite what I thought it would be and is more pink, but I do like it and I think it looks lovely. Hats off to Bruce and Gi, of course, for doing such a good job. There's just the exposed stonework at the bottom of the wall to work on.

After

Monday 28th July 2008

When the seven days were up, I went back to the hospital, had the plaster removed and another plaster fitted with a hard sole This now allows me to wear the sexiest looking moon boot. Not! It's a ghastly looking thing. Gianni has found a wheelchair for me, which will enable me to go to the village fiestas. On Saturday night Bruce wheeled me to the Piazza to watch the parade of matrimonial dresses worn by the girls of the village. Exquisite vintage and modern wedding dresses. I was surprised by the level of attention I received from everyone gathered for the event. They were curious and wanted to know what happened to my ankle and how did I break it.

Bruce is quite moody and appears to have the blues. Things aren't good between us.

Friday 1st August 2008

I've been resting and B is working on the exposed stone and painting the iron balustrades on the front of the house.

We had a long, enlightening discussion about our relationship and where it's heading with this new life and it seems we have reached a watershed in our marriage. After twenty years of constantly thinking about various businesses that we've set up and sold and the eight or so houses we've built or renovated, we've decided this is to be our last renovation. We realise how '*all encompassing*' and '*consuming*' these ventures have been and haven't left any time for us. We've had very few holidays over this period, so we've decided everything is going to be different now.

We're going to devote more time to us.

Thursday 7th August 2008

My Uncle has given me the name of an old friend, Rose, who just so happens she'll be in Cortona, Tuscany, attending *'The Tuscan Sun'* festival. I've made contact with her via email and we've arranged to meet on the steps of the Cortona Theatre. Cortona is only 3 1/2 hrs away and it's a great excuse to visit the region, now that we have a car. We're driving up tomorrow. Even though I am still hobbling around, I'm sure I'll manage to be a tourist. I've read about a group of quilters in Stia, a small village north of Cortona, so we'll drive up there and try to find them while we're in the area.

Sunday 10th August 2008

'The Tuscan Sun' festival is on in Cortona at the moment and Rose's friend from New Zealand, now living in London, is organising the whole shebang. Unfortunately, because we're late in booking, all accommodation is taken, so

we've managed to book a small country hotel in Farneta, fourteen kilometres away in the beautiful Tuscan countryside. Each morning it's a delightful drive into Cortona. As a newcomer to this area, the initial impression of this famous region is almost overwhelming in its beauty. Notable for its sprawling, green rolling hills, the views are superb.

Standout views as you drive through the Tuscan country-side.

On arriving in Cortona, driving through one of the main gates of the wall surrounding the town, you soon realise you are entering a timeless place.

Cortona is everything and more. Naturally, I'd read the book, *'Under the Tuscan Sun'* and nothing compares to Frances Mayes's descriptions of this region and her amazing house renovations *'Bramasole'*. My story and my house renovation are most humble in comparison. But to actually be here in Cortona, an enchanting, medieval, walled city is a beautiful experience.

It was lovely to meet Rose after all these years. Our paths hadn't crossed even though she doesn't live far from Uncle and he had often spoken of her. Our days were spent exploring the town, shopping, chatting and going to dinner each evening. Visiting art exhibitions, the most exciting was Sibylle Szaggars. She was in town along with her partner Robert Redford as part of the festival. And while we're name-dropping, Rose sat next to Anthony Hopkins at the grand dinner. No, I didn't get to see them, but a great time to be here.

Happy to be in Cortona.

Monday 11th August 2008

Yesterday we drove to Stia, an hour and a half from Cortona and what a gorgeous drive it was. This is the region, it seems, for growing apples and other fruit. My mission in Stia is to find the quilting group in the town. I'd read somewhere about a group of about twenty or so ladies in this area. I thought they may help me in my pursuit of quilt supplies in Italy and just generally want to meet some other quilters of the same ilk. We arrived in Stia around lunchtime and had lunch at a quaint family restaurant. I started my task by asking the owner, who spoke English if she knew of a group of women who did traditional American patchwork. No, but she rang a friend. No, they didn't know of anyone who did this. I can now see what a naïve notion it was to think that if I mentioned quilters or patchworkers to a few people around the town, they may know of someone, as I'm pretty sure if someone asked in my village they would point them in my direction. But, then this town is bigger than I thought. Never mind, we wandered around the old part of town, asking at various shops to no avail. We drove to another village to see some sights, still asking. But as the hours went on the search proved fruitless. We had a very pleasant day, and what a great excuse to see this part of the country, but now it was time to return to Cortona.

Dining amongst the ancient architecture, on a warm summer's evening.

We dined with Rose and her friend and it turns out Rose has a couple of weeks in limbo before going on to her next adventure in the UK, so she's kindly offered to come and stay with us in Introdacqua. She wants to help me in the house with cooking and such and maybe do some painting on the house. Serendipity is at play again! In a few days, she'll come by train to Rome and then train to Sulmona.

We're looking forward to showing her our part of Italy and having her stay with us.

We're heading home tomorrow.

Chapter 19 - We broke down on the Autostrada

ROSE COMES TO STAY.

"Art is the stored honey of the human soul."
Theodore Dreiser

Thursday 14th August 2008

We left our Hotel Farneta early on Tuesday morning. On the autostrada and only about thirty minutes from home we noticed the red light on the dash of the car came on, so pulled into a lay-by. I rang Gianni, giving him our GPS co-ordinates. Luckily we had insurance which covered us to be picked up from the autostrada. After some time the rescue truck came and loaded the car onto his truck and took us to his little village, where the mechanico looked at the engine to survey the damage. It wasn't good. Something to do with the alternator. We were driven back to Sulmona in the tow truck with the Fiat on the back (not a pretty sight) to Mateo's garage, where he and Gianni were there to meet us.

Friday 15th August 2008

Michele came by in the morning to start putting up the steel frame for the veranda on the back terrace.

Rose missed a couple of connections from Cortona, but finally arrived late yesterday afternoon. After a shower and freshening up, she joined us in the garden for a pre-dinner drink, prior to one of my favourite Italian pasta dishes with mushroom sauce. Bruce helped with the preparation. After dinner, we wandered down to the Piazza. It was in full swing with a band playing.

Sunday 17th August 2008

Yesterday, Rose and I went to the market on the bus, whilst the car was being repaired and it was awkward to manoeuvre myself around in between the crowds, but I enjoyed showing Rose this part of Sulmona.

Sulmona market

Bruce and Michele continued work on the veranda. In the afternoon Rose tidied the garden and cooked us a lovely dinner. Each evening after she's cooked us a fabulous dinner, we stroll to the Piazza where, during August, there's so much happening. For Italians, the outside world is forgotten and time doesn't count. It's all about forgetting the long, bitterly cold winter and enjoying the music, dancing and talking with friends, neighbours and family.

Our lunches on the back veranda are long and leisurely - in typical Italian style.

Enjoying the Fiestas in the Piazza most evenings
- broken ankle or not.

Monday 18th August 2008

Last night, a deliciously warm evening, we queued in the Piazza for a ticket to buy our traditional Italian meal and to eat al fresco. Row upon row of long tables with colourful paper cloths. On the small stage beneath the church clock tower, the good 'ol boys were playing traditional Italian music from the 80's to a packed audience.

The scene before us was like a multi-layered stage show. It captured the essence of everything you've ever dreamt of or imagined Italy to be. This evening, this picture, with no pretence, encapsulated all that was Italy.

The Piazza is bordered by a backdrop of ancient, medieval buildings which appeared mystical as the festive lights gave an eerie glow. The age-textured homes, the cobblestone streets, throngs of villagers chattered and laughed and old people clapped in time with the music. Long rows of tables weighed down with traditional food and wine, aromas from the cooking taking place behind the screens, flower filled balconies, tubs bursting with a riot of geraniums, teenagers enjoying being with their families, decorations spanned across the street, the lights lighting the night sky. Even a full moon came out to join us.

Dining in the warm night air with my new family and new friends. This evening will forever be etched in my mind. It summed up everything I had inadvertently imagined, but thought could not possibly exist in real life. It has given me a sense of belonging that I hadn't experienced before.

Tuesday 19th August 2008

Rose prepares a hearty breakfast each morning and then it's downstairs for me as I'm experimenting with a variety of art techniques. Bruce is helping Michele and they're nearing the completion of the veranda over the back porch. Rose is painting the rusted wrought iron balustrades white and they're coming up a treat.

About Michele: he's a widower. For many years he nursed his sick wife before she succumbed. I thought he may have taken a shine to Rose, as she's so vibrant and attractive. But, he hasn't shown any interest.

Being on crutches doesn't deflate my mood. I find that I can slide up and down the stairs on my bum. I whizz around the kitchen and lounge on my office chair with wheels.

Thursday 21st August 2008

Every night there is a different band playing in the Piazza. We stroll into the square and have a good time chatting, singing and dancing. Or we may go later and have a gelato.

It's all party, party, party and happy times.

Saturday 23rd August 2008

At eight am, there it was – Boom, Boom, Boom – the ground literally shook, and the windows rattled like crazy. It caught us off guard, a real heart-stopper. I've never experienced anything quite like it. Turns out, it marked the beginning of yet another fiesta. The sky was ablaze with fireworks, and it was daytime! The booming cannons added to the spectacle. Not to be outdone, the three churches chimed their bells, and a lively brass band paraded through the village. From my balcony, the whole scene unfolded before our eyes. Those colossal booms? They came from those cannon-like fireworks. And let me tell you, they didn't hold back on the fireworks – it was an impressive display throughout the day. All part of my learning curve of living in another culture. Well, we got a culture shock this morn.

Sunday 24th August 2008

I rested my leg today. It has swollen with the heat and is quite painful. The fiesta celebrations keep on going. The square was packed with people from all over the district for the concert last night. We have to get there early tonight, so as not to miss a good position. The village is awash with music, fun and people.

A first-rate Italian show band from Rome - in our little village. It was superb!

We've met Aussies, Irish, Americans and English, as most return to their family roots here each year, or have a holiday home here.

Bruce has been working so hard in the heat, but the roof of the veranda is now finished. It was quite a mission to find the clear plastic sheeting. It's similar to corrugated iron, only in plastic to let the light through. We finally found it at another hardware store a few miles away. It is going to be wonderful when it rains and snows, as the porch will stay dry and the furniture can remain undercover.

Wednesday 27th August 2008

Rose is leaving for London today. She'll be there for a few weeks visiting friends, then is returning to New Zealand. Michele offered to drive Rose and I to Pescara airport. No, he didn't have much to say to her, so not much going to happen there. I thought it might have been a good match. He has a nice house here and they could live happily ever after, but no, not to be. Ahh, a person can dream, can't they?

Saying our goodbyes was bittersweet, as we'd shared wonderful moments and she's been a great support, especially with her culinary talents that gave us delicious meals. We were going to miss her dearly.

Thursday 28th August 2008

Only two more weeks and my plaster will be coming off. Thank goodness.

In my studio, I'm only dabbling. With so much happening on the house, it's difficult to be creative. Bruce has outlined the exposed stone by painstakingly etching each rock. The front of the house looks really good now.

Monday 1st September 2008

I've been hobbling around in what I call the shed. An area under the downstairs veranda, shifting things around and cleaning it up. It's an area we haven't looked at yet. I think I'll be able to manage to paint it. It's going to be an ideal workspace, giving me an extra area, especially as it has hot and cold running water. Ideal for washing brushes and a wet area for future felting projects.

We still have to finish the garden. We're going to buy some paving stones and sand to lay them next week. It's challenging to get the products we need without the car.

Tuesday 2nd September 2008

I've finished painting the shed and have put it back together. There was a long length of marble leaning against the wall, which has made a really good bench.

We had a huge thunder and lightning storm. Forked lightning flashed across the sky and torrential rain for three hours.

Maybe we'll get the car back today.

Our roofing material has arrived for the main roof. Gianni helped Bruce stack all the sheets on the top balcony until he returns next year to install it.

Wednesday 3rd September 2008

Gianni took us up the mountain for dinner at a very rustic restaurant. My God, the health authorities would have a field day here at this very basic, but oh so rustic, restaurant. Their clipboards would be filled with the likes of bare concrete floors, corrugated iron roof and walls. But it was clean and the food was extremely good. Arrosticini were delicious, as was the porchetta. The guy who owns it is Gianni's friend, but then everyone is Gianni's friend. I'm not surprised at how popular my Italian brother is. Everywhere we go it's Ciao Gi. He knows everyone. He is the male version of "Pollyanna". How lucky we are to have him as our friend. Quite frankly, I don't know how I would get by here without his help. After the meal, in true Italian style, the bottles of drink were put on the table.

Ratafia has become my drink of choice at the end of the evening. It's made from cherries and is very moreish.

Chapter 20 - Summer Time and the Livin' is Easy

OUT AND ABOUT AT DIFFERENT FIESTA'S IN THE AREA.

"The object isn't to make art, it's to be in that wonderful state which makes art inevitable". Robert Henri

Saturday 5th September 2008

We have our beloved car back and it's going beautifully. Oh, the joy! So the first job was to head off to Scannelli's for building products and the rest of the day was spent working around the house.

Tuesday 9th September 2008

On Sunday afternoon, we drove to Lake Scanno and you can understand why it's such a popular destination for picnics and swimming. Around the shore-line people were gathered in pockets, absorbed in their own family activities - swimming, sunbathing, reading and savouring meals cooked on BBQs. It was an atmosphere of pure relaxation. After a couple of hours, we ventured to the village and had a beer in the main square taking in the locals chatting and ambling around.

Italians enjoying Lake Scanno

Friday 12th September 2008

My plaster cast was removed the other day and I was surprised at the mess of my lower leg. It was red, swollen and the skin had become dry and wrinkled! It was difficult to walk, as the tendons were stiff and tight. But, it was a relief to have it gone.

Yesterday was the seventh anniversary of 9/11.

Seven years. It's hard to believe that it was so long ago. It seemed like yesterday when Bruce rang from the fast-food business we had at the time, to tell me to turn on the TV and watch the incredible drama playing out from New York. It affected me terribly, as with all people across the world.

A Previous Life.

After the we sold the our Nursing Home, Bruce set up a fast food business, we built another house, then once again it was time for me to think about my next business venture. For a year it was a bit of a roller-coaster, trying a variety of different ideas. Shopping tours around Christchurch for tourists. I bought a really nice touring van, a people mover and spent months studying for my special driving licence to carry passengers. My self-styled uniform was a lime green coloured jacket and tailored skirt. A magnetic sign attached to the van, with a comical picture of women hanging out of the windows with bags of shopping they'd bought. I then placed brochures in every hotel and accommodation units throughout the city.

My first booking was from a couple with a four year old child. Well, he did nothing but whine and whinge the whole time. Taking them to factory shops was OK, but I didn't like waiting the three hours for them in the outlet stores. So, that was my first and last customer. This was not for me!

My next venture, to make use of my special licence and people mover van, was to branch into taking tourists around the South Island.

That seemed like a good idea at the time. New name for the business. More new cards and brochures placed in the city hotels and I made a new website. My first booking, I picked up a lovely American couple from their hotel for a day trip to Kaikoura. They were booked to go whale watching. Great, away we went. It's only a two hour trip. On arrival in Kaikoura, I escorted them to the Whale Watch office and they were gone for the most of the day to watch whales. I'd already been on this amazing trip, so I knew they'd have a lovely day.

But, what was I to do while they were at sea? I hung around and generally didn't know what to do. I read. In hindsight, I most probably should've taken some handwork to do. By the time they got back from their day trip, it was getting dark. The drive back to the city was awful. It was about then that I figured I didn't like being responsible for people on our New Zealand roads. Our roads are OK, but they are only two lanes and they're just not up to par, especially at night time as there are too many trucks and impatient drivers passing you when they shouldn't. (Not like the four lane autostradas here in Italy.) There are never enough passing bays. Nope, this isn't the business for me. That was my last job in that line.

Next. Remember that store I was telling you about in the first chapter, well this is where this silly idea originated. Maybe a woman of my ilk would do OK in a lovely, shabby chic style home-interior store. I'd taken an interior design course a few years previous. There was a good-sized shop available for lease in the up-market area I wanted to be. It needed a lick of paint, which we did in no time at all. Bruce made some super shop fittings.

Then, I was off to the Gift Trade Fairs in Melbourne and Sydney in Australia. What could be more fun than getting all dressed up and spending the day looking at gorgeous stuff, chequebook in hand, buying and ordering. And it was fun. I met a couple of like-minded women. We'd meet for drinks and dinner at the end of our days of buying. I returned to New Zealand to finish the shop interior while I waited for the gorgeous products to arrive. A few weeks later the large cartons and boxes were duly delivered. With ohhhs and ahhhs I unpackaged the boxes and started to set the shop out in a stylish manner. This was the most satisfying part. The night before opening day, all my friends, relatives and a couple of local newspapers came for a viewing and a celebration dinner.

The first few days were wonderful. Lots of people and many products were sold. It was all good, except I was trapped. I was here all day. This is not looking good!

I employed a person to come and give me a break once or twice a week, so I could have some time to get other things done. That was OK, but I soon became tired of the monotony of retail. I just didn't like the whole thing. I was wholly sick of people coming in "for a look" "just looking" they'd say, "what a lovely shop" "It does my soul the world of good coming to look in your shop" Yes, but it doesn't do my bank balance any good, I wanted to reply! "I'll be back", yeah right, I know, I've said these very words myself.

After a month I put it on the market. It took a while to sell, but when it did, I decided that even though I've set up and owned a variety of businesses since I was twenty, with the most successful and profitable being manufacturing and exporting sheepskin jackets and coats, renovating houses and selling them, B&B, restaurant, and fast food. At one stage owning a nursing home, but retail and my short-lived driving tourists around were not cutting the mustard for me.

"Bugger it!" I said, "I'm just going to concentrate on my art"! That's when, funnily enough, I received the email from the Florence Biennale committee inviting me to exhibit in Florence.

All these experiences I've had over the years, some wonderful, some not so, but hey, there is no shame in trying new ideas and if they don't work out, that's alright. Don't be afraid to try things now and then. Have a go. I've always believed 'Life is what you make it!' which has led me here - in Italy, looking at being able to fulfil a dream of becoming an artist.

Who knows where that will lead?

Some years ago, I wouldn't have admitted publicly that I had tried all these things for fear I would be judged - indecisive, changeable, inconsistent, erratic even. But, I'm none of those and I know this now, so I've come such a long way since I wrote that journal entry. To have the confidence to follow your own path, no matter what people may think, is true freedom.

Sunday 14th September 2008

Back to Italy and every day is consumed with working on the house. I'm learning to walk again and exercising my ankle. It's slow going. Bruce is busy working in the garden. Big Lorenzo helped yesterday to bring the gravel and sand in from the street, through the gallery and studio, and then out into the yard. The paving stones are being laid for the outdoor table and chairs. It doesn't leave time for playing or sightseeing.

*The stage is being set for long Italian meals in
the garden.*

Gianni invited us to his hometown for the Bagnaturo Fiesta on Friday night. It was a pleasure to meet his parents and many of his close relatives. They made us feel part of the family and the local food, particularly the delicacy Arrosticini. Lamb, sprinkled with delicate herbs and BBQ'd on sticks. The fiesta went until the early hours, with plenty of music and dancing.

Friday, September 19th 2008

An eventful week. Michele finished the remaining bits of the veranda and plumber Davide put the spouting (guttering) on. He has also extended the upstairs veranda roof by a foot and added spouting to that veranda too. Now there won't be a huge noise and waterfalls when it rains.

The finishing touches have been added to the new bathroom and it's a dream. From the shower the view out the back, over the fruit trees and gardens, to the row of ancient houses and the forest backdrop is superb.

Bathroom after.

Bruce has changed his flight ticket back to New Zealand and we'll have an extra five days together to make sure the house is ready for winter. He's added insulation in the attic over the coved ceilings. When I bought the house, there were a few very old bed quilt covers in a box in the cantina, but they are so heavy you couldn't possibly sleep under them and they're musty with age. So instead of throwing them out, we've put them on top of the insulation batts in the ceiling for added warmth.

Monday 22nd September 2008

A day out to Lake Bomba.

It was a few hours' drive away through truffle country, though we didn't find any for sale. When we arrived, we couldn't find a way down to the lakeside and had to view it from a distance. It was very pretty and the scenery on the way to the lake was beautiful. We drove back home through Pescara, stopping at the beach for a while, had a gelato and walked the promenade. It was beneficial to get away from renovating for the day.

Thursday 25th September 2008

The house is a shambles as we tackle one job after another. We seem to be forever at the hardware stores. I've been painting the back wall of the top balcony, the same colour as the front of the house.

The other day we met a couple from Aussie, Brian and Pat and went to dinner with them. They're staying in their friend's house up the road.

We've been cleaning the house, as Bruce leaves on Sunday. He's been here for nearly three months. The backyard and garden look great. It is going to be a lovely space to retreat to. I have plans to plant vegetables in spring.

Monday 29th September 2008

The day had begun with a 2 am wake-up call for the drive to Fiumicino for Bruce's flight. Watching as he checked in, there was a shared moment when he took the time to reassure me about the life we're building here. He reminded me of the cosiness and warmth of our home, the idyllic location, and the kindness of our village neighbours. In those quiet moments before departure, it became clear to both of us that this was more than just a place; it was our sanctuary, and that, despite the physical distance, we were firmly in this venture together. A reminder too, that home was not just a physical space; it was a feeling of belonging and contentment that we had discovered right here in the heart of Italy. Everything here was perfect, he assured me, except for one thing – he couldn't work here. His job demanded his full attention, and with the house now in order and my happiness assured, he was keen to throw himself into his work. It was a moment of shared understanding, a recognition that we were both in the right place for our respective pursuits.

A big hug, kiss and he was gone.

The day after – the house was empty. I made a coffee and sat out on the top balcony to write this journal entry in my pyjamas in the sun. I polished off the sweets Maria had made. I'm feeling a bit lost and sad, not depressed, just sad and blue. It'll take a while to get used to my own company again. I'll go down into the studio and start working on a project.

Because of the sacrifices we've made, I have to make this Italy thing work!

I have a list of jobs I need to do before I can completely concentrate on my art.

Clean the shed and stack the wood

Clean the studio

Make curtains for the lounge and all bedroom windows

Paint both internal art gallery doors

Paint guest room headboard

Paint all internal doors and architraves white and get rid of the horrible dark brown colour.

This list of jobs will keep me going for another couple of weeks.

Chapter 21 - Finally, it's here this

THE START OF MY ARTISTIC LIFE!

"Every artist was first an amateur." Ralph
Waldo Emerson

Tuesday 30th September 2008

The doorbell rang and surprise! A girl holding a beautiful bunch of flowers. They were from B, who had secretly collaborated with Fiona and the florist across the road to have them delivered to me. It was a lovely gesture and I had a little weep.

Wednesday 1st October 2008

I may have overdone things on the cleaning front yesterday, as my ankle was sore and swollen. When is it ever going to heal? Bruce rang from LA, he's fixing his sister's house for a week before heading to New Zealand. He said it's very hot there and told me the sad stories of people as the American share market crashes. It doesn't sound good.

The trees here are starting to turn yellow. Looks beautiful. Still not able to go walking in the woods as my ankle has still not healed enough.

Davide, the plumber, came to complete some work. During his recent family trip to Croatia, he brought me a tray of Croatian sweets and told me about the country; it sounded like a neat place and worth exploring. Of course, the plumbers back in New Zealand never come bearing sweet treats – it's a unique touch that added a bit of Croatian to my day!

Saturday 4th October 2008

I finished some small painting jobs, a headboard and a couple of lovely old chairs, given to me by a friend of Fi's. The range hood arrived, and I expected the guy who delivered it to install it, but no, he just left it ."non comprendi", he said.

I went to dinner last night at friends Fabrizio and Gemma's house. They're from Ireland and have a holiday home here. He's a superb cook and it took my mind off being on my own again.

Monday 6th October 2008

Saturday dawned an achingly beautiful day, so I decided to go to the market in Sulmona. Again, I make a beeline to the linen stalls, where I bought quite a few lovely old crocheted doilies. I'm sure I'll be able to incorporate them into my artwork in the future. My idea is to breathe new life into these treasures, as so much work has gone into making them and they give us a window into the past.

Clean second-hand linen at the market.

Sunday, I cleaned the house from top to bottom, changed my room around a little, aired the bed, put on the winter bedding, and made curtains for the French doors.

Wednesday 8th October 2008

I've been painting the doors and the architraves upstairs. I still have two more to do. Honestly, it's the worst job I have undertaken. Well, it's probably not the worst, but it is right now! I've come to loathe renovating. Renovating sucks! It doesn't leave you any time to be creative at all, as you're always in a mess and your thoughts are all about the job in hand and buying more supplies to keep you going. So, this is it, finito! No more renovations.

Next week when it's all finished it will look lovely and I won't be so tired all the time.

Friday 10th October 2008

Bruce is still in LA. He changed his ticket again, as his sister wanted him to do more work on her house.

I'm spending a bit more time down in the studio, experimenting with new techniques while listening to my Learn Italiano CD's. It's still some time before I'll be having a proper conversation with an Italian who doesn't speak any English at all. It would be a game of charades, I'm afraid. Maybe I'm one of those people who just can't get a handle on another language at all.

Wednesday 15th 2008

I ran into Richard in the street here. He bought his beautiful white Abruzzi dog, Shana over to be put with Marco's big male dog, Zorba. I haven't seen Rich for a while. He'd been back to London and then busy setting up his new B&B. Gianni keeps me updated on his progress. His breed of dog are specific to this region. They're big, noble-looking, white Maremmano-Abruzzese Sheepdog, and are used by the shepherds to mingle in with the sheep to protect the flock from wolves. Yes, there are wolves and bears in them thar hills which surround the village. We have two local shepherds around our village. Such a wonderful sight to see the flocks of sheep and goats grazing on land on the outskirts of the town. The sound of their bells is delightful. Each flock have three or more of these dogs protecting from wolves and helping the shepherd with the flock.

We had a coffee and he invited me to go to Ortona War Cemetery with him and a mutual friend, Sue, next month for the Armistice Day event there. I said yes.

Friday 17th October 2008

Bruce rang. He's back in New Zealand after an extended time in LA working on his sister's house. We talked for hours, as we have very cheap calling cards now. While he was in LA, he bought himself a fabulous new keyboard as he's started playing in his brother's band, *'The Beagle Boys'*. They're a really good blues band. So while he was on the line, he played for me and sang. He sounded so good. It's been a long time since he's played seriously and even longer since I've heard him sing. I fell apart and tears welled up, as I realised he was so far away, on the other side of the world and what the hell was I doing here anyway!

He managed to calm me down and reminded me of the rocking chair test and that we were both on this adventure together. I was to push on and do the art I wanted to do, and he was also benefiting from this experience. Travelling more, being able to buy his fabulous keyboard from the States.

I've become friends with an American woman, Jean. She has a holiday home here and spends more time here in Introdacqua than most of the overseas people. We're having dinner tonight at the local restaurant, La Trota, it's a wonderful place. The owners are from Naples and even though Naples is only around three hours, it's like they're from another country. On the weekends the large homely restaurant is almost fully booked, like tonight. People wave or pop over to our table to welcome you. Because Jean has been coming here every year for a long time, she knows a lot of people. I love the ambience of the restaurant. It would be typical of the traditional family restaurants throughout Italy. There are about four TV's around the walls, all tuned to their favourite sport, football.

It's interesting to note the contrast in the dining culture between New Zealand and here. Most restaurants at home don't feature TVs, but it's an entirely different story here. The Italians, being passionate conversationalists who express themselves with dramatic arm movements, manage to eat and talk, all while keeping one eye on the telly. Tonight, the restaurant is bustling with activity, and the air is charged with excitement, because of a football match. Carlo, the owner, takes such pride in his business, as he tries to chat and welcome everyone who enters, but tonight he's very busy. His son, is a real artisan, as he makes his pizza bases, not too thick, not too thin. He deftly tosses them in the air as he coaxes them into the required shape and thickness. It's a sight to behold.

My other favourite is Salmone Farfalle, a bow-tie, shaped Italian pasta, which is pretty much as it sounds. Pasta al dente, done in a rich creamy sauce drenched in flaked salmon. The bread is the best Italian bread. It is baked every afternoon in the same wood-fired ovens. They have a very good house wine, though of course there is a superb wine list of wines from the region. We settle for the house wine and the cost is minuscule.

Sunday 19th October 2008

Yesterday Jean and I went to the market. On the way home the car developed a problem. The smell of diesel was very strong. When I arrived home I parked the car and a large pool of diesel developed on the street. I rang Gianni and he and the lovely Matteo came to fix it. It needed a new hose line or something.

I've arrived!

Monday 20th October 2008

Wait for it!

Finally, it's here this very day. It is such a memorable day. This is the beginning of my real journey. It seems like all my life I've been working toward today! I've had this yearning to be at home and work on art.

Yesterday, I finally finished painting all those blasted internal doors. I got rid of all the dark brown in the house. The whole house is fresh and light. What a relief. I washed my paintbrushes and rollers, put away the drop cloths, threw out the rubbish and cleaned the house and windows. The house is sorted and has a real 'girls house' feel about it. The microwave is in its new place, the other cupboard arrived last week, so too has the dishwasher. One complete kitchen. The car is sorted, as is the phone, even though I only have dial-up internet and it's very slow, still, I'm grateful to be online. The gas boiler and all the radiators are working, so I'm going to be warm this winter.

To have my place. To be able to spend whole days in my studio doing stuff. I was never sure what it was, or even what I'd do, but to have a large space in my home dedicated for my work. Not to have to clean the table or clean the guest room out for guests, but to have this dedicated space where I can work each day and night and not have to worry about the mess. Now, that's a luxury in itself. I have nothing to do now from here to eternity. I can go down to my studio happy in the fact that I have no other commitments to either house or kin. To have no guilt about "I should be doing this or I should be doing that.". From now on, no guilt. I've earned this.

This is what I do and I don't want any distractions.

All is well in my world and the anticipation is delicious.

It's amazing how the stars have aligned, leading up to this one day in time when I can confidently declare, "This is the day." No more excuses, no holding back. I finally have the opportunity to pour as much time as I want into my art. I'm looking ahead, excited about the fascinating people I'll meet – both online and in person. I'm equally thrilled about the artistic journeys that lie ahead. This is a career path I won't simply stumble into; I'm taking charge and embracing it wholeheartedly.

I can name the day I began and it is today 20th October 2008.

Already, I have a day and a goal to work toward. November 9th is only a couple of weeks away. It's a yearly event here. Ringraziamento: a Thanksgiving day where artisans come from all over the region to display their wares and demonstrate their craft. The locals who are organising the event have asked me to take part. How exciting. I'll need to make some art and make a few signs directing people to my galleria.

So, the big question is, what will I create? Where will this art journey lead? My new motto is 'Have a Go'.

Chapter 22 - And so, the Art Journey Begins

BUT...I DON'T KNOW WHERE TO START!

"An artist requires the upkeep of creative solitude, the healing of time alone. Without this period of recharging, we become deplet-ed" J Cameron.

Tuesday 21st October 2008

Well, after yesterday's hype, I'm off to a slow start. Quite frankly, I don't know where to begin. Maybe I should keep some to-do lists and not stress about the open day that I'm planning for the Ringraziamento day on the 9th. Just 'enjoy the journey.' I'm always saying that, so I should take my own advice! I'll do some experimenting with small textile art pieces. I have enough stuff to put out on the open day. I make a note to enjoy the freedom of my new life as a studio artist.

It's easy to get caught up in other people's ideas of things, instead of going down my own path. You can lose focus, just like that! Example: meeting Jean and becoming involved and caught up in her world. The key is to stay focused - try new ideas - don't hurry - be relaxed - enjoy - enjoy - enjoy and it will all come together.

Notes to self:

Pay for another year's subscription on my website.

Write some 'to try' lists.

Don't think about the 'open day' until next week.

Concentrate on various techniques - painting pictures with fabric and silk.

Go for a daily walk.

Make my fruit and vegetable juice each morning.

Have a good night's sleep - I've had great periods of sleep lately - I'm taking my hottie (hot water bottle) to bed as my feet are getting cold.

Thursday 23rd October

I've been playing around with a new technique with fabric pictures, printing them on the printer. They came out alright, though my values around the tower are too similar. Being able to concentrate on art, has changed everything! Relaxed lunches in the garden, thinking and taking notes, being inspired by the magazines I bought with me, such as '*Quilting Arts*'.

Michele came to put in my new intercom system. Now when someone comes to my front door I can ask who it is and push a button and the door opens. This saves me from running downstairs and letting them in.

With the change of season, the autumn colours are glorious.

Friday 24th October 2008

Bruce rang yesterday, it was great to hear from him. He didn't sound too happy about his debut night at the tennis club. But I bet they loved him playing the piano, and listening to his singing and joking. Apart from this gig, he's also been out playing his new keyboard with *'The Beagle Boys'*. They played at an Ashburton hotel and they're playing down there again on Sunday night.

He was telling me how large businesses are going broke in New Zealand, due to the 2008 financial crisis. Even though I haven't been living in Italy for very long, I've noticed a different perspective when it comes to homes. Over in New Zealand and other Western countries, we tend to place a lot of importance on houses as a way to make money. I have to admit, I've been part of that too - buying and selling houses for profit, and we've done pretty well with it. In fact, it's allowed me to establish myself here. But in Europe, there is a different psyche. Their homes are for shelter and comfort. A place to live for most of your life and not as a source of making money and then moving on. I think it makes for a more stable life.

Monday 27th October 2008

One month since Bruce went back to New Zealand and twelve months since I settled the house sale.

I'm finding it difficult to stay focused - as I'm continually bombarded with other people's ideas or their perspectives on what you should do or how you should live. Looking at their lives - I have to remember to live my own life and not listen to them. For instance, folks are constantly asking about sales and how will I sell my art. What they don't understand is, it's not about selling. Yes, of course, it would be marvellous if I sold my work, but that isn't my motivation. My motivation is to get through each day being totally happy with what I am doing, and where I'm at. My level of contentment and joy is what's important to me now.

Really, what I need to do is to concentrate on learning new techniques. Devising a portfolio together so that I can teach, whether it is here or in America is irrelevant. I have to have time to evolve into my new life. That alone is going to take time and solitude.

As the open day approaches in just two weeks, the tasks seem like an ever-growing mountain, yet excitement for the event is growing. It's a challenge to get everything in order, but the idea of displaying three traditional American-style quilts that I bought over from New Zealand, for just such an occasion gives me hope that some of the ladies from the village would like to learn how to make a traditional quilt.

Feathered Star quilt - machine pieced and hand-quilted. A traditional American-style quilt.

Back in another life prior to the Rest Home business, I used to teach quilt-making classes. I was so hooked on quilting in the mid 1980s, that we moved to the country and built a red American-style barn, just so I could have quilters come to stay for retreats and classes. The old story, 'build it and they will come.' And they did. Every year we would host a Quilter's Gathering. Quilt-makers came from all over the region to share the day in the country.

Not only did we host quilters gatherings, but each week I would teach quilt-making classes in our purpose-built lounge. We became known for hosting Probus and garden clubs from the Christchurch and Ashburton regions. Bruce would play the piano and sing all the old-time songs. Having busloads of groups coming for the day was born out of necessity. Building the barn house was a big project and it became a massive money pit where our money was sucked into and we had to find ways to make it pay. I must say having large groups of people coming to your house every other day kept you on your toes. That and over two acres of new gardens to keep tidy and lawns to mow.

We'd installed a massive open log fire. So big, we always said, you could fit at least five or six bums in front of it. In the kitchen sat pride of place a large black, Shacklock double oven coal range. How I loved it. For two buckets of Giles Creek coal, I could cook a roast meal for fifty people.

Anyway, I digress, so, back to my thoughts: live a simple life, don't get caught up in the lives of the Americans and the Brits that live here for part of the year. There's quite a large population of expats in our village, hence, it's easy to get caught up in social events or have dinners at each other's homes, etc.

One big challenge is to keep on trying to learn the Italian language, which I've found really difficult. My brain doesn't appear to retain or process the language very well.

Tuesday 28th October 2008

Yesterday, I zapped and painted baby wipes (mmm, sounds strange. They're unused) Interesting effects were achieved. It made a texture similar to moss. I was able to incorporate it into a piece I'm making, featuring the Introdacqua Tower.

Worked in the studio until eight o'clock.

Thursday 30th October 2008

Apart from working in the studio each day and I may add, it hasn't been that easy. Most of the time I mope around. All these years I've yearned to have the time and the space to be an artist. Now I have it all and for the life of me, I don't know where to start or what to do. I dabble a bit here and there. I lurch from one technique to the next, not knowing what type of art I want to do.

I've shipped my hoard of vintage and quilting fabrics over from New Zealand and I've been accumulating vintage doilies and linens from the markets each week. How to use them, and how do I incorporate these into my work? Too many questions and not enough answers, that's the quandary I now find myself in.

On my daily walks around the village, I come across people in the street chatting and talking, hands waving around in expressional speech. There's always a "Ciao Eva" 'Come Stai" how are you? It's the people of course, so happy and friendly. Here in this region, right in the heart of Abruzzo, families seem content and solid. I might have mentioned this before, but it's a wonderful place to simply "be". There's no constant urge to be on the move, to see every sight, or no pressure to always be busy. It's perfectly alright to unwind and not feel obligated to always be on the move. If you know what I mean.

I'm confident that as time passes, I might find a more concise way to express what exactly makes Italy so darned liveable.

Chapter 23 - Ringraziamento and Studio Work

STILL TRYING TO FIND MY WAY.

"Creativity takes courage". Henri Matisse

Sunday 9th November 2008

Ringraziamento - craft day in Introdacqua and my first open day. Gianni came to see if he could help out and before the main crowds came we down to the Piazza for a quick coffee.

The main street was alive with activity and stall holders. Most of the crafters and artisans were mainly men and they came from all over the region. One man was carving the most beautiful houses and small villages from ancient olive tree roots, it was fascinating to watch. Another is carving Saints from limestone and he was also demonstrating a wheat grinder for making flour, but the grinder nor the flour were for sale. There were leather carvers, basket weavers, potters, artists, and food stalls providing soups and stews made the old-fashioned way. A delightful surprise as I came across a group of women lace makers from Scanno, a region renowned for its exquisite lace. Their nimble fingers were creating the most intricate and delicate patterns passed down through the ages. Goldsmiths showcased their craft, turning raw materials into gleaming works of art.

Quite a few people meandered into my gallery during the course of the day. Even though he didn't have much idea about what I was doing or why I do it, Gianni was a big help and I appreciated it. I gave demonstrations and I'd organised my little galleria with what I thought were appealing pieces, with three of my large American-style traditional quilts, plus I had plenty of books and magazines to browse. A few women were mildly interested, but really, no one wanted to learn how to make a quilt. Oh well, never mind, there's always next year.

Richard and his handsome Abruzzi dog popped in to say hi. Even though she's still a puppy she's grown quite big. He reminded me about going to the Ortona War Cemetery on the 11th for an Armistice Day ceremony. He knows I have a strong interest in the history of New Zealand soldiers who were here in Italy, in WWII. I offered Richard to leave the dog in my garden, but, no he insisted on bringing her with us when we went to the Piazza for lunch. By this time the crowds had arrived and you could barely move. Well, the poor dog froze in fear. The last time I saw Richard, he was disappearing down a side street carrying his large dog. Anyway, Richard is a whole new problem and even though he's a very nice gentleman, he makes me feel gloomy. I'm not sure why. He never laughs and is just so sombre. I suppose that comes from his military background.

Around four o'clock, I closed the gallery and went to watch the parade. It was bone-chilling cold, but there were still plenty of people around. I ate ten arrostici-ni. I finished off at the bar, where I chatted with a few locals. There aren't any ex-pats around now, as they've returned to their homes whilst Italy is shrouded in winter, except for Jean, but she left the Piazza early and has retired home. I ended with a Sambuca coffee. Then it was home to bed. I was exhausted from the preparation, the constant talking and explaining. I was done.

The main parade.

When the sun goes down behind the mountains, around 4ish, it is cold, so cold.

Tuesday 11th November 2008

Armistice Day. Well, I should be off to Ortona with Richard today, however, the heavens opened and it was freezing. He rang early and cancelled the trip due to the change in weather. I was relieved to be home in the warm, so I spent the day in the studio. Bruce rang and we chatted for a long time. He's not coping well with the separation and is thinking of coming over for Christmas. That would be good.

Wednesday 12th November 2008

I went to bed early with a cuppa and some art mags for some brainstorming! It worked and I came up with a couple of good ideas, starting with painting my fabrics, then adding collages. Paint the old crocheted doilies and linens I buy at the markets, making sure to keep the pristine pieces as heirlooms for a future shop on Etsy or something. It will most probably take six months to find the art media I'm most comfortable with. At the moment I'm all over the place. Fabric, acrylic paint, oil paints, silk, collage, printing on the computer. The list is endless.

Contemplating the concept of happiness, I found myself grappling with what defined happiness? Was it a place where you lived? I'd never been totally at ease living in the city, yet it was necessary for my business. I never felt like I fit and instead yearned the open spaces and the quietude of the countryside. There, the connection to nature and the unhurried pace of life felt more like where I belonged. It's a reminder that happiness is a deeply personal journey, and the place we choose to call home can play a pivotal role in that quest for inner contentment.

Sunday 16th November 2008

I keep reminding myself how lucky I am to be diving into these new experiences. It's a chance for me to really delve into various art techniques and let my creativity flow. I've realised that being an artist requires a certain level of relaxation – it's kind of like learning to play golf. If you're all wound up, your swing just won't work and you won't hit the ball in that sweet spot. You've got to consciously ease up and let things happen naturally. I can just imagine my family rolling their eyes at this type of conversation. You know how it goes? Who does she think she is? I think that's a pretty common scenario in most families from my era. But for some reason, I've always had this desire to stay home and be creative. Back when I was making quilts it was seen as a hobby, but now I'm aiming to step it up a notch, and because in my immediate circle or family there are no artists or creatives and I find it a bit daunting. The Internet, though is a great source for meeting and learning from others.

Taking a little break from the world won't do me any harm. I actually enjoy the luxury of not having to rush to work or worry about house renovations. When I reflect on my past, it strikes me that I've had some pretty remarkable experiences over the years.

One time during a three month extended holiday, our first in over a decade, we embarked on a road trip along the entire East coast of Australia. Our journey took us from Noosa to Melbourne, then onto South Australia and Adelaide, all in search of the perfect place to settle down. As we travelled down the coast, I made a point of swimming in every beach we came to. It added another dimension to our trips as I have a genuine fondness for Australia. Queensland holds a special place in my heart, particularly the Sunshine Coast towns along the beaches. From the charm of Caloundra to the beauty of Noosa, the pristine beauty of Mooloolaba Beach. Back in the '80s when I lived in Brisbane, I would often escape for weekend getaways to Maleny, nestled in the hinterland, inland from Noosa. The hinterland villages that dot the landscape around the Sunshine Coast are quaint and back then, unspoiled by the waves of tourists who eventually discovered this hidden treasure. The scenery is lush tropical green, with the Glasshouse Mountains standing tall – a sight that's simply breathtaking and magical.

Glasshouse mountains, Sunshine Coast - Australia

Shifting gears a bit, we were captivated by the State of Victoria and its array of country towns and bustling cities. One standout is Ballarat, a city that beautifully intertwines the old and the new, offering plenty of places waiting to be explored. Our day at the tourist town *'Sovereign Hill'* a living museum, which represents the story of Ballarat as a gold rush boomtown. Gold was discovered here in 1851, triggering the greatest gold rush the world had ever known. Stepping onto its streets was like going back to that period – it felt like time travel, as the experience was so real that it's etched in our memories and we talk about it to this day.

Then there's the Yarra Valley, just an hour out of Melbourne, a region with its own unique charm. South Australia also has its allure, with the stunning Barossa Valley stealing the spotlight. The picturesque country towns around Tanunda and Angaston add to the area's charm and make for delightful places to explore.

We stumbled upon a small country town, Strathalbyn. On High Street were a number of antique shops and I was in my element. We became chatty with a couple of the store owners and they invited us to their fish night on a Wednesday night at the local pub. We've never laughed so much. It was like being on the set of the 'Carry On' movies. They were so funny as they recounted stories, like when bus loads of pensioners come to town from the city for the day. Each shop owner quickly phones around to the other shops and they bolt their doors and head for the hills. You can't blame them. Pensioners pick everything up in the shop, "Oh look, I had one of these" etc, and they tend to be a bit mean - they don't buy anything in the town except a coffee and will share a muffin between four of them.

Plenty of memories with the Aussies. But I digress (again). See how quickly I become distracted.

Tuesday 18th November 2008

On Sunday I worked on Tara - a piece I had taken a photo of prior to the renovation. I've been transferring photo images onto fabric. There is a variety of different methods for doing this. One is to put an edge of glue onto an A4 sheet of paper, then lay the fabric, cut to the same size, onto the paper and print onto the fabric directly from the printer. Or print the image onto paper. Spread glue onto the image and the fabric you are going to print on. Lay the image face down on the fabric and press hard with the back of a spoon to transfer the image from the paper to the fabric. For this piece, I printed the image directly onto the fabric. I'll most probably use it in conjunction with a collage and then stitch into it. I liked the effect of this technique.

Jean and I went to dinner on Sunday night in Sulmona, as La Trota, our local restaurant was closed. Sulmona Corso was full of people out strolling even though it was wet and cold. We had a lovely dinner. We finished quite late and as we walked out into the cold misty night into a dark alley, at the end of the street, a group of teenage boys were milling around under the light. They looked menacing. As we walked past they all smiled, "Buona Sera" "good evening" they said. Such polite teenagers here. Now, if this had played out in a New Zealand city, I would've felt quite intimidated, scared even.

Wednesday 19th November 2008

What a struggle it is for me to find a style that I'm happy with for this Swiss competition that I have decided I may enter. At this stage I'm not very good at entering competitions - so this is a real challenge. I might just throw in the towel before I start. The design I worked on yesterday is too disjointed. I'll have another

191

go at it tomorrow from a different angle. Meanwhile, with such a heavy frost this morning, I'm worried that the car doesn't have enough anti-freeze. Hopefully, it'll be OK until I get some more in.

Thursday 20th November 2008

Still struggling with this Swiss art piece. Then guilt sets in - this is one of the things I wanted to do - now I can't even get started!

Still haven't heard from Bruce for a while.

Friday 21st November 2008

Not a very good week this week. I haven't accomplished a bloody thing! Yep, this week I've been down. I don't think it's because Bruce hasn't rang - it's mainly because I'm not sure what direction to go. I wanted to enter the Swiss competition, but I'm running out of time.

Jean has invited me to the American Thanksgiving next week. This is such an occasion, with many people flying back to Italy to be part of the event, as quite a few are stationed at an American air base somewhere in Europe.

Saturday 22nd November 2008

Bruce rang and we talked for a couple of hours. He was telling me how the economic downturn is affecting the country. Quite grim, with businesses closing down, people not able to sell their houses, building industry slowing down, collapsing almost, in this very bad economic depression! He has plenty of work which is good news.

I should've been down in the studio, instead, I was Internet surfing (time-wasting and procrastinating!) But interestingly, I came across the Shackleton Centennial expedition, led by Henry Worsley MBE. The three team members are descendants of Sir Ernest Shackleton and other members of the team he led in 1915. This is all pretty exciting for me, as it relates to my hero, Sir Ernest Shackleton. Plus I have an interest in adventures in the Antarctic.

Taking a leap back to 2004; I hopped on a flight to Wellington to visit the Shackleton Exhibition held at Te Papa, New Zealand's National Museum. The exhibition showcased an impressive array of documentation and captivating photographs, and what a treat it was to hear the genuine voice of Shackleton himself. But the real highlight for me was to see the actual 'James Caird' – the boat that those brave men dragged for miles across the frozen terrain to the edge of the ice and set sail, eventually reaching Elephant Island.

From that icy island, Shackleton and a small team rowed the *James Caird'* an incredible eight hundred miles to reach South Georgia, leaving behind twenty two men to await their return. It's a tale of sheer determination that continues to amaze and inspire. Weak with hunger, they landed on the wrong side of the South Georgia Island, which meant they had to climb a huge mountain range to finally get help from the whaling station. The weather was so bad that it still took four or five trips by sea to try to get back to Elephant Island and rescue the stranded men. Finally, after the failed attempts they managed to get back and miraculously, every man was still alive. Not one life was lost in this unbelievable journey. So, I'll be keeping up with this Shackleton Centennial Expedition led by Henry Worsley as they trek across the Antarctic.

A collage I made in honour of Sir Ernest Shackleton. With an image from his log book.

Chapter 24 - And just like that! I booked

STRIVING TO OVERCOME THE VOICES IN MY HEAD.

*"You must do the things you think you can-
not do". Eleanor Roosevelt*

Monday 24th November 2008

Saturday was spent in front of the fire, the first one this year. It took most of my wood supplies, but it was delicious. I popped up to La Trota and bought a pizza take-out for dinner.

A couple of weeks ago Robyn enticed me to book a day trip to Naples, a city renowned for its enchanting *"Christmas Alley"* displays. But, she's unable to come as she's not well, so I'm on my own with a bus full of Sulmonians. The excitement was palpable. On arrival in Naples, we visited three large and prominent churches. This led us to Via San Gregorio Armeno, a narrow cobbled street, free from traffic. It is lined on both sides with small shops that spill their wares out onto the street. The street was full to overflowing with an array of cribs and mangers, all handmade by generations of traditional artisans. There are also large choices of hand-made tambourines depicting local scenes, as well as statues and figurines representing famous Italians, be they politicians, singers or footballers. You could also watch the making of these nativity scenes in some of the little squares, leading off the main road.

Naples Christmas Markets.

The streets were so crowded I could hardly move. I didn't like the crowd-crush sensation at all and made sure I held my bag close to my chest, though there were plenty of police stationed every so often. I'm not saying there were bag thieves around, but I don't think I've been in such a scary, overcrowded situation before. I was separated from the others, but I managed to navigate my way through the narrow streets, and with Peter Sarstedt's song *"Where do you go to my Lovely"* playing in my head, I caught up with our group. Back on the bus we went on a short tour of Naples. For lunch, we stopped at a fairly sterile restaurant for a pretty mediocre lunch. By now it was 2.30pm and we were famished. The small mussels and squid with salad didn't cut the mustard. Dessert was a sorbet gelato and really didn't go anywhere near to filling the gap. After lunch, we had a tour around the bays for some photo shoots. We left for home at six o'clock arriving back in Sulmona around ten. It was a long but interesting day.

Tuesday 25th November 2008

In order for this new life to work, I have to get things sorted. Initially, I thought I'd simply go into my studio each day and work on my art. But, and surprisingly, it hasn't worked like that at all. Instead, I do everything but make art or make a start! I'm putting myself through constant pressure because it hasn't happened as I expected - is it that I'm still in my hobby frame of mind? I'll need to find a way through this if I'm going to get off the ground.

Ideas: Looking to set up a professional website, keep experimenting on new techniques - with an eye to finding my own voice. Just keep doing the work, even if nothing is working for me at the moment.

Picked up Jean and we went grocery shopping. Wet and cold today. Wrapped up with boots, gloves and a warm coat.

Saturday 29th November 2008

What a delightful evening the Thanksgiving dinner was. I didn't realise there was such a large contingent of American expats who live up near the Tower. Claire's house was packed. It was a very traditional evening, with a large log fire roaring in the corner. A splendid turkey surrounded by goodies came out on a platter. It was cooked to perfection. We sang and danced. It was an evening to savour. A wonderful opportunity to meet new people.

Yesterday, while working on the computer, it kept freezing up. I'm still only on dial-up, which is very slow. I lost my temper and slammed my hand onto the keyboard!

I think I've killed it! My laptop! It was with a woeful expression on my face as I presented my dead PC to Donato at the local electronic store in Sulmona. I'm hoping he'll perform a miracle and bring it back to life!

Rose rang last night from New Zealand. What a pleasant surprise - we chatted for nearly an hour.

Monday 1st December 2008

Donato informs me I'll need a new hard drive. Hopefully, he'll be able to save all my stuff.

Jean has asked me to go to Rome and spend the day with her, as she's heading back to the States. She wants me to go today and stay the night, but it's not possible for me to go today. I'll go tomorrow on the bus and meet her there, do some Christmas shopping, then come home in the evening.

Wednesday 3rd December 2008

Well, the heavens opened yesterday whilst in Rome. My first job was to buy an umbrella. Jean is staying near the Pantheon. We ventured over the river and checked out the area in Trastevere. Even though the weather was atrocious, I fell in love with this fascinating and very old part of Rome. I came across a textile artist, so we stayed and talked with her for a while. It rained all day, with thunder and lightning. Walking around was difficult, but we managed to find a lovely lunch in the Jewish Quarter. Then a quick hug goodbye and I had a mad dash back to the train station, and back to Sulmona, where I'd parked the car at the station. It was very late by the time I got home and into bed.

Friday 5th December 2008

Well, the prognosis on my laptop is not good. It looks like I need a new one!

Robyn has organised a night out with the girls. It was last night. Most of them are expats, married to Italians and some have lived here for over thirty years. There were about nine of us. We went to a popular restaurant in Petorana. And you know what it's like when a bunch of gals who've had a few drinks. We were loud, raucous and laughed ourselves silly, great fun. We've all agreed to get together at a different restaurant each month. Now there's something to look forward to. God help the restaurant.

But it's the turmoil I'm going through in the studio that has my hopes and dreams dashed! I just can't seem to get out of my head! I wonder if other artists suffer from their mind telling them:

You're not good enough!

Who do you think you are?

You know you can't draw or do anything that's real art!

Nobody is going to like it!

Or even understand it!

I have all the stuff to make art, but instead, I look through magazines trying to become inspired, or I'll clean the house, work in the garden, or go for a walk. Oh well, if I don't know where to start, it's cold, so I'll light the fire and knit. Every day is now a constant battle of trying to begin a piece, then not sure where to go with it. I cry, I shout awful things to myself. I'm in total despair. It's cold, the dog over the back has started barking again and I'm a miserable mess! This is not at all what I envisaged. It's been like this for weeks now and everything considered, has come to a debilitating climax! And even though I did manage to get enthused to work on a collage, a collection of memories from our past twenty years of marriage for our upcoming anniversary, it's OK, - but it's not what I want to do!

So, just like that, I booked my ticket and I'm going home!

I'm leaving for New Zealand tomorrow. When I get to Fiumicino Airport, I'll go on standby. Even though I'm booked I want to get on the earliest flight.

Crikey! I'd better get packing!

Thursday 11th December 2008

I managed to get a flight on Emirates. Two days and here I am back in New Zealand. Bruce is working about three hours north of here and most nights stays on the job, so he won't always be around.

We've opted to come and live on Bruce's parent's property. When he was a young apprentice, he built a very large room, which they called the poolroom. With some re-organising, it can easily accommodate us. The room is sectioned off with partitions into spaces. One space for the computer/office, another for a couple of dressers and a wardrobe for our clothes. We have a small lounge with a TV in the corner and another area for the bed. We even have a space for his keyboard, and there's room for a sewing table for me. It'll work out alright, as his parents are getting older and will be quite helpful for them to have him around for a few months each year. While I'm here I'll be on cooking and cleaning duties.

Friday 26th December 2008

I haven't been journaling these past couple of weeks. Not sure why.

Today is our twentieth wedding anniversary. Still ghastly weather. There is a strong, cold Easterly wind howling outside and it's going to rain. Not at all like our wedding day, which was hot and beautiful. We were married at our house. We'd only just finished renovating the night before! It was the first renovation of many that we were going to undertake over the next twenty years.

It was a large two-story character home, which had become derelict, with creeper growing through the old weatherboards. The house was huge and the renovation was costly even though we did everything ourselves. Windows were rotten. Everything needed replacing, apart from a few tiles in the Welsh slate roof. It took a couple of years to complete the job. On the whole, we had a lot of fun, but I wouldn't recommend living in the house when you are trying to remodel the kitchen.

We did for a while, then hired a caravan to use for cooking and eating and to have some respite from the chaos inside. From memory, we only just finished the lounge and furnished it on Christmas Eve. We had a house full of family and friends staying. It was just marvellous to be married at home and to have an intimate amount of guests.

Today, in our tiny abode, we lazed around reminiscing and answering text messages from friends back in Introdacqua. I rang Fiona. She told me they both had a happy day yesterday. I texted Gianni and thanked him for all his help over the past year and for what a special friend he was.

Christmas Day was very special this year. I rose early, showered, prepared the turkey, and other titbits and off we went to his brother's for dinner. Taking the turkey to share.

Lovely family. Their two boys getting their scholarly degrees and they are also very good musicians. Such a happy environment. So coming home at short notice and spending a heap of money on the airfare has been well worth it.

Sunday 4th January 2009

What a busy, though relaxing time we've had. Our friend Vonny, has let us live in her apartment for a week, while she is away. So, it has been a rare treat to experience living in the city. Very handy to walk out the door and mosey a short distance to the trendy cafes and shops. She has Sky, so also a novelty to sit up late and watch movies. Rising late and having a chic brunch at a stylish restaurant close by.

On New Year's Eve, we drove up the coast to spend a few days with Bruce's cousin Peter. I could write a book about him. Interesting fella. He has no concept of time - quite refreshing - meals late into the night, like the Italians. He's a great cook - passionate - with lots of stories to tell. Then out came the fireworks. A terrific show for just the four of us. The next day he took us up the mountain, very scary, to check out the view over the farm and ocean. It is beautiful. Then it was back to the city.

Thursday 8th January 2009

BBQ last night at our friends. It's great to have this unplanned trip back and to be enjoying a New Zealand summer.

I met another friend, Shirley for a coffee. From there we went to explore some art galleries. The galleries in this city are always good value, where we studied some of the art in minute detail. From there to an art shop to load up on supplies. An inspiring day.

We've been out walking each day for about an hour. Days spent on the Internet. Still working on my website.

I bought a new laptop on the 26th, Boxing Day sales. (It's a New Zealand thing)

Tuesday 13th January 2009

'The Beagle Boys', Bruce's brother's R and B band (Bruce plays the keyboard) are playing at a popular holiday resort on Saturday night. We drove the four hours on Friday. Driving through the beautiful scenic Lewis Pass to a town near Nelson. Stopping to have nature bathing (new term) in the rainforests along the way.

The resort is set in a beautiful spot, right on the banks of the Buller River. The river was crystal clear. I took the opportunity to have my first swim of the year. Quite refreshing!! But wonderful to swim in such a gorgeous place.

We had a meal at the local cafe that evening and sat around chatting and drinking, of course with some fairly laugh out loud moments with the other members of the band.

We had a look around the town, with a bit of shopping at the antique shop. The museum was interesting. There were photos of my relations and their ruined houses during the 1968 Inangahua earthquake. And it bought back awful memories. I'd been living in Inangahua with my first husband and baby, until six months prior to the earthquake. We had married young and it wasn't long before I found out he was a boozer and a wife beater, as his father before him. So, a year after my son was born, and with the help of my kind neighbour, we, my son and I, had to sneak out of the village in the morning when he had left for work. I was in fear of our lives from this cruel man. I was pleased to leave the museum and the memories that had flooded back.

When we got back to the venue, the boys started setting up their equipment for the evening's gig. An hour before they were due to play, it began raining! We were hoping that all the campers and others staying in the camp would come and hear the band play, plus the residents of the town.

Not many people came. Most probably put off by the rain, though it was only drizzling. Disappointing for the owner, as he was at least hoping to recover costs. The next morning, we were all pretty slow. But, the owner Peter, cooked us the most wonderful breakfast of bacon and eggs with, dare I say, whitebait patties! What a really decent Kiwi bloke.

We left the others and headed onto Spring Creek, to see my brother, his wife and two lovely kids, Bryce and Rose.

I bought some kites. So we were kept busy running around the whole afternoon with them. We finished the day making interesting figurines with good old-fashioned plasticine. We stayed the night. Graham is such a funny guy. With some robust stories to tell from the region. He has made a fabulous job of building his house, even making the doors with deer antler handles and a beautiful hand-hewn sideboard. A real credit to him. Their little farm is a delight with small horses, goats, chickens, kittens and a raft of other critters.

It was pretty late when we arrived back home, Bruce is working in the morning.

Chapter 25 - Back to Italy

WITH A QUIET DETERMINATION AND NEW INSIGHTS.

"Whether you succeed or not is irrelevant, there is no such thing. Making your unknown known is the important thing".
Georgia O'Keeffe

Tuesday 21st January 2009

Being back in New Zealand has been beneficial in many ways, for instance, I can now see our point of difference and our Kiwiness, I suppose. I appreciate it more and I'm viewing everything through a new set of eyes. Maybe because I've learned to slow down and have become more mindful.

The days drift by without too much drama. We have a nice routine. Bruce heads out to work each day and I study various artists on the Internet or go to the library to borrow books, mainly about artists. We live within biking distance of the Mall, library, second-hand shops, post office, banks and most importantly an art supply store. So, I don't need a car while I'm here, I jump on my bike and I'm there within ten minutes.

Have bikes, will travel. We travelled the South Island a few years ago and it is truly one of the scenic wonders of the world and even more so when you can enhance the experience by cycling around beautiful places like Arrowtown, with its old-world charm and lovely miner's cottages - Queenstown, on the shores of Lake Wakatipu and the same cycling around stunning Lake Wanaka. You are rewarded with spectacular mountain scenery and little towns like Naseby, St Bathans and Cardrona with their quaint pubs to stop and have lunch. On the trip home, we cycled around the old-fashioned town of Oamaru, with its wide streets and striking, Palladio-styled architecture, built from local limestone.

Saturday 24th January 2009

We spent the day in town shopping, then a spot of lunch at one of the restaurants along the Strip, where there is a variety of restaurants and cafes. Situated on the banks of the river Avon, which meanders and winds its way through the heart of the city, passing picturesque character buildings, through the park and botanical gardens along the way. Later, we went to dinner at a friends house for a whitebait dinner, too many drinks and dancing to ABBA. I only mention this as whitebait in New Zealand, is considered, by some, to be a delicacy. It's a very small fish, that is scooped up in large handheld nets. Growing up near the magnificent Buller River, I fished off the rocks down by the wharf. I loved it. Getting up early, depending on the time of the tide, I'd pack my lunch, and load my long scoop net, spotters, buckets, thermos and gumboots into the car. Spotters are long sheets of painted, narrow iron. These, you slip into the water, then as the shoals of whitebait swim across, you can spot them as you guide your net and scoop them up. They're cooked in a thin batter of egg, flour and milk, called a whitebait patty. Whitebait are sold by the pound.

Some years ago we spent a week fishing at Gentle Annie, on the Mokihinui River, with our two dogs Meg, a white West Highland Terrier and Mac, a Black

Scottish Terrier. Bruce never did get over that trip and could not see the fun in standing on a river bank looking at a couple of spotters in the water for hours on end. The dogs and I loved it, though we didn't catch a lot!

"Coasters and their bloody whitebait" he'd scoff.

Whitebaiting a few years ago on the
Avon River.

I've been following the recent spate of bushfires in Australia. I looked up Marysville on the Internet and it was such a lovely little town. Now it is destroyed by the fires and many people have died. It seemed like a neat place to live. It's near a Lake, and ski fields - a place I might have wanted to visit in the future.

My heart goes out to the people who live in these areas.

Back in Italy.

Tuesday 10th February 2009

I arrived back in Introdacqua the other day. I'm endeavouring to change some habits, an ongoing process for me. The idea is to channel my emotions into my art for a month to see what will happen. I'm amazed at how much I seem to change when I'm here in Italy on my own. My thoughts are different. I'm more aware, more in tune.

This is a plan of work I have set up.

From now on each work is set down as a project. It has a title and time limit - theme - materials - each piece is to be documented, like a journal. Techniques, materials used, thoughts on the pieces and what I'm feeling, plus anything else that might be relevant.

Friday 13th February 2009

Bruce rang the other day. It's taking me a while to adjust to being on my own again. I still only have dial-up internet! No Skype yet!

I'm mad at myself at the moment, as yet, I'm not motivated to start a project in the studio. I had a plan, but instead, I've been on the internet reading about the bushfires still raging in Victoria and the stories of the people trying to escape. Just the most horrific thing - I've been crying off and on for days. The animals, koalas, alpacas, and people's beloved pets. Most probably the saddest and worst disaster in my lifetime. Well, close to home.

Monday 16th February 2009

It has snowed these past two nights and I've woken to a winter wonderland; I reminded myself again of how I appreciate this time of solace - and how I'm beginning to enjoy my solitude again. It's snowing very heavily now.

I've started to work on my website again and have it up and running. I found this quote to put on the home page

'It is required of man to share the passion of his time – in peril of being judged not to have lived' Oliver Wendell Holmes Jnr

Tuesday 17th February 2009

I went for a long walk up to the tower. The pathways have been cleared of snow and ice and it felt wonderful to be out walking around the village again. Shapes and designs are now outlined by the snow and the chimneys are highlighted. I can see there is a series of just chimneys. I still have a creative block at the moment. But it will pass. Something is holding me back - I will detail this for the future - I think it's a matter of being patient and letting it find its own way, as things do in this country - it is one giant test in patience, living in Italy! Even waiting until your muse returns.

Wednesday 18th February 2009

Wake to snow again this morning - quite heavy. So, that means I won't be getting my new battery for the car until next week.

Snowing heavily. This is my track to my wood in the back yard.

I'm discovering more acutely, since my return, the different lifestyle here, which soaks in after you have spent a decent amount of time. It's a state of just being - instead of always doing or going. In New Zealand, people ask questions like "What do you do?" or "What are you doing?" or "What have you been doing?" "what are you going to do?" These two words, 'going' and 'doing' tend to be common, whereas, here in this village, you don't have to be doing or going to do anything. Here, you just be. No, questions asked. I don't have to DO anything, or GO anywhere! That is freedom! Though it does take a bit of adjusting to.

Saturday 21st February 2009

Still mucking around my website.

Monday 23rd February 2009

Still, I work on my website. It's all about having a B&B. I can't seem to get it how I want it. Put in a new page about the Abruzzo region, plus generally wasted time, tidying paragraphs and making them sound right. It doesn't help that the broadband is so slow! (All before I found out about Airbnb)

Made bread, a bit soggy in the middle, but OK with jam.

Thursday 26th February 2009

Well, I've been back for twenty days and still, I have difficulty getting something going in my workroom. Though, to be fair I've spent a lot of time on the PC. Now all the computer work is done, there's no reason why I can't knuckle down and get busy. A question I asked myself - was I pushing the envelope with my 'artists life' type requirements?

Saturday 28th February 2009

The month is over already. I start my Introdacqua Quilt tomorrow. I'm going to send it to New Zealand for the twentieth anniversary of our Quilting group.

But, that's a long way away.

A good day working on my quilt. Robyn came over. She's organised our group of expat women, to go and see *'Slumdog Millionaire'* at the cinema near Corfinio. Should put our knowledge of the Italian language to the test, as all movies are dubbed into Italian.

I read the New Zealand papers occasionally on the Internet and I see that many people are losing their jobs, due to the world economic situation caused by the greedy US banking conglomerates.

Saturday March 7th 2009

I basted my quilt, ready for stitching.

Rain, rain, rain. So much rain lately. Roll on primavera (springtime).

What I have to learn is to just 'be', as I've said before, it isn't easy to change habits of a lifetime, rushing around with deadlines and all the trappings of being in business. I thought I could just flick a switch and convert from one life to another, just like that. But no, I can see now that it takes time and these things happen incrementally when you're not looking!

Sunday 8th March 2009

Beautiful sunny day. I'll finish putting the quilt together and go for a long walk. I'm loving my long walks and feel they are helping me to keep a positive mental attitude. One of my favourite pastimes is to hand quilt out in the garden and I'm ever hopeful that soon I'll no longer be at the beck and call of my whimsical mind and *"will be more in control"*.

More thoughts from May Sarton, *'Journal of Solitude'*.

The things I cannot stand are pretentiousness. She says, *she hates small talk with a passion, along with coarseness of soul and vulgarity!*

She goes on:

Why? I suppose because, with any meeting with another human being is a collision for me now. It is always expensive and I will not waste my time. It is never a waste of time to be outdoors and never a waste of time to lie down and rest, even for a couple of hours. It is then that images float up and I plan my work. But it is a waste of time to see people who have only a social surface to show. I will make every effort to find out the real person, but if I can't, then I am upset and cross - time wasted is poison!

Pretentious - defined as: pompous, phoney, smug, arrogant, artificial, conceited, inflated, showy, entitled, privileged, ostentatious and shallow.

And for the record, in my view, the English tradition of handing out Knighthoods to members of our society, (even in New Zealand) such as rock stars, film stars, sports people and some (most) politicians is abhorrent. It sums up the pretentiousness of the British hierarchy. Enormous respect and kudos are more likely given to those who, over the years have turned down Knighthoods and other self-effacing decorations. David Bowie, Albert Finney and John Cleese to name a few. John Cleese summed it up, "*it is silly*". Dawn French and Jennifer Saunders said there were others more deserving. John Lennon sent his award back!

I don't buy into these outdated traditions and will call them out at every opportunity I have!

My neighbours here and the people I've met to date in Italy, are never pretentious.

Chapter 26 - Enjoying the Isolation

DISASTER STRIKES! THE L'AQUILA EARTHQUAKE!

"An artist cannot fail; it is a success to be one". Charles Horton Cooley

Tuesday 10th March 2009

Yesterday turned out to be somewhat of a watershed moment. In those quiet hours, my thoughts took a reflective turn focusing on the appreciation I have for Bruce and the life we've built together. Sometimes you need a bit of distance before you see the things that truly matter. Adapting to life on my own took some time. The winter in this part of the world is long and cold, and it feels like the people here are in a state of hibernation. Yet, in a surprising twist, I now cherish the moments of solitude. It was during these stretches of quiet, during this period of reconnection with myself, that I discovered a certain peace and tranquillity I hadn't known before.

There was a newfound joy in these solitary moments, a sanctuary within myself that had patiently waited for me to uncover it. It came as quite a revelation, as I had never expected to reach a stage in life where there wasn't a whirlwind of activity. In my previous life, I was a bit of a chatterbox and my home was a revolving door of people coming and going. Whether it was the hustle and bustle of work or the incessant ringing of the phone, there was always a sense of constant activity surrounding me. Not anymore.

Friday March 13th 2009

A big day today. I finished the quilt I've been working on, *Images of Intro-dacqua'* which is to be sent to New Zealand for the twentieth anniversary of our quilting group.

'Images of Introdacqua'

We had another girl's night out. Again a lot of laughter and a reasonable cost too - €10.00 for pizza and wine. This time we went to Pacentro. A most beautiful village. Last night's conversation was centred around how they, the girls, have assimilated into the Italian community. The outcome was interesting. Carol, is from the UK and married to an Italian. They have three boys and she told us it doesn't matter how long you live here, you will never be *one of them'*. She continued, saying it didn't matter how good your Italian is, or how much you try, you'll never be accepted and you'll never fit! She should know as she's been here for nearly thirty years! So, that was interesting. The other girls, who have also been here for over thirty years, and there are quite a few in our group, agreed with her. This is why contact with other expats, even though we don't get together often, is so important to them.

Saturday 14th March 2009

At the Sulmona market today, I found another great haul of vintage linens, doilies and bought home a bundle of them. *"I'm in heaven"* song on my mind. Even though they're clean and not at all smelly, I'll still wash and starch them when I arrive home.

*Rummaging through the many pieces
of linen.*

Sunday 15th March 2009

Lazy day. However, I did venture out for a quick-paced walk up the hill to view the beautiful scene down to Sulmona. Breathtaking.

Monday 16th March 2009

I had my last open fire last night, as I've used all my firewood. I made Bruschetta - toasted bread over the hot embers, tomatoes and mozzarella cheese. Dozed.

It's while I stitch by the fire, I know a secret comfort and a personal peace.

Tuesday 17th March 2009

My cousin, Mike, who I hadn't seen or heard from for a number years made contact and we reminisced for a couple of emails.

An earthquake during the night! About a 3.5. Then there was another smaller one. Very scary.

Thursday 19th March 2009

Spent the day working on my mannequin series, which I'm really enjoying. Gi rang to see how I was.

Snowing again.

Saturday 21st March 2009

Still snowing and becoming quite deep.

Tuesday 24th March 2009

Gianni and Matteo came and fixed the car and a new battery €130.00

The snow is melting.

Wednesday 25th March 2009

Another light dusting of snow overnight. It's still three months before Bruce comes over from New Zealand. I hope I'm not a mental case by then.

Started working on a paper art collage yesterday. I'm happy with it and continue to work on these types of projects all week.

Saturday 28th March 2009

A very productive day. I painted a huge amount of painted tissue paper with a wash of acrylic paint. These will be used in future art projects to be stamped and stencilled then decorated with gold leaf to be made into collage pictures.

Tara and Poppies.

Painted tissue

Paper Collage

So, I feel as if I'm starting to gain traction and it's taken me over three months to really get going with any sort of confidence and enthusiasm.

Sunday 29th March 2009

Actually, I have a news deficiency now as I don't read the newspaper of course, and then I don't understand what they're saying on the telly. I must admit it is liberating, how I love it. And I've discovered drinking red wine from an ordinary glass tumbler as the locals do, as opposed to a stemmed glass, is just as liberating.

I continue working with my coloured tissue papers. The colours are fab and I have no idea where I'm going with this line of art.

L'Aquila Earthquake!

Monday 6th April 2009

Earthquake! It was around 3:30 am when the ground heaved with a tremendous force. The jolt rattled not just me but everything in the house. In those initial moments, panic gripped me, as I jumped out of bed and rushed to the safety of the back veranda.

Outside, I discovered that the power was out and the darkness added an extra layer of dread. I stood there for a while, the aftershocks continuing to unsettle my nerves. It was a harrowing experience and I eventually mustered the courage to return to bed. Daylight brought with it a reassuring calm after a long night of anxiety. In the light of day - news of the earthquake had spread already and I was contacted by relations and friends from New Zealand who were concerned for my welfare. It turns out the epicentre was in the heart of L'Aquila city, which is about forty five minutes from here. The city has been totally destroyed and sadly, many people have died. All day I watch the events unfolding on TV. Such widespread devastation.

Our village and Sulmona have sustained some damage, though nothing to comment on. Gianni popped out to see how I was. Fiona and my other neighbours have been rallying around and we've been chatting over the fence. Thankfully the power is back on.

Easter Monday 13th April 2009

The huge aftershocks cause uneasiness and people are continually on edge. I'm a total wreck. Routines are all to hell. No exercising, no juice. It has been a week of misery. Easter celebrations around the Province have been cancelled. Around three hundred people were killed in the quake.

The devastation left by the quake.

My god, that is awful. So close to home.

Well, it's certainly been a time of high drama and trauma. It's not easy for me right now and I'm finding it difficult to get back to a routine. I haven't been eating or sleeping. To top it off, Bruce has informed me that he's thinking of putting his trip back a month. What!! Telling me last week how he now knows that I'm his soulmate, yet doesn't mind me waiting a whole month for him to come over. Men!

Yes, I know, I've made our life difficult by coming to Italy on this adventure.

Today I went back to work in the studio. The garden is all done - it took four days to get into shape and to plant the wildflower seeds.

So, it's back to work.

Wednesday 15th April 2009

An Aussie woman Shirley has befriended me. She's a reporter for a newspaper in Sydney and has a house here in the village left to her by her father. She was here for most of the afternoon checking her emails and generally using my computer. The problem is she never stops talking. She has eight children and some of them are sickly – on and on she goes.

I'm having mixed feelings about Bruce at the moment regarding his trip here in July. He has clouded the issue by wanting to stop over in LA for ten days. Ten precious days he could be here with me! I'm not quite sure how to handle it at the moment.

Anyway, I've had enough of soul searching and past issues. Now I just want to concentrate on life here.

Sunday 19th April 2009

Apart from heading into Sulmona market to buy some plants, it's been an uneventful couple of days. I'm waiting for Bruce to ring to tell me what he's decided about his trip. The weather has been cold and grey, which is adding to the oppressive air that now surrounds the quake news.

Around 40.000 people have been left without a home in L'Aquila and are now living in tents. The weather has become overcast and wet adding to their misery.

Tuesday 21st April 2009

These past few days have been a continual stream of rain and I'm thankful for my warm, cosy home and that I can keep myself busy in the studio to take my mind off these trying times. I find myself in an ongoing search to uncover my true forte and admit to dabbling in and around various ideas. Immersion into a substantial, worthwhile project is constantly on my mind, but the path to get there remains elusive. I suppose, like many things, it will come to me in its own time.

Yay, Bruce's decision is to come directly here, and no, I didn't resort to any dirty tactics.

Wednesday 22nd April 2009

Shirley's son became very sick, so I was called upon and we had a mercy dash to Pronto Soccorso, the hospital emergency. He was admitted overnight and the next day, thankfully he was OK. He had eaten something that hadn't agreed with him.

Since I'm not making headway in the studio I've started to revamp the back veranda and turn it into a lovely sunroom. A few weeks ago I'd bought twenty metres of white thermal-backed fabric from the market for only €1.00 a metre and will be ideal for the curtains.

Saturday 25th April 2009

Nights are still spent with some anxiety, as you never know if there is going to be another earthquake. There was a large one the other night, with an epi-centre in Sulmona. A bit close to home.

Finally, the sun has started to shine.

Chapter 27 - Getting over the L'Aquila Earthquake

RICHARD DIED - SUDDENLY!

"One can have no smaller or greater mastery than mastery of oneself". Leonardo da Vinci

Sunday 26th April 2009

These past few weeks since the earthquake have been filled with sadness and heartbreak, as we witness survival stories and funerals each day on TV. So as a way to numb the pain, I went through and chose my favourite coloured fabrics, silks, braids, buttons, bits and pieces I've been collecting for years. Stuff, I was always going to use one day!

Well, one day was here!

This little project will be my way of dealing with the upheaval and perhaps will chase my blues away. My aim is to stitch this assortment of fragments into a cohesive piece of wall art. Recently I've discovered that making art isn't just about finishing the piece, it's more about the process and embracing the therapeutic means of crafting as a journey, where the act of creating itself becomes a source of solace and meaning.

There are still strong aftershocks, so the authorities have set up fourteen tents down at the Sportiva (football stadium) for people and families in the village who are scared of being in their homes at night. These stone houses don't bode well in earthquakes. I hope things settle down soon.

Fi and I went for a walk up to the tower. There's a garbage tip up in that area and the pickings are generally not bad and this visit didn't disappoint! We found an old cupboard with nice glass in the doors. With a bit of sanding, a lick of paint it'll come up quite smart. So we scurried off back home to get the car, then back up the hill to push and shove it into the boot to haul it home. We find such good stuff and have a lot of laughs in the process.

Tuesday 28th April 2009

So to sum up this April 2009: the earthquake, the awful weather, and the feelings of isolation all took their toll, so jump-starting my creative juices by working on these small blocks, was what was needed. I love the look that comes about by zapping tulle with the heat gun and along with this technique I'm adding embellishments, such as gold leaf and beading. The evenings are spent quietly hand embroidering. I've left each piece in its organic state, rather than squaring them up perfectly, as you would for a traditional quilt. The music I listened to while I worked was a mixture of Sarah Brightman, Pet Shop Boys, Russell Watson, Supertramp and Dusty.

*This is an example of the six inch blocks
I made during this time. From there I
stitched them to the blue background. I
made sixteen small blocks in total.*

Wednesday 29th April 2009

Michele finished the electrical wiring in the guest room. Now I can start to titivate the room to be ready for guests.

Gianni took me to a family run factory to buy a new mattress for the bed in the guest room. It was interesting to find how they make their mattresses and not only did I buy a mattress, I came away with a bag of cleaned, long, chunky wool, which the company use as their fillings. I'll incorporate it into my felted wall art.

Saturday 2nd May 2009

I've discovered, quite by accident the type of organisation which I'd been hoping to connect with and I've decided to become a member. It's an online group based in the US called SAQA. Studio Art Quilt Associates.

Monday 4th May 2009

A clear sky this morning, maybe the weather will settle down now and will start to warm up, as it's cold for this time of the year.

Saturday night on one of my rare visits to the Piazza, I ran into Marco. He told me about the charity jazz night they were having tomorrow night for the victims of the earthquake. I went along to listen and it was lovely to be out socialising with my new friends again.

Sunday 10th May 2009

I'm putting the finishing touches to the curtains for the outdoor sunroom. It turned out to be a fairly big project and it's satisfying to see it completed. We now have a sunny, private area to have our meals.

Thursday 14th May 2009

While in Sulmona the other day, I popped into the Police Station to renew my Permesso Soggiorno. My permission to stay here in Italy. A long procedure, which I have found to be of no benefit at all, except for buying a second-hand car.

Shirley has been dropping in quite a lot to use the computer to send her articles back to her Sydney newspaper and to check her emails. She was telling me how she believes everyone should have as many children as she has, as the population throughout the world, particularly Italy, isn't keeping up with the number of old people left to look after themselves. On and on and on she went. She's on a crusade to convince the world.

Well, good luck with that, I say.

Tuesday 19th May 2009

Richard died!

Gianni called me and explained the surrounding events that caused his death. Apparently, he had a brain tumour. Struggling from his bed, he staggered out-doors for help and sadly he was found lying in his garden. I am so sad. He was a kindred spirit and he had so many plans and dreams for his B&B and his classes for people who wanted to study Ovid. What a shock. You'll remember I met Richard on my trip to London. We were introduced by Lucia and sat next to each other on the plane, where he told me of his plans for his property. He came over to the village for Ringraziamenti with his lovely Abuzzi dog who had frozen in fright, due to the crowds of people and the last time I saw him he was carrying his dog from the festival to his car. I was expecting him back to have lunch with me. I never saw him again. Gianni heard the news on the radio that he had to be airlifted out to Avezzano Hospital. He died a few days later. His daughters came to take him back to the UK.

So sad - he was only 58.

Thursday 21st May 2009

Talking to Bruce the other night, we've made a decision to explore Europe while we're living on this side of the world and figured the best and cheapest way would be to buy a van similar to the one we have in New Zealand. For many years now, Kiwis have been able to buy very good, cheap second-hand Japanese imports. A Google search showed they also import used cars from Japan into London. I've found a dealership in Dagenham that sells Toyota Lucida's at very reasonable prices. It'll be ideal for touring and camping. Without further ado, I've booked a Ryanair flight to London in July. The air tickets didn't cost anything, just the taxes. €55.00 for both of us one way of course, as we'll be driving the van back to Italy, via France. Doesn't that sound exciting?

Bruce emailed his nephew, Matt in London and told him we were coming to buy a Toyota van. He wrote back and offered us to stay at his flat, though it will be too crowded, so we'll stay close by in Earls Court. He's looking forward to us coming over.

The weather has been beautiful, hot with no wind. The garden is looking good. I've been buying geraniums for the tubs on the balconies. They're so neat. So Italy.

I haven't been in the studio for a week or so now, what with one thing and another.

I've invited Susan and Roger for lunch on Sunday.

Saturday 23rd May 2009

Only a month before Bruce arrives. I'm in the process of researching really good cameras, as I'm buying one for his birthday in the hope that he'll renew his love of photography and record our travels. Photographing and documenting Italy and the places we visit - capturing the essence of the country. I'd like in the future to have an exhibition of our work. His photos and my artistic interpretation of them.

Started a new series *"Moving Forward"*. It relates to living your dream. Moving forward in life - conducting your life in a manner that will lift your spirits - as Richard was doing - my thoughts continually wander to him as I'm working. Pursue your passion - make it happen. Each piece will have a theme script on it, such as, "go with your hunch" - "just do it" - listen to your inner person - "I want to be free" - "turn me loose" - "it's the journey", etc.

Every now and then I lose the plot. I don't stay focused. I won't go into the studio - I drift - clean the house - clean all the bedding - tend the garden - daydream.

But is that losing the plot or merely regrouping, gathering strength and making plans? It appears to me that some of the traits I've inherited from my mother are not all bad and it does help to have my house tidy, clean and presentable. Though I'm not as fastidious as she, and she was always quick to remind me how much like her mother I was. Nana, it seems, was a bit slapdash and would only clean up when things got messy and that sounds a lot like me.

The mattress arrived, so now the B&B guest room is set up, bedding and everything is in order.

Guest Room - ready for guests.

The huge amount of documentation of the Permesso Di Soggiorno, has been a real challenge.

Meantime, I've been thinking about our new vehicle that is going to take us around Europe and planning the trip to London, all the while trying to keep my weight in check, by walking up the hill most days.

Tuesday 26th May 2009

Our lunch on Sunday here at home with Sue and Roger was a great outlet and we all ended up pretty merry! Just what we needed to let off a bit of steam. I'd prepared some Italian dishes, prima patti of prosciutto, with tomatoes, basil and mozzarella cheese, then a secondo of pasta with fungi (mushroom sauce). We had some laughs and some sad moments, as we discussed the passing of Richard. Sue was closer to him, as they shared an interest in stage shows and went to various events these past few years.

Friday 29th May 2009

Bruce rang and told me he's booked his ticket and will arrive on 1st July. Great.

Monday 1st June 2009

I've fallen in love with the art of felting and it is lovely during the day working out in the wet room. It's sunny and I enjoy looking out into the garden and the mountains.

Rose is coming back to Europe and asked if she could stay. I emailed to say we would be in London for a week or two, but she's most welcome to the house while we were away.

Sunday 7th June 2009

Fixed up my website. Quite happy with it now.

Still not confident about having a blog. The question has been lately, 'to blog, or not to blog'.

Very, very windy today. Quite scary. Blowing my new outdoor room and curtains to bits.

Out with the girls the other night. We dined at La Trota and I did enjoy it. I hadn't seen them for ages, though some of us keep in touch by phone.

Monday 8th June 2009

It seems I've learned a valuable life lesson. I have a whole new outlook on life. I've overcome the want or the need to be with people all the time. I can honestly say I'm over it, whatever IT is.

There's a difference between being alone and being lonely. More and more I sense being alone, but I don't feel lonely. This newfound awareness has brought me an inner sense of well-being and happiness that's hard to put into words. It's like a heavy burden has lifted and finally feel like I can move forward. Learning to find contentment and happiness regardless of the weather or external influences has been a real turning point for me. I've seen how some people fear being alone, even for a short while, and the idea of having to entertain themselves seems daunting. I find the notion of just "filling in time" or "killing time" without purpose can leave us feeling pretty empty as if the moments just faded into the background noise of life.

Tuesday 9th June 2009

After the wind blew my outdoor sunroom to bits, I've managed to get it back into shape.

I had a delicious morning devouring my recent SAQA magazines in the garden. I'm excited to discover an inspiring group of quilt/textile artists who are pushing the boundaries of their art.

This has indeed lifted my spirits to a new high.

Chapter 28 - Finding the secret to a happy life

WELL - FROM MY POINT OF VIEW.

"There is no must in art because art is free".
Wassily Kandinsky

Friday 12th June 2009

During my daily walks around the village, I notice some doors are adorned with little pink cards and delicate flowers. It's an indicator that a new baby girl has arrived, or if it's blue signifies the arrival of a baby boy. On the other hand, the presence of white ribbons tied in a sombre bow tells of a recent loss in the family.

I cross paths with some interesting locals, like the other day I met a friendly lady sitting on her well-worn chair outside her home. Most homes have chairs or benches outside their homes. This is where the owners can sit and enjoy the last rays of sunlight and catch up with their friends. She had a lovely smile and invited me in for coffee. The house, a traditional family home with the obligatory religious icons dotted around the walls, was a home that had been well lived. She shared a slice of her homemade cake and we chatted, though not really able to understand each other, we got the gist and a genuine connection was made. As I left, her hug spoke volumes. A simple yet profound meeting.

This house, my house, with its cosy spaces, brings me a sense of harmony. Despite its compact size, it works amazingly well. Just outside the studio in my open shed, everything I require is within arm's reach – hot and cold water, a generous sized bench at the perfect height. It's open with a view of my cottage garden, yet sheltered from the elements and is shaded by the now, vigorously growing fig tree.

Wednesday 17th June 2009

The weeks are flying by. In two weeks I'll be going to Rome to meet Bruce at Fiumicino Airport.

It's become very hot, so I keep the doors and windows closed and find the house stays cooler.

Friday 19th June 2009

After eating salads, exercising, particularly my upper body, doing girl press-ups and strength training for my arms, I'm starting to see and feel some good results.

Today I found an outdoor table and two deck chairs, thrown in the garbage, which I'll give new covers and a lick of paint.

Saturday 27th June 2009

As a founding member of the Quilting group back in New Zealand, the committee has asked me to write a speech for the forthcoming twentieth year celebrations they're planning. Here is part of my letter which will be read out to the group at the celebrations.

'The setting up of our Quilters group, was relatively straightforward, compared to some ideas I've had over the years. The problems arose from the fact that there were no role models or guidelines on how to set up a group. I started by placing a couple of small ads in the local paper, asking if there were other like-minded people who were interested in forming a quilt group.

Well, there were plenty. Our first meeting was held in a little room above Jan's quilt shop and it was soon bursting at the seams with enthusiastic, keen quilters. The actual meeting is a bit of a haze now, because we were so overwhelmed by the response. I recall a couple of us stammered our way through the next hour or so and gave out handouts explaining when and where we would meet in the future.

Our first meetings were held in the church hall around the corner from where I lived. We sort of bumbled along to start with. There were many different ideas and opinions on where we were going, what our aims would be etc. My initial vision was to get together with a few other quilters and quilt together in a hall each week or whatever. The next thing I knew there was talk of a president, secretary, treasurer, committee, subs, and a library.

It went something like this, 'Well, you started it, you be president' 'Oh, OK'

It didn't really matter what I had envisioned for the group, because after the first few months, it gathered speed and had a mind of its own.

It took off. We had committees, sub-committees, quilt shows to organise, quilts to raffle, quilts to donate. We established a great library, had some wonderful guest speakers, and lots of classes for beginners. The retreats were great fun.

When Bruce and I shifted to the country, a few years later we held 'The Quilters Gatherings' for six years and many quilters from the group would come down for the day to attend this annual event. Actually, I haven't met any quilters here in Italy yet, lace makers, but not quilters.

Our Quilters group has become a huge organisation. It has helped and inspired many of the remarkable quilters who belong to the group. On reading your last newsletter I was amazed at the variety of topics and events planned for the future.

I am very proud of the way it has gone from strength to strength. I wish you all the best for this weekend and also for the 20th celebrations in September.

I will be thinking about you all. Have a good time.'

Monday 29th June 2009

I haven't been this excited for ages. Bruce leaves New Zealand tomorrow and will arrive here in a few days. It's quite a mission for him, as I'm not there to help him. He's helping his mother, as his father has recently had a stroke and now needs to go into care. This has been very stressful for everyone.

I digress:

So many people don't have a hobby or a passion - I think the secret to a happy life is to sort out your passion and a hobby and see where it leads you.

My advice to would be creatives is to 'just do it'

I'm always surprised by what I create. I use a variety of techniques and materials. I get a run on something. I might spend a week or a month, say creating felt or art collages or whatever It depends on the weather. If the weather is lovely I can go out to the garden and make felt.

Creating stuff takes me into a different realm. I don't need to be entertained by TV or have the need to go out.

This is why I'm happy doing art here in Italy. I have no distractions. I don't have the need to join any clubs. There was a time, last year when I thought about becoming more involved with the local groups. There is a lovely band of ladies who gather to organise the fiestas and the food stalls. It would be an ideal way to meet everyone and hone my language skills, but I decided to concentrate on my art, as I felt if I became involved with community happenings it could lead to distractions on many levels, hence my decision. But I may do later on.

Have I really arrived?

I feel I have arrived at a place, mentally speaking, a place that many strive for, but often struggle to reach. It hasn't been an easy path, and it has taken time for me to navigate the many bumps along the way. It's a state of being where guilt, anxiety, and the longing to be elsewhere have simply melted away. Creating art makes me feel good. When I'm in the zone, I don't have the need to be anywhere else or to go anywhere. I am already here - exactly where I want to be.

Electing to move to Italy, was risky and it could've gone either way. I was warned by a woman in Florence when I told her of my adventure here, she said, "Oh, I don't know about long distant relationships. It has been my observation, that they don't work in the long run". Well, I hope she's wrong, but in hindsight, I don't want to be apart for this length of time again. Five months has been a long time, eight or ten weeks is long enough.

OK, enough daydreaming and analysing!

I was trying to write an artist statement. I'll work on that again later. Right now I have to get into the shower and wash my hair - get everything organised and tidy for his homecoming.

Bruce will notice a few changes, not just in the house, but in me as well. I've undergone a transformation, becoming more serene and at peace with myself. After spending five months in relative isolation, the prospect of heading out occasionally is an exciting prospect. Yet, the incessant need to be out and about has lost its grip on me and I'm just as happy to be at home.

Wednesday 1st July 2009

I spent the day cleaning yesterday. It was such a long day. I'm always anxious when he is in the air, twenty five hours, it's a long flight from New Zealand.

I'm off to Rome in a couple of hours, then out to Fiumicino.

Sunday 5th July 2009

On Thursday while in Rome I managed to do some shopping in Nazione Avenue. I was mainly looking for cameras to compare prices with the one I have put away in Sulmona. I didn't see a camera shop.

I caught the Leonardo Express out to Fiumicino. I was late and Bruce had already come through the big sliding doors and was waiting to one side of the crush of people. Such a busy place, that it was hard to spot him at first. He hadn't been waiting long. We had a big kiss and cuddle, as you do.

We needed to divert to the unaccompanied baggage department in another part of the airport to retrieve the bag he had sent unaccompanied. But, the bag wasn't there. So much for the staff at our airport telling him it would be on the same flight and he'd be able to pick it up at Fiumicino when he arrived. We have to come back on Monday. Shades of my lost artwork came to mind.

So we caught the train back to Sulmona, where Gianni picked us up.

Days pass and compared to my normal routine there was much catching up to do. It's all so exciting.

On Friday, while he slept I popped into Sulmona to pick up the camera.

Here I go again, I thought, organising Bruce's life. I bought this camera for him to document our travels. For me to do art pieces from, with the idea of one day of having an exhibition together.

Chapter 29 - Off to London to buy a van

AND WE MEET GUIDO.

"If I could say it in words there would be no reason to paint". Edward Hopper

Monday 6th July 2009

To celebrate Bruce's birthday, on Saturday night I chose Vecchio Muro for a romantic dinner, where I presented him with his camera, a Nikon DSLR. I'm not sure if he was pleased with it to start with. I shared the vision with him and as the evening progressed he loved his camera and the idea of recording our adventures. So much so, on returning home, he'd quietly put the camera in our bed. You're going to think this is strange! As I got into bed, there was the camera. A secret 'thing' we have shared ever since either one of us bought something we loved and wanted to take to bed. For instance, his new skill saw would end up in bed, or my new shoes, or whatever. Always a good joke and made us laugh.

So, here was the camera. A sure sign that he loved it.

Today we went back to Fiumicino in the car, which went really well for a long trip. We went first to the airport then had to backtrack to Cargo City, which brought back memories of my trip to find my art crate. The place is huge, but it's surprisingly organised. We handed over our documentation and were summoned down a hall into an office, where the Italian official only wanted to know about the '*All Blacks*' and '*Lord of the Rings*'. Italians associate these two things with New Zealand. Bruce has often had to do the Haka in the strangest places (but not here, thankfully). After a lot of laughs with the boss, who spoke very good English, the bag duly arrived in the office. B signed a heap of documents, and after lots of handshakes, we left happy. The Italians are just so nice when you are doing business with them.

I love 'em.

On the drive home, we stopped in at IKEA. It was our first time at IKEA. No, we don't have one in New Zealand. It was amazing. Love the concept. Bought a few things.

Had a great day.

Thursday 9th July 2009

Sent the letter (email) off to Roz at the Quilters group. I nearly forgot, as there is so much going on lately. She's going to read it out on Saturday night at the Quilter's meeting.

Friday 10th July 2009

In the evening, we went into Sulmona for a stroll, passeggiata, along the Corso. We ran into Gianni and stopped to have a Prosecco with him before going into Garibaldi Square. There was a pizza night and music going on. While we were standing in the queue, we met a charming man. He heard our English voices and introduced himself. Guido (Guy) and his daughter Nancy, husband Pino and their daughter. We ended up dining and spending the evening with them. Guido had lived forty years in Melbourne working for a shoe company and singing on cruise ships doing Frank Sinatra and Tony Bennett. A real crooner it seems. He returned to his home here in Italy many years ago and bought a small ski resort, restaurant and accommodation at Passo San Leonardo. Which is way up past Pacentro on the other side of the valley.

It was an evening to savour and as we said our Buona Notti's, we promised to drive to Passo San Leonardo and visit him.

Top of mind is our trip to London. This will be our first trip to the UK together and we're making plans to see as much as possible while we're there. Driving back to Introdacqua through France and Switzerland will be the highlight. I have a list of things to do, like visiting art supply shops and art galleries, but first I need to research car dealers.

Sunday 12th July 2009

I've been working on small pieces for the 'White' series of felted merino and silk tops, with French knots and other embroideries. I framed them in white box frames bought from IKEA. They look delicious, even if I do say so myself.

A night out in the Piazza last night was a jazz evening, part of the jazz fiesta going on this week. It was good to catch up with many of the locals I hadn't seen for a while.

Monday 13th July 2009

Beautiful sunny day - we strolled to the Piazza for a coffee. Home for lunch in the garden - talked - drank - laughed, then went for a long walk around the village and up to the tower. Gianni came out for a visit and chat. Bruce rang his mother, who is in LA staying with his sister.

Think about this and let's be honest – when was the last time, in your hometown, did you do these things? Stroll, passeggiata, pizza in Piazza, an evening walk to the main street and meet with others for a chat? Well, it doesn't happen where I come from! Yet here, it happens in a way that is so natural, so normal, that you could be fooled into thinking this way of life happens everywhere, but we know it doesn't. That's why we came here. To experience it, to live it and we leave richer for having known it and tasted it.

Tuesday 14th July 2009

Today we are packing, as we're off to London tomorrow. Rose rang to say she would be here on the 23rd. I thought she would've jumped at the chance to stay in the house while we were away. Not as adventurous as I thought.

Gianni is picking us up at four in the morning to drive us to Pescara airport. He's been panicking about this for days, worried that he'll sleep in.

Wednesday 15th July 2009

Well, he duly arrived really early, as we knew he would, but we're grateful he's driving us to the airport. Such a wonderful friend to have.

We arrived at Stansted Airport, UK and because I was with my husband, there was no dispute over my entry into the country, this time! We caught the bus to Strathfield and then the train to Dagenham East to the car dealers.

A very friendly Indian fella picked us up (already arranged by email and phone) from the station. We looked at a couple of Toyota Lucida/Estima, eight-seater vans they had in the yard. Their choices didn't look as good as portrayed on their website. Why does that surprise us? But, they did have one van that looked OK. It was up on the hoist, as they were working on the motor. We could come back and have a look at it tomorrow. We left there and went to Earls Court station. I'd booked into a hotel around the corner. The room was small and dank and we were here for five nights! That night we met Matt for drinks and an Indian meal. He helped us with buying our Oyster card for travelling on the train.

All good.

Thursday 16th July 2009

Up early and caught the train back out to Dagenham East to see if the van was ready to take for a test drive. It wasn't. So the ol' uncle took us to a local shopping centre where we could fill in the time shopping while we were waiting. After a few hours he came to pick us up, but the car still wasn't ready, which meant we had to come back in the morning.

Friday 17th July 2009

I was up early to spend an hour or so on the Internet looking for more vans for us to check out. We found one that sounded really good. I rang the guy, and yes, it was a good van for the price. With great expectations, we set off on the train and as luck would have it, it was in the same direction as Dagenham. Our confidence for the underground is growing and our Oyster card is doing what it's supposed to. Steve picked us up from the station.

Well, what a disappointment! The van was filthy and reeked of cigarette smoke. We thought there may be a possibility of getting it professionally cleaned, but then we saw things were falling off it, we bolted. Thanks, but no thanks.

We scurried back to the station and then to the other car to take it for a test drive. Yes, it was ready and had been cleaned. Compared to the last one, it was pure luxury, no cigarette smoke in this one and drove like a dream. Bruce was happy with the way it handled and the fact they had spent quite a bit of time and effort on reconditioning the engine and it was diesel. We have the same van model back in New Zealand, but it has a petrol engine and is more expensive to run. So, yes we'll buy it for £1500.00. It's great to have another Toyota Lucida in the family. There are curtains on the windows and they're clean and intact. The seats fold down to make a very comfortable double bed. It's just the ticket for seeing Europe, which will start with our trip home through France and into Italy.

The air-conditioning unit needs tweaking, so we'll come back on Sunday, pick it up and drive it home.

A huge thunderstorm late today. We ate British fish 'n chips for tea. Stayed in for another early night. Clambering onto trains and getting around London is exhausting.

Saturday 18th July 2009

Organised insurance for the car, which almost cost as much as the car! Then it was off out to explore London. I found an art supply shop and bought what I needed. We had an enjoyable time at Madame Tussauds wax museum, taking our photos (with the camera) and posing with famous people, especially Jonah Lomu, a very talented New Zealand rugby player. He became the youngest ever All Black when he played his first international in 1994 at the age of 19 years. Sadly he died in 2015.

Later, we walked around Leicester Square to check the shows on offer for tonight. We bought tickets for *'We Will Rock You'* concert. Shopped in High Street. Covent Garden is a wonderful surprise. And what about Harrods? Even before entering, the exterior is beautiful with its famous green and gold signage and featured window displays.

Harrods is one of the most iconic and prestigious department stores in London, if not the world, it's history dates back to 1834 when Charles Henry Harrod opened a small grocery shop and is now a grand emporium that spans seven floors and covers 4.5 acres of retail space. It is renowned for its lavish interiors, especially the Egyptian Escalator, adorned with ancient Egyptian decor. The store is divided into a variety of departments, offering everything from high-end fashion and accessories to fine jewellery, home furnishings, cosmetics, and gourmet food. Our favourite of course, was the Food Hall, where we *'ohhhed and ahhhhed'* over the exquisite foods and delicacies from around the world. We bought some goodies for our trip home and other treasures to remind us of our visit to Harrods, where it wasn't just a shopping experience; it was a journey into the world of opulence and style.

Loved the Harrods experience.

Sunday 19th July 2009

'We Will Rock You' the concert last night was brilliant. We're huge fans of Freddie Mercury and Queen. Brian May came on stage at the end to play his guitar. We would love to live in London for a while to experience more shows. Next time, we'll stay longer.

This morning we were up early and headed for Westminster, but the Abbey, unfortunately, was closed for repairs. Next on the list, the London Eye. I wasn't keen to go on, as I'm not good with heights, but with Bruce's encouragement I ventured and I'm glad I did as the experience was just lovely. A complete rotation takes about thirty minutes and it was slow and smooth allowing us to capture stunning photos and enjoy the city from various angles and views for miles. From there we went to Tate Modern. Such a pleasure to visit art galleries, especially the

Chelsea area. There was so much more we wanted to see and do, but time was against us, so it was back to the hotel, gathered our stuff, then out to pick up the car and start our drive back to Introdacqua. It was around four o'clock.

Mission accomplished.

The Van.

Monday 20th July 2009

We drove to Maitland, where we stayed overnight in a lovely hotel. This hotel had a policy: *if you do not have a quiet night, we will refund 100% of your money.* Well, with our track record of noisy nights in hotels, we couldn't go wrong, right? Wrong!

We were well and truly awakened at three am by people on the floor above us stomping around and playing a base guitar. Un - bloody - believable! We rang the desk. But for some reason, the noise continued for a while longer. Seems no matter how hard we try, we are destined to be woken. This was made more palatable with our refund, though I would've preferred a good night's sleep.

Tuesday 21st July 2009

Stopping at Maitland, quite a large and lovely English town, where we came across a well-stocked tile shop and bought some tiles to use as a splashback behind the bench in our kitchen. Arriving in Dover, we booked the ferry bound for Calais, France.

Yahoo, France.

Calais captured my heart the moment I laid eyes on it. The architectural style – it was simply, well, French! And the meticulously laid-out gardens were a sight to behold. To our surprise, there was an incredible photographic art exhibition display in the park. This exhibition introduced us to the work of *Yann Arthus Bertrand*. The park was adorned with a breathtaking collection of his photographs from around the world, all captured from unique aerial perspectives, which showcased Yann's distinctive artistic approach. It was a truly enchanting experience.

We were transfixed until almost dusk.

As the sun dipped below the horizon, we arrived at our hotel in Saint-Omer, yet another picturesque town. It felt like a whole new world had opened up before me. I couldn't help but fall in love with these French towns and their traditional architecture. I guess you could now call me a devoted Francophile.

After a quick refresh at the hotel, we ventured out into the warm night air for a stroll around the town. Finally, we settled into a restaurant to savour a wonderful dinner.

Chapter 30 - Driving Back to Italy, Via France

HAVE VAN - WILL TRAVEL.

"I found I could say things with color and shapes that I couldn't say any other way—things I had no words for". Georgia O'Keeeffe.

Wednesday 22nd July 2009

From Saint Omer, we drove for a while on the main toll routes, then realised we would capture the essence of France by driving on the untolled 'B' roads. We drove through and stopped at some quaint villages, having an ice-cream or coffee, or melt in your mouth croissants. Our lunches each day consist of a French baguette laden with ham, cheese and tomatoes, which we devour at a picturesque spot on the roadside, surrounded by the gorgeous French countryside. What's not to like?

French Countryside.

On arriving in Strasbourg, we booked into an Ibis hotel. This chain of medium priced hotels has become our choice of accommodation while in France. We've had a couple of quiet nights and the breakfasts were good.

We dined under the beautiful Cathédral Notre-Dame de Strasbourg. It's quite a sight to behold. French poet and playwright Paul Claudel called the Gothic edifice a "pinky-red angel hovering over the city." Goethe declared it to be "composed of a thousand harmonizing details". And I must say, he is not wrong.

It was spectacular. The cathedral's grandeur was enhanced by the special lighting that, on this particular night, synchronised with the music of a symphony orchestra performing nearby. Such a mesmerising evening, combined with a delightful dinner. Undoubtedly, a magical experience in the heart of Strasbourg.

Strasbourg Cathedral

Thursday 23rd July 2009

I had a text from Rose. Gianni picked her up at the Sulmona station and took her to our house.

The drive from Strasbourg to Milan took us through the Alps, and I must admit, going through a long, single-lane tunnel in those towering mountains was a bit nerve-wracking. The tunnel stretched for seventeen kilometres, and the queues were incredibly long. It felt like an eternity before we finally entered the tunnel and once inside, the speed limit was quite slow. I breathed a sigh of relief when we eventually emerged on the other side.

Driving through Switzerland was like stepping into a childhood dream. The scenery was nothing short of spectacular with towering mountains, vast meadows, charming farmhouses and chalets scattered across the landscape. I half expected to see Heidi herself sitting in the meadows among the daisies, surrounded by the iconic Swiss cows, which interestingly still had their horns intact. In

New Zealand, for some reason, they tend to remove the horns. Switzerland truly felt like driving through scenes from a picturesque calendar. Our lunch stop in Zurich was a delicious yet budget-busting experience. It's no wonder people here are so slim; dining out can be quite an investment. Switzerland, while breathtaking, does come with a price tag. France, in comparison, is a bit more forgiving on the wallet.

On arrival in Milan, once again we stayed at hotel Ibis. OK, but just not as classy as the French chain.

Friday 24th July 2009

Exhausted from this leg of our trip, we decided to skip dining out and settled for a quick snack nearby before heading straight to bed. The next morning, we had a hearty breakfast before catching a bus into the city centre. My God, the Duomo di Milano is breathtaking. It's an exceptionally large and elaborate Gothic cathedral on the main square of Milan and of course, is one of the most famous buildings in Europe. The Duomo is so lace-like and had obviously been cleaned recently. It was the most magnificent thing of beauty I've seen to date.

Duomo di Milano

It was a beautiful morning strolling around Cathedral Square and in the drop-dead, gorgeous Vittorio Emanuele Gallery. The gallery is renowned for its amazing architecture, characterised by a glass-vaulted roof, ornate mosaics and intricate ironwork. In the mosaic floor of the Galleria, there is a famous image of a bull. According to local tradition, spinning on the bull's genitals with your heel three times brings good luck. Though I didn't witness anyone spinning around. Leaving Milano just after lunch, we embarked on a long yet pleasant journey on the autostrada and as we drove hilltop medieval villages passed by in the distance, with Florence on the horizon. Our goal was to stay the night in Florence, but made the decision to press on, and we arrived home around eight o'clock. One thing that was noticeable during our travels around Italy was the Abruzzi landscape is the most spectacular. With huge mountains, coastal sea towns, medieval villages atop giant craggy peaks, valleys of farmlands, olive groves and villages nestled in the landscape. It is exceptionally rugged, yet picturesque.

Even though it was eight o'clock, it was still extremely hot, around 40°. The van performed really well and the air conditioning was a Godsend.

Rose was there to welcome us home and had prepared a pasta meal, which was swilled down with a red Montepulciano while we bought Rose up to date with our latest adventures.

Friday 31st July 2009

Monte Cassino

We've been back from our trip for a week now and Rose is enjoying her stay. As usual, there's much to catch up on, and we've been sharing plenty of laughs. The other day we went to Monte Cassino, a rocky hill about 130 kilometres southeast of Rome, two kilometres to the west of the town of Cassino and 520 mtr altitude. It is a few hours drive from home. Monte Cassino is best known for its historic Abbey. The history here is quite poignant for us Kiwis. During WWII in the battle to take the hill, 343 New Zealanders were killed and are laid to rest in the war cemetery here.

This huge beautiful abbey has been completely restored to its original state, after it was bombed to smithereens during the battles of WWII. The order to bomb the Abbey was given, due to the Generals believing the Germans were holed up in there, but they weren't. As you proceed through each chapel and space, you are in admiration and amazement of the task it must have taken to accomplish such a feat as this complete rebuild. The mosaics of gold and blue set in religious icons are truly a wonder.

We had our picnic lunch on a lovely outcrop overlooking the valleys far below, with the distant hills away off in a beautiful Italian haze. Delicious.

We drove down to the Cassino War Cemetery and upon entering, you're immediately overwhelmed by the sheer number of white headstones. They're laid out meticulously in neat rows, surrounded by beautifully manicured gardens.

The rows stretch into the distance creating a profound sight. However, it's when you start reading the names and ages on each headstone, especially those of the young lads who lost their lives, that the tears start to flow. Standing there, in the very place where it all happened, you can't help but feel a deep sadness for those boys, so far from home in the midst of a cold, miserable winter in these rugged, unforgiving mountains.

Cassino War Cemetery

This area saw some of the fiercest action among the battles of the Italian campaign. The Cassino War Cemetery is the second largest Second World War cemetery in Italy. More than 4,200 Commonwealth graves are located here. We found the New Zealand contingent. Also in the cemetery is the Cassino Memorial, unveiled in 1956, which commemorates the more than 4,000 Commonwealth war dead of the Sicilian and Italian campaigns that have no known grave. The names of 192 Canadians are inscribed on its 15-foot high slabs of green marble.

The War Cemeteries are very well maintained by the Italian Government. It is a very peaceful location.

At Roccasecca we had a gelato, while I asked some locals about a New Zealand woman, Kaye, who lived in the area, but no one here had heard the name. We asked again at another bar and, yes she was in the next village. Compared to our village, it appeared not many people spoke English at all.

Finally, we located her. She was surprised to find three Kiwis on her doorstep. I explained that I'd read a newspaper article about a New Zealand artist living in this area, and on a whim, I decided to try and find her. She welcomed us in but unfortunately, she was on her way to Fiumicino Airport to catch a flight.

We only managed a quick hello, exchanged contact details and we were off again, but not before Franca, her friend, took Bruce on a fascinating short tour of the local church and showed him how the automatic bell ringer in the church tower worked.

We finished a fabulous day with a pizza and too much wine at a restaurant in Pettorano, close to home.

Slept well.

Saturday 1st August 2009

Lazy morning yesterday - cleaned the house while Bruce and Rose went into Sulmona to buy Rose's rail ticket.

In the afternoon we went to Pescara shopping - managed to buy a few things we needed, sun umbrella, ladder and a cabinet for the bathroom.

We ate gelato and walked the main corso.

Sunday 2nd August 2009

Today, we drove up to Playa restaurant on top of the mountain at the back of Introdacqua. We had arranged to meet Gianni. Maybe we should've gone to a more civilised place, as this is pretty rustic, to say the least, but the owner is a mate of Gianni's and we wanted to thank him for taking care of us. We filled up on arrosticini. Arrosticini: consists of cubed chunks of lamb on skewers with a maximum length of 10 cm (4 inches). They originate from the shepherds and other inhabitants of the mountainous areas in Abruzzo.

The evening was really good fun.

At the end of our meal a couple of bottles of Grappa and Limoncello were plonked on the old plastic table for us to have a few for the road. Most of the old family restaurants do this. It's a sort of tradition. Grappa is ghastly, but I'm starting to get a bit of a taste for it.

Bruce never will!

Monday 3rd August 2009

I've been doing some deep thinking about my insecurities and I must admit, I'm not completely over the feeling of being judged or not measuring up, even at my age! You'd think that with the successful businesses I've had over the years and the image of self-confidence I portray, these feelings wouldn't plague me. But when I'm around people from home these old insecurities resurface and it's a struggle to shake off self-doubt. Interestingly, I don't experience these feelings when I'm here in Italy on my own. I revel in being different and yes, I'm a bit rough around the edges. But hey, I come from the Coast and I was a wild child back in the day.

Damn it all, I refuse to be pigeon-holed - I don't have any airs and graces - I like who I am! This line of thinking came from a throwaway comment made by Rose about me growing up on the Coast.

Thursday 6th August 2009

Bruce has bought himself a bike and he intends cycling each day.

We had a hilarious night last night at the new restaurant in the village, Carzillo's. It was Rose's last evening.

We got a fit of the giggles. It was one of those rare occasions when the least little thing would set you off into a round of uncontrollable hysterical laughter. It was while we were discussing different ways of making money. One of Rose's ideas was to teach widowed or divorced men how to cook. She would teach them in her own home, as we agreed there were so many men out there who have no idea of how to get around the kitchen if they are left to their own devices. Anyway, it was when she started telling us how she'd get the word out about this venture. Went along the lines of *"Cooking classes for chaps on their own"* or *"Chaps cooking classes"* It was the word *"chaps"* that made us collapse in a heap. *"Chaps"*, such an old-fashioned, typically English word. It conjures up all sorts of images. An elderly gent with grey hair, handlebar moustache, smoking a pipe. Then it was the nice *"chap"* in the tweed jacket, leather slippers - and it just went on and on. Luckily, there weren't many patrons outside where we were seated.

After we wiped our tears and regained our composure, we finished the meal and moseyed on with a stroll up and down the Piazza. Stopping later at the bar, where we ran into Michele. He introduced us to a couple of Brits, Carol and Ivan. We had a drink and we were chatting away, as you do. We exchanged our stories about how we ended up in this village. They'd bought a house up by the tower about eighteen months ago and it was being renovated at the moment. It was Tara! I explained that agent Giorgio had taken me to see the house, how I'd fallen in love with it and was starting to make some art, inspired by the ruin.

During the conversation, Ivan told us Michele was doing some work for them and he thought he, Michele was a really nice "chap." Well, we three, looked at each other and we couldn't help it, we just collapsed again! We tried to suppress it, but that was worse. We just gave in and roared with laughter. Poor Carol and Ivan wondered what the hell was going on. We tried to enlighten them between uncontrolled spurts. They explained that they'd also been at the restaurant and recalled how these 'unruly' people - us - were in fits over something and now they were pleased to find out why. Though, not sure they really understood. But, a bloody good night all the same.

Friday 7th August 2009

Sad today, as we said goodbye to Rose as she went off on the train to Rome. From there she'll go on to London.

Bruce goes biking every morning to Bugnara. Quite a ride.

He's fixing the tiles to the back of the kitchen sink/bench, as a splashback. These are the tiles we bought at Maitland in England. They look really good.

We went to a fiesta over in Pacentro. What a delightful village. One of the girls from our restaurant group, Myra lives here and by chance, we ran into her. She accompanied us during the festival and introduced us to her friends.

Chapter 31 - Festival Season in Introdacqua

IT'S ALL ABOUT BEING WITH FRIENDS AND MAKING NEW ONES.

"It is only when we are no longer fearful
that we begin to create". J. M. W. Turner

Sunday 9th August 2009

An Argentinean band has arrived in Introdacqua at the bequest of the bar owner, as he is originally from Argentina. So along with wonderful music and dancing were the huge cuts of beef steaks on the BBQ. We sat with a couple we had met in Pacentro on Friday night. The band was wonderful. All this free entertainment they have here every August is amazing.

The Argentinians have arrived!

Today we walked up to Playa restaurant and it was a long hike. The whole village has gathered here today, though most of them drove up. Anyway, it's a picnic day up here in this gorgeous spot under the pine trees. It's another village event and we'd arranged to meet Carol and Ivan. Roberto is busy as usual, cooking the locally made sausages and putting them in a bun and there is Arrosticini along with local red wine.

Afterwards, Carol and Ivan came back to our house and coincidently, I was working on a small piece, which their house, Tara, is the subject. I was telling them of my love affair with their house from the time I started going for my walks last year. They were amazed that I had done so much homework on their house and they liked the name I'd started to call it 'Tara'.

There was music again in the Piazza tonight, so we're back out and meeting with them and Sue and Roger.

Wednesday 12th August 2009

When we're not out mingling and socialising, I'm dedicated to putting the finishing touches on my art. August is undoubtedly the time to be in Italy. Everyone is on holiday, and the atmosphere is absolutely infectious. It's a time for reuniting with old friends and forging new ones, dining outdoors, and relishing various genres of music. Each night brings a different band, all of them exceptionally talented and quite classy.

Friday 14th August 2009

I've been experimenting with gelatine plate printing. I made the plate using around four packets of gelatine dissolved in water, then poured into a shallow tray. When it is set and firm, you spread the surface with paint, then place leaves or stamps and press with fabric or paper. These can be used in your art pieces. Interesting technique and I have yet to discover more of what it can do for my art.

The day was absolutely stunning. We prepared a picnic, and with eager anticipation, we drove over to Bugnara to pick up Sue and Roger. They kindly offered to take us on a local hike in the picturesque hills around Anversa. There's something truly rejuvenating about being in the heart of nature, and this day was no exception. We returned home both refreshed and pleasantly tired, having basked in the beauty of the outdoors. The jazz festival has started. I'm not really a fan, but Bruce will most probably go most evenings, but even he said a lot of the time it's mainly for the purists.

Saturday 15th August 2009

Today is Ferragosto and it's a public holiday. It originates from Feriae Augusti, the festival of emperor Augustus, who made it a day of rest after weeks of hard work in the agricultural sector. It became a custom for the workers to wish their employers "buon ferragosto" and receive a monetary bonus in return. Families tend to go for picnics.

I'd heard of a village called Caramanico that had thermal pools. So, we decided to go and find them. It was a fairly long drive, up past Pacentro. Along the way, families were picnicking under trees and on the side of the road near Passo San Leonardo. We called into Guy's establishment, but it was closed until next month.

The road to Caramanico, was long and quite windy and I wasn't feeling very well by the time we got there! We couldn't find the pools, though the village was lovely and we stopped for our picnic at a place where we could view the valley below. We had another try at finding the pools to no avail and then became trapped down a very narrow street! It was difficult to turn the van around, though we did eventually, but frustrated we headed back home.

Having the van has made such a difference to our lives here. The Fiat is my little run-around car for popping into Sulmona. It's not suitable for long trips, and moreover, it doesn't have air-conditioning! We use the Toyota van for our longer trips out of the district, as it's far more luxurious.

Monday 17 August 2009

On Sunday we cleaned out the room that used to be the old kitchen in readiness for turning it into an office.

We had a very long lunch - the days are long, lazy days.

Tuesday 19th August 2009

Bruce has been putting new cupboards up in the studio, which is just the ticket for my collection of fabric and stuff. I'm a fabricaholic - a term used to describe a person like me who has loved fabric since I was a young child. I was always buying remnants of fabric at our local fabric shop, Dellaca's and now I have a vast collection. The tables and benches have been painted white and while it wasn't necessary, they make the studio look streamlined.

Wednesday 19th August 2009

Life is continuing on with revamping the studio, boiler room, outdoor wet room and finishing off the office. Plus, we go into the Piazza most evenings to join in the fiesta's. We had a spur of the moment jaunt to Pescara to buy an office desk, shopping at the huge Castronama, in awe of the number of products this store has. Around five o'clock we headed to the beach for a swim. North of Pescara, we found a pretty little spot, Pineto. It's a public beach, where you don't have to pay and it's easy to get to. We were almost the only ones in this particular area. I think we've found our favourite beach and the village is a gem.

Pineto Beach, this was a great find.

Friday 21st August 2009

How time flies when you are having fun. The studio is looking amazing. All the hard work has paid off now the tables are all painted and it's well laid out. It will be a pleasure to work in.

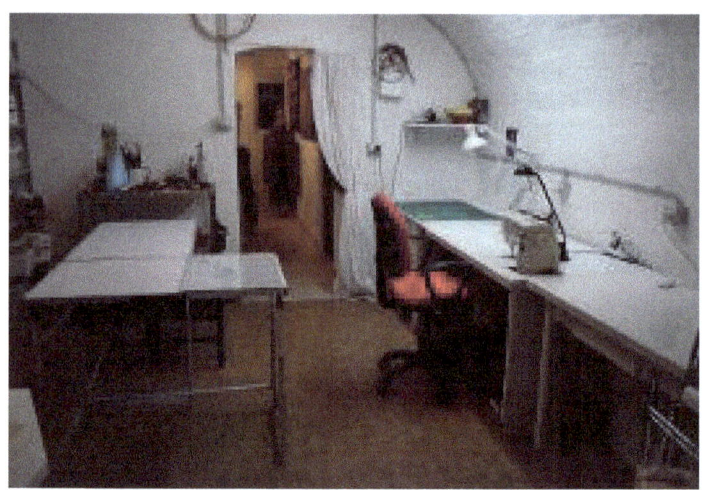

Studio - workroom

Saturday 22nd August 2009

This weekend brass bands from around the region congregate in Introdacqua. It's colourful and joyous, as they march around the streets for two days, adding another layer to the festive atmosphere here every August. We are fortunate to be part of such a neat, lively little village.

Today Bruce is concreting a new step that leads down into the studio, so there will be no possibility of me missing steps and breaking any more ankles. Once the work was done we cleaned ourselves up and headed into Sulmona to participate in the passeggiata along the Corso. We ran into Gianni and had a Prosecco with him and more of his friends joined us. When we arrived back in our village, there was a show band on stage. The gorgeous *'Fabiana'* and her band from Rome. She sang and entertained for over two hours. Our village is well known for having the best entertainment during Fiesta time.

Monday 24th August 2009

We worked on the new office set-up. Then in the evening headed for the Piazza. We enjoyed dining alfresco and music, music, music and a concert on the main stage. Tonight is the final night of the fiesta month.

It finished with a BANG, literally! After the concert, the crowds moved into a circle in the lower Piazza. This is the grand finale.

The local band marched in front of a very large, giant puppet lady. (il ballo della Pupa) A man was inside the steel frame, which was in the shape of a woman. She has been lovingly decorated by my friend in the village. Maria has adorned her, the *Pupa* (puppet) with colourful crepe paper and has a beautifully made-up face, with braids of long hair, also made from crepe paper.

The man underneath supports the frame on his shoulders and dances a jig in time with the music. So this huge puppet, surrounded by the band, dances its way down the steps and into the throng of excited people.

It is then, wait for it, she is set alight! Sky rockets protruding from various parts of her body explode into the air. The *Pupa* becomes an enormous raging inferno, still dancing around and when you think the guy underneath is surely roasted to within an inch of his life, he throws the burning effigy off his shoulders, which miraculously, misses the people standing close by. It burns out of control until it dies down.

Finishing with a bang!

Our health and safety officials would have a field day here. From there we followed the townspeople to the sportiva grounds, where they held the fireworks display. Twenty minutes of incredible fireworks. The best display I've ever seen. Spectacular - stunning.

A disco followed, with everyone joining in even Carol and Ivan.

Wednesday 26th August 2009

I have been feeling a bit listless these past couple of days. A combination of late nights, too much drinking, lots of laughs and fun, but draining. It has become necessary for me to have some early nights.

We're still fixing up the office. Finished painting the old shabby tiles on the wall. They look fresh and crisp with the new eggshell blue colour.

Finished office.

Thursday 27th August 2009

I slept for twelve hours, so feeling refreshed today, and ready to get back into the studio. A traditional roasted chicken with roasted potatoes and veggies for a nice long lunch.

Sue and Myra, who we'd had an evening with at Pacentro, came over for a cuppa and chat.

Monday 31st August 2009

A busy weekend working on the house and garden.

We went to the Cantone Porchetta Fiesta, where we ran into some friends, Rosina and Luigi. They have inspired us to get serious about learning the Italian language. I must admit we've been a bit slack. In the beginning, I studied regularly, but found my retention levels weren't the best!

We line danced, along with hundreds of locals en mass, to another fabulous show band from Rome.

Thursday 3rd September 2009

Our Italian lessons are now in serious mode. Each day in the studio w study with the help of the Italian Language CDs we bought at Dubai airport. Seem pretty good.

I have (avere) started work (lavoro) again in the studio, though I don't know what direction I am (sono) heading in.

Chapter 32 - Amalfi Coast, Here We Come

AN ITALIANO BAPTISIM

"If I create from the heart, nearly every-thing works; if from the head, almost noth-ing". Marc Chagall

Sunday 6th September 2009

The days drift by in a sort of lazy hazy days of summer, so to speak. Bruce is just adding the finishing touches to the laundry room, which when finished tomorrow, will herald the completion of every room in the house.

Most evenings we pop into Sulmona to partake in the passeggiata. Stopping to chat if we come across anyone we know, or we dine at La Trota, a favourite place for us, as it's an easy walk from our house. And so it goes, this lovely life. We've cut our drinking back to three nights a week and then only one or two glasses.It's a tough life.

Gino, Bruce's brother in law, rang from Castellammare di Stabia. He's in residence at his apartment and has invited us down to stay with him. He's married to Bruce's sister and they live in LA, but he comes to his family home each summer for a couple of months. The town is on the outskirts of Naples, close to Pompeii and the Amalfi coast. We plan on driving down next week.

I'm working on a new project in my newly painted studio. It's a series '*Introdacqua Chimneys*' I used a special vintage wheat bag for the background. So precious, it's been carefully mended and loved. I'm not sure in New Zealand if we were ever this poor and I find it very humbling when I come across these treasures from the past. The women of the village have started to drop these jewels at the door of my studio.

'Introdacqua Chimneys"

After dinner, evenings are spent practising our Italian lessons. We listen and then write the words. It seems to be working and we're starting to get quite a repertoire of Italian words and we are even able to string some short sentences together. It is just a matter of retaining what we learn!

Mornings and Bruce is still biking to Bugnara and back. Quite a haul.

Tuesday 8th September 2009

The air is becoming cooler, which means autumn is nigh, though it's still warm enough to head for the beach at Pescara. While we're there, we'll go shopping. We need a shower door and a few other things. It's a big city with some huge shopping centres and plenty of very large Brico (hardware) stores. Later on, we'll go to our favourite beach, Pineto, a sweet little town with a real beachy feel and the pretty main street runs parallel to the beach. The main city of Pescara, unfortunately, it was heavily bombed during the war. Subsequently, the buildings are quite bland compared to other old medieval cities in Italy. We swam, then lazed on the beach reading for a while before heading home with shower door and other goodies in the boot.

Thursday 10th September 2009

It was a beautiful drive down to Castellammare. What a sight Mt Vesuvius is. Once spotted, as you drive closer it looms large and menacing. It towers above and is the backdrop behind Naples city. I'm not sure I would like to live so close to a volcano with such a reputation. We drove past Vesuvius and onward toward the coast where after three hours from home, we pulled into a car park in Gino's hometown. We rang him to get directions to the apartment. His mate found us outside the railway station and we followed him to where we could park the van while we were here.

After climbing three flights of stairs, we were welcomed onto this expansive, open-air balcony terrace with a jaw-dropping panorama over the Bay of Naples to Naples and Mt Vesuvius. The balcony was at least ten to twelve feet wide and ran for the length of the building. You could access four apartments from the balcony. Such a warm communal area with street sounds drifting up from below. It was the hub. This is where everything happened. The views of clear blue sky, the crystal waters of the bay, are all dominated by the distant volcano vista.

Hugs and kisses all around, as we were welcomed warmly by Gino's family. Salvatore, the dapper, was charming and is always dressed to go to a wedding, jokes Gino. Having grown up here, Gino and his brother were fortunate, as in this area there was a training school for boys to learn to become ships crew, boiler makers, engineers and all sorts of trades related to the shipping industry. Later, they both found good jobs on the cruise ships and they cruised the world until he retired to LA. With the money he'd earned over the years, he was able to buy this apartment here in his hometown He had met Bruce's sister, Jan, many years ago and they married after a short whirlwind romance, settling in LA. They have two lovely boys.

Lina, a wonderful cook, had prepared a delicious Italian meal for us, four courses! We ate late and were joined later by their two adult children. What a treat it was to eat out on the well-used balcony.

Gino's apartment was typical Italian style, with tiles and marble everywhere. The kitchen and bedrooms were large and airy, the doors opening out onto this wonderful balcony.

View from the veranda.

We were in for a fantastic week.

Friday 11th September 2009

Today we went by train to Pompeii. It was only two stops away. We chose to have a guided tour with Franco. He made our day and showed us everything and it was most worthwhile to have a guide, as it enabled us to understand the tragedy of Pompeii in more depth. I took many photos in anticipation of doing some art pieces from our trip. It was a wonderful day and brought back memories of my Interior design diploma. I had chosen Pompeii as my project to study art and buildings. Now to view them in the real world was very special for me.

Textures and colours of Pompeii

Even though it was stifling hot we spent all day there. It was a wonderful experience

On the way home, we decided to have a look around Naples. Some areas were dilapidated and run down, with rubbish piled high and stacked up everywhere. We decided to catch a suburban bus to see some sights but ended up miles out of the city and hopelessly lost. A bit scary, but we managed to get another bus back to the city, and then the train home.

That evening, another wonderful meal. Gino told us Lina was happy to cook and loved to cook for the family, so we must accept that as the norm each night and not offend her by eating out. Lina had no understanding of English, but Salvatore was quite good and had a great sense of humour. He scolded us for not knowing Italian. Now and again he would say things like 'the Bee Gees' or 'Bar-ry White' or 'Bar-ry Manilowww' emphasising the syllables. He and Bruce would discuss music and musicians, as they both had a love of music and we all enjoyed the discussions they had. And as the evenings wore on he would think of other names to throw in, then we would get in on the act. You had to be there, really.

Saturday 12th September 2009

Sorrento was on the agenda for today. It's just a few stops away by train. Sorrento is truly stunning. I was captivated by the narrow alleyways lined with little shops. The linen clothing was irresistible, and I ended up buying a few pieces. I couldn't pass up the beautiful Sorrento sandals either. Despite the crowds and the heat, it was an incredible day. The views from the town and the train ride were picturesque. Before going back to the apartment, we strolled the streets of Castellammare di Stabia and bought food and wine for our picnic lunches. Most of our lunches are packed picnics.

Arrived home to another fabulous Italian meal and more laughs. Each evening, Gino goes into the town to walk and talk with his friends, leaving Salvatore and us in stitches over something he and Bruce were discussing. In the distance were the twinkling lights of the huge city of Naples nestled under the ever-present Mt Vesuvius, reflecting over the bay, with constant splashes of fireworks reminding us of people celebrating life in the city.

Sunday 13th September 2009

Exciting day today. We've been invited to go to Gino's nephew's son's baptism in Sorrento. Luckily I bought my new linen clothes, just what I need to wear on a hot Italian day. It was a long process, as there were three other baptisms that day and we either waited outside or in the ancient, cool surroundings of the church.

At the Baptismo.

Finally, it was our family's turn. After the ceremony, we walked to the home of Gino's brother, where there was an elaborate spread of food and drinks. Everyone was friendly and curious about these Kiwi folk in their midst and wondered why we would want to live in Italy. The younger ones wanted to know about New Zealand, the All Blacks, the New Zealand national rugby team, as always a hit and Haka renditions were performed hilariously. Lord of the Rings is next on the interest list of New Zealand. We told them that we used to live close to where they actually filmed some of the scenes in the movie. New Zealand is high on their list of places to live or visit.

It was a very special occasion, especially as it was their first boy, where the baby would be endowed with many gifts of gold trinkets.

Monday 14th September 2009

Our adventure today takes us to Positano and Amalfi. The drive along those narrow, winding roads was challenging. As we navigated the twists and turns, I was taking in the breathtaking views, the spectacular scenery and the lemons. They were everywhere, Bruce, you keep your eyes on the road!

What can I say about Positano, definitely my pick of all the places on the Amalfi coast.

A summary of the Coast:

Quaint Streets: Positano's narrow, winding streets were a delight to explore. They're lined with boutique shops, art galleries, and local restaurants, making it a fantastic place for a leisurely stroll.

Culture and Art: you can find galleries and artisan workshops showcasing local art and crafts. And artists painting on the beach.

Positano Fashion: The village is famous for its fashion, particularly its linen clothing and handcrafted sandals. You can find numerous shops selling these stylish items.

The Beach: Crystal-clear waters of the Mediterranean lapped the shore of the main beach, Spiaggia Grande, which is covered in small pebbles. We admired the paintings of the artists who were capturing the wonderful seascapes and scenes of people walking along the boardwalk. I didn't swim there, but I swam on the way home in the Bay of Naples. Isn't that a neat thing to say...."I swam in the Bay of Naples" who'd a thought, little 'ol me.

Swimming in the Bay of
Naples

Back at home once more, we gathered on our super-sized balcony for yet another delicious Italian meal. The group enjoyed hearing about the adventures of our day out. I shared the story of my refreshing swim in the bay, which they were surprised by, and then I forgot to ask why. I hope there aren't sharks! I insisted that I prepare a meal for the last night tomorrow night. But, I was cried down and Lina wouldn't hear of it. She is so used to cooking all the meals I guess.

Tuesday 15th September 2009

The Isle of Capri was on the list for today, as the ferry leaves directly opposite the apartment, but we rose late and so in love with Positano, we decided to go back. We asked the gang to come, but no the folks didn't want to come.

This time on arriving in Positano, we took the time to take in all the loveliness of this picturesque town. Gorgeous pastel-coloured houses, and balconies draped in petunias and geraniums, perch precariously on the hillsides. More art galleries to visit. I ended up buying another linen frock. A girl can't have too many. Lunch was a leisurely picnic on the beach, with our wine. We had a snooze, then I went in for a dip and had another swim on the way home in the Bay.

Another perfect day and evening with the family.

Tomorrow we heading for home.

Wednesday 16th September 2009

We're back in Introdacqua. We arrived home tired, but happy. It had been a beaut week. The van performed well. We're so grateful and lucky to be able to do all this.

We hadn't been home long when Bill, a member of the band that Bruce plays in New Zealand, rang from Provence. He's staying with a friend in France and has invited us to come and stay for a week. Can we come? Can we come, of course we can!

Yay O Yay, Provence, France, here we come.

We leave Friday morning.

Thursday 17th September 2009

Apart from Bruce putting the shower door on the shower, we've been getting ready, washing and ironing clothes for the next trip. The van is coming into its own as we can head off at a moment's notice. Exactly the reason we bought it. On this trip, we intend to sleep in it, pulling into camping grounds on the way to and from France. We'll make the bed up in the back by laying all the seats down, then throw our suitcases and other things on top. Packing the food into a chilly bin and picnic basket.

Chapter 33 - Road Trip to Provence, France

AN AUTHENTIC FRENCH HOUSE - FRENCH MEALS - THE REAL FRENCH DEAL!

"I have already settled it for myself, so flattery and criticism go down the same drain and I am quite free". Georgia O'Keeffe

Friday 18th September 2009

It was a thrilling prospect to return to France and to explore the picturesque South of the country; As you know, Provence is widely known for its landscapes, including rolling vineyards, lavender fields, olive groves, and charming villages. So, with an early start, we finished packing and organising the van, entered our destination into the GPS, and took off towards France. Our first stop was Portofino.

On arrival, yes, it was a beautiful tranquil place, however, we soon realized there was no place to camp there. So, we drove back around the peninsula, whence we came and found a camping ground. A fine drizzle had settled in, which didn't help matters, but close by was a restaurant that served delicious pizzas and we enjoyed our meal, happy to be on the road again.

Saturday 19th September 2009

We had a great sleep, as the bed in the back of the van was very comfortable and I have a feeling that these vans are insulated, so it was warm and cosy. We left the camp early and travelling on the autostrada (highway) it allows you to cover the distance relatively quickly, but you miss the coastal scenery. Through the 110 tunnels from Genoa to Monte Carlo, we pulled into a picnic area to stretch our legs and have lunch, then found a far better vista to take photos with an awesome view of Monte Carlo along the road high above the city. Monte Carlo, the name alone conjures excitement and anticipation. We found a park and wandered through the town, stopping for a well earned coffee. The shops, of course, were fabulous, but, I'm afraid I would have to take a mortgage out just to shop here.

Monte Carlo, Monaco.

It was starting to get dark when we arrived at our destination, Saint Maxime. It took a while to find the exact place. It was in the countryside, where Bill's friend (we're not sure what the relationship is with Susan!) owns a small winery, not quite a Châteaux. It's what they call a Domaine, where they produce their own wine. When we finally drove up the long driveway to the house, my first impression was – 'Get outta here! It is drop-dead gorgeous'!

The large two-story house is cream coloured with it's pale green shutters is dripping French provincial. Susan wasn't home from work, so we had a cuppa and a walk around the grounds while we waited for her. She arrived home looking stunning. Introductions over, wine comes out as she proceeded to quickly and efficiently prepare a simple, but delightful French meal.

The French live to eat, while we Kiwis' eat to live, (just a generalisation, really) so I was taking everything in and aware of whatever she was doing in the kitchen. We chatted while Susan, who speaks fluent English, gathered the meal together, as she explained the two family businesses she's in charge of, including keeping her eye on the farm and the vineyard. Dinner and chat went on until around midnight, so we were more than ready to turn in.

Sunday 20th September 2009

We started our day bright and early, heading to the nearby village of Saint-Max-imin-la-Sainte-Baume. As we arrived, there was a small market underway in the ancient part of town. There was a distinct upscale charm and character here, compared to the markets in Sulmona, though no better nor worse, just quite different. They were visually striking, the fruit and vegetables were displayed with flair, as were homewares and antiques. A broad selection of second-hand and new clothing. The vast array of breads, cheeses were impressive, as was the fish.

The buildings of Saint-Maximin are painted in pale dreamy French colours. Blues, pinks, greens and cream. It has a population of 14,000 and is very pretty. Everyone, it seems, is walking around with their baguettes. Even the men on bikes have their baguettes tucked under their arms, along with their morning paper. The French language is a problem for us and not many speak English.

We arrived back at the house, with a couple of baguettes and other stocks, wine, cheese and meat for the home larder - a quick nutritious breakfast, packed a picnic lunch and off we went. Susan is taking us hiking and we're heading for the coast to Calanque Blanche National Park. Pure white limestone spires.

An awesome region. It was quite a trek up to the top lookout, but the views were spectacular and they were an unexpected surprise. We ate our lunch while surveying the white cliffs shimmering in the bright sunlight, with crystal clear blue waters below. Then once finished, we quickly made our way back down the steep grade to the car, as they were going to a rugby match in Marseille. The match was between rivals, Toulouse and Toulon. Thankfully, they only had three tickets, which counted me out. I was free to explore the city, as Susan gave me the use of her four-wheel drive.

Calanque Blanche National Park.

I drove right up to the top of the mountain to view the magnificent Marseille Cathedral Notre-Dame de la Garde. What a place to have this huge Cathedral. It overlooked the whole of the Bay of Marseille. I was inside for a long time, so much to take in. The size inside made you feel so small.

From there I continued around the seafront to go back to the stadium.

Wrong turn, I was lost! I mean, I was really lost! I ended up down a very narrow one-way street right in the heart of the city, though it was suburban. I had to keep going down as there were no turning points. Then I reached the end, still nowhere to turn! I had to back this big 4-wheel drive machine all the way back up to the top!

Christ, it was narrow, with twists and turns. Near to tears, as I was sure I was going to scrape Susan's car along the tall, whitewashed walls, or worse end up in someone's garden below. I tried to remain calm and to not panic and prayed no one was going to come down behind me. I had no idea where I was and couldn't believe people could live in areas which are so difficult to manoeuvre a vehicle.

After what seemed like an eternity, I eventually backed my way up to the top where I could turn around. It had to be one of the worst experiences of my life. I emerged from this area onto what I thought was the main road. I was still in the city, but I had no idea where the stadium was and the game was due to finish soon. They would be expecting me to be somewhere near where I last saw them. I drove around, by now there was traffic everywhere and people were starting to surge across the streets.

Finally, not sure exactly where I was, I found a clear spot and pulled in. I was able to contact Bruce on the phone and lo and behold here they were coming out of the throng. I gladly handed the reins back to Susan. To this day I haven't told anyone about this incident.

We left the car there while we went for a beer and waited for the traffic to clear. Four beers €25.00...$50 New Zealand dollars Mmmm, pretty expensive to drink here! From there, Susan took us on a tour and history lesson around the greater Marseille. I mentioned to them I'd been up to the Cathedral up on the hill. They were impressed.

Back home and we witnessed another lesson on cooking French style. Bruce was given the job of trussing the chicken. As he turned it over, he gave a yelp and jumped back. It still had its head attached to its body. In New Zealand, the heads are cut off. We all had a laugh, as Susan took the chicken and shoved a heap of Provencal herb branches in its rear end with onion and garlic, then threw it in the oven. The herbs were retrieved from the large French dresser in the pantry. The drawers are full of dried herbs, sending a delicious aroma around the kitchen. Next was the chard, our equivalent of silverbeet, washed and thrown whole into the pot to boil. Fennel bulbs are sliced and added to the potatoes to roast with the chicken. We relived the events of the day, well most of them, while downing a few lovely French wines as we waited for dinner to cook. What a feast and experience. It was delicious.

Darn French, they can cook, eat and drink, with seemingly no effect, while we stumbled off to bed.

French kitchen.

French Kitchen.

We had a similar experience with a French couple many years ago.

As I've mentioned before, we built this big red American-style barn B&B in the New Zealand countryside. Well, out of the blue, this French couple turned up on the doorstep wanting to stay for a week. Andre and the beautiful Annie.

Yes, come in. I showed them to their room and wondered how they'd found their way here, as coming from the city, we weren't easy to find. Anyway, he was in New Zealand to learn English and she was his tutor. Mmmm, a bit fishy, but never mind, Annie could speak English, but Andre's was limited, as he was learning.

Each day they would drive into the city, (over an hour) to the English language school and would return late afternoon weighed down with food and wine. Andre was an excellent cook. It was wonderful. He'd roast the lamb, and when the meat was falling off the bone he then proceeded to bash the hell out of the bones to retrieve the marrow for the gravy, broke my trendy wooden breadboard in the process, but a minor detail, as he went on to cook the most delicious sauce. Reducing, reducing, as he explained to Bruce, how important it was to reduce the sauce and the red wine. While all this was going on, we were all drinking up large! Later we would be treated to a wonderful meal. It was after midnight before we had finished, and then it was time to relax with a couple of dark and stormy's. A concoction of rum, dry ginger ale and ice. Then this most gorgeous blonde French woman, Annie, lit up a huge, fat cigar! What a sight. I almost fell off my chair!

What fun. Naturally, I couldn't let her smoke on her own.

The stereo blasted out the CDs they'd bought with them, rock and roll, romantic tunes, and French music. We danced and danced and had the most wonderful parties. This format went on for most of the week. When it came time to say farewell, we all cried and hugged, tears streaming down our faces.

It had been a remarkable week. I am not sure we were crying - because they were leaving or because we were totally exhausted from all the drinking, eating, dancing and late nights. A lot of both, I think.

Monday 21st September 2009

Back in France...

Up bright and early Bruce, Bill and I are off to St Tropez. We stopped at the local bakery, which was to die for, and bought our baguettes and other yummy treats for our picnic lunch. Do you believe the absolute yumminess of (I know that isn't a word), there isn't a word to describe French bakeries. We threw in a few, melt in your mouth, croissants and sweet tarts.

French Bakery

Now to stop at the deli for some ham to add to leftovers from last night's meal, then grab a few vinos from the wine shop, done. Gorgeous lunch sorted and tucked into our picnic bag.

Have I mentioned my picnic bags? A lovely bag, that can be carried as a backpack, if necessary. One large insulated compartment for the cold food and drinks, the middle section has cutlery, plates, wine glasses, chopping board, even a tablecloth and napkins for four people. A one-stop shop, ready to go on a picnic in a jiffy. It's my can't live without item. I have one here and another in New Zealand.

We stopped and strolled around a couple of charming villages en route. I met and chatted with a local artist who had a lovely gallery and studio which opened out onto the quaint street. Warm and sunny. We wandered around taking photos.

Beautiful villages.

From there, Bill, he was more or less navigating, said to take this turn-off. Well, we ended up going around this bloody mountain and peninsular. It took forever! I was getting hungry and wanted to find a place to have our picnic. Preferably on a beach at St Tropez. Christ! Bill never shuts up. Talk, I've never heard anyone talk so much.

Finally, the road was so windy and I was getting grumpy, trying to find out where we were on the map and Bill yapping about nothing. I finally just turned around and told him to shut up! I know, I was sorry about it later, but it just popped out of my mouth. He did, but not for long. He's one of those guys that is impossible to offend. We found a white sandy beach, an ideal place to finally have our picnic near St Tropez. After lunch, the guys went off to find a bar and I went in for a swim, then snoozed until they came back. We stayed in St Tropez for the afternoon, strolling along the waterfront, taking shots of the luxury yachts berthed in the marina, hoping to spot someone rich and famous. We chatted with some of the many artists who were painting along the boardwalk. We wandered up into the old part of town, it was stunning, colourful, and clean. We ended the day at a very nice bar where we were being very French, sipping our drinks and people watching. Bill still yapping away.

We arrived home in time for another French dinner by the marvellous Susan. She was interested in what we had been doing while she'd been at work. Tomorrow, she is taking Bill on an excursion to one of her business enterprises in another city for a couple of days, leaving the two of us in charge of her amazing Domaine

Chapter 34 - Avignon, via Aix-en-Provence

A SURPRISE TRIP TO ARLES

"He who works with his hands is a labourer. He who works with his hands and his head is a craftsman. He who works with his hands and his head and his heart is an artist". Saint Francis of Assisi

Tuesday 22nd September 2009

A quiet day. We're staying around home, popping into town to rummage around the second-hand shops I'd spotted on the way in.

Wednesday 23rd September 2009

Today a day trip to Avignon through Aix-en-Provence is on the agenda. It's about an hour and a half drive and as usual, we stopped first to stock up the picnic bag with, what has become a staple, our baguette, cheese and croissants. How will I get by without these when I return to Italy? The Italian made baguettes don't quite cut the mustard for taste and texture. There was quite a large market going on in St Maximin, so we were distracted for a while. I couldn't resist a few fabric remnants and also a couple of round, brightly coloured tablecloths.

Driving through the French countryside was an absolute delight. The grand Plane trees lining the road created a stunning effect. We found a spot for lunch on a grassy verge, overlooking a stream, before passing through the gates of the walled city of Avignon. The ancient wall was well-preserved, and Avignon itself was a picturesque medieval town. We explored the historic town centre, which was enclosed by its medieval ramparts and I even stumbled upon some fabric shops, where I couldn't resist adding to my fabric stash. I found some lovely Provencal fabric that I plan to use for making matching placemats for our tablecloth. Additionally, we picked up some Provencal herbs and spices, including those big bunches of dried herbs that will go straight into our kitchen drawer when we return home. We also bought a couple of yellow pottery jugs and some large soup mugs with saucers, typical of this region.

All these things will be reminders of the wonderful time we're having here. We opted not to go to the Palace. It was a bit expensive. We took in the history of the city especially, the Ponte d' Avignon on the mighty river Rhone.

On the way home, we drove to Arles and checked out the city.

There were some surprises here, such as The Arles Amphitheatre. This two-tiered Roman amphitheatre, which thrived in Roman times and is probably the most prominent tourist attraction in the city. Built in 90AD, it looks very similar to the Coliseum in Rome and can hold 20,000 people. I was also interested in the life of Vincent Van Gogh while he lived here in the 1880s. His house was bombed during the war, but there were reminders of him and a small gallery, which was closed today.

It was getting late, so we headed for St Maximin.

Thursday 24th September 2009

Today we're exploring the mountain area of Moustiers St Marie.

On the drive to this mountainous region we passed through some very pretty towns, stopping occasionally to have a stroll and browse the little shops, or if there was a market taking place.

Our lunch break took us to the picturesque shores of Lake Sainte-Croix. This vast, man-made lake came into existence between 1971 and 1974, transforming what was once a quaint, original village into a submerged memory. The lake's colour is truly breathtaking, vibrant shades of emerald, blue, and turquoise all in one mesmerising blend. I couldn't resist a refreshing paddle in the crystal-clear waters of this beautiful lake.

Moustiers

Here I am again, head over heels in love with another French village. Nestled in the Alpes-de-Haute-Provence region of south eastern France, this historic village is renowned for its scenic location. Perched on the side of a limestone cliff, which creates a breathtaking backdrop against the surrounding mountains and the Verdon River canyon. It's famous for its artisan ceramics, which have been crafted in the village for centuries. We explored numerous boutiques and workshops showcasing these beautifully hand-painted ceramics.

The historic centre in the heart of Moustiers features charming narrow, cobblestone streets, medieval architecture, and quaint squares. The village is characterised by its distinctive star hanging between two cliffs, which is linked to local legends. The brochures outline the many outdoor activities the surrounding area offers. Such as hiking, rock climbing, and water sports. Moustiers is also a popular starting point for exploring the nearby Verdon Gorge, known as the "Grand Canyon of Europe. As we were also in the high country area where the Provence lavender is grown. Only remnants of the past season, from June to August, remain in the outstretched fields of cropped lavender. One can only imagine the beauty prior to the harvest. Smartly dressed locals going about their daily business, such a joy to be here to experience this time. We sit in the café and observe the comings and goings of the townsfolk.

We drove a different route on the way home, taking in the stunning Gorges of Verdon. We stopped, of course, to take in the awesome beauty. The drive home was a very long route, which meant we were pretty tired by the time we arrived and it was straight to bed. Exhausted. Tomorrow we are heading back home to Introdacqua.

Gorges of Verdon.

Provence is so beautiful. Perhaps I can come and live here when I've finished my stint in Italy, though the language is more of a barrier here in France than in Italy. The French don't have the same patience with us "English" as the Italians. When we mention to the French we're from New Zealand, the tone changes, as they have a high regard for us Kiwis. Memories of the two wars.

Friday 25th September 2009

This morning we had hugs and kisses with the lovely Susan and Bill, and off we went. These past few weeks on the road have been a dream come true for both of us. We've had a wonderful time here and all thanks to Bill and especially Susan, who was so generous with her time and her knowledge.

I make a note to make her a piece of art to show our appreciation when I return to my studio. We've packed everything into the van. What a treasure it is and drives like a charm, it's economical and has all the bells and whistles.

We took the motorway to Cannes, where we dropped down into the city and had and a quick look around, before getting back onto the motorway until we reached the outskirts of Nice, where we did the same. Taking in the fabulous wide streets of the never-ending boardwalk, that ran for miles along the beachfront. The elegant apartment buildings, where the rich and famous hangout, was a perfect backdrop. We had our lunch on the beach.

Through the many tunnels, until we were back on Italian soil. We drove on and on looking down from the autostrada to the city of Genoa below. Rushing past olive groves, high on the hills above. Becoming sick of the constant driving, we decided to stop off by a beach. Bad idea.

Monterosso ended up being miles from the highway, but lovely when we finally got there. I immediately changed into my togs and went in for a swim. It was heaven. Bruce, even though he was annoyed that it had taken precious time to get down to the town, was happy to be having a sleep on the beach. We had to drive all the way back to the highway, from whence we came, but we were now, at least, refreshed. We had planned to spend the night in Florence, but decided to keep going. Arrived home at 10.30 that night. The trip was 950 kilometres and had taken 13 hours. Bruce did a great job of getting us there and back. The cost of diesel and road tolls was around €400.00 return. Approx $700.00 NZD

Saturday 26th September 2009

A little bit hard to wake this morning after our long drive home yesterday. We have to get all our holiday gear packed away and the house ready for the B&B guests who are arriving later this afternoon. Alison and Kevin, from Dunedin in New Zealand, are travelling around the Abruzzo and found us by talking to someone in Sulmona. Our guests arrived on schedule and I was able to show off my new French cooking skills that I'd observed from Susan.

I think they were quite impressed with the way we casually trussed the chicken with a whole onion and a handful of branches of dried herbs, with twigs poking out the rear end. We had chicken and vegetables in separate courses, beginning with the Swiss chard, which had been thrown into boiling water, whole leaves, then dished up casually with a dash of olive oil and a few chilli flakes. Just like Susan had done.

When vegetables are eaten on their own, as is the French and also the Italian way, you get the full flavour of that particular vegetable or meat dish. It also allows for a more relaxing way of having a meal with friends. Next, we had fennel bulbs sliced and cooked in wine, with roasted (skin still on) garlic bulbs. The garlic is then sort of squeezed into your mouth with your teeth. Finally, the chicken dish with a reduced red wine jus and a few roasted potatoes. All swished down with a few hearty Montepulciano's.

Wonderful to entertain in our revamped kitchen.

Sunday 27th September 2009

We all rose late this morning. We have breakfast and chat for a while out on the balcony. It is lovely and sunny. The guests have a rental car and are driving up to Scanno for the day.

We mucked around the house, pleased to be home after our travels these past few weeks. I tidied the studio to get ready for the next project. I'm planning to enter a SAQA exhibition, titled *'Science to Art'*. It has to be entered by the 12th of October, maybe I won't make it in time.

In the meantime, while I think of how to portray the theme, I made six Provencal-style placemats with the fabric I bought home from Avignon. I cooked another Provencal-style meal. Directly from the beautiful recipe book I've had for about fifteen years and only occasionally attempted any of the mouth-watering dishes, now I can't get enough.

I invited the guests to join us and we had another fun night of laughing and chatting.

Monday 28th September 2009

Our lovely new friends (now) are departing this morning. They seemed genuine when they said their stay here had been the highlight of their trip. And we enjoyed their company also.

They were hardly out the door when Sarah and Andrew dropped by for a cuppa. They're staying up at Carol and Ivan's house. Andy is doing some work on the house and wanted to borrow a few tools.

The rest of the day was spent cleaning and then a couple of hours in the studio. Sarah and Andrew popped back in later. Stayed for a drink, then another. They finally ended up staying for dinner. A casual affair. Luckily I'd made soup, so there was plenty for everyone.

Tuesday 29th September 2009

As you can most probably tell by my tone I am over all this tripping around. Touring, travelling, sightseeing and entertaining can leave you emotionally drained. So I'm overjoyed to be back in the studio today working on my new project for the SAQA competition, while Bruce is pottering around on something on the house. A quiet relaxed day. We went to Sulmona for some groceries.

Wednesday 30th September 2009

In between working, I head off up into the hills for a quick jaunt. Trying to lose some weight, as I have my sixtieth birthday coming up in December.

Saturday 3rd October 2009

I've asked Bruce if he'll cook all the meals next week, as I'll be busy with my Science to Art project. He said sure, but I can see he's a bit anxious about it. Secretly, I think he'll enjoy it.

I've decided to make a piece depicting the birth of a star. I found an image on the NASA site, which I manipulated in Photoshop. It's quite involved.

I began by cutting twenty pieces of black fabric into 5" x 6" squares, then proceeded to add bits and bobs, dyed silk, and tulle, which I zapped with a heat gun, painted lace and I've embroidered these pieces. I'll set all of the twenty different pieces 1/2 an inch apart onto a black background with a thin backing of padding and a black backing. Then machine stitch over the whole piece.

With so much going on these days I find that I don't see or hear much from Lucia; she's fully consumed in the bar and café she runs with one of her sons, and I've been diving deeper into my art, house renovations and travel. It's similar with Gwen – after I bought my house, our paths didn't cross again, just the occasional chat when we see each other at the market. Sometimes that's just how it goes with people you meet along the way. Life pulls you in different directions and you lose touch.

Chapter 35 - Passo San Leonardo

FINISHING OFF MY ART PIECE

Sunday 4th October 2009

Today we drove up to Passo San Leonardo for a picnic lunch. We found a large beech tree to set up our picnic. It overlooked a vast spread of green fields that go for miles into the far off hills, dotted with oak and beech trees.

It was idyllic sitting doing my embroidery under this gorgeous Copper Beech tree. Listen, the soft sounds of jangly bells coming from herds of animals that roamed free up here. Donkeys, horses, cattle, sheep and goats. The next thing a cluster of lovely donkeys moseyed close by with bells clunking beautifully as they grazed. Then came the cows and water buffalo. Off in the distance, were a herd of horses. We had our picnic and a couple of wines. Time for a snooze and a cuddle. What a magical place. It is for sure our favourite area.

Picnicking at Passo San Leonardo

Then a little later, a swashbuckling shepherd came by on his horse overseeing his expansive flock of sheep and goats. His unexpected arrival added a touch of adventure to our day and as he stopped for a chat, we were taken with his impeccable English. Concealed amongst the flock were four or five formidable Abruzzi dogs. Their role is to safeguard the sheep from the ever-present threat of wolves. The shepherd didn't mind us taking photos, allowing us to capture this serendipitous moment and offered a glimpse into his rugged yet captivating life he led amidst these rolling hills and open skies.

When I first experienced shepherds who tended their flocks for the whole day, I couldn't believe people actually did this day in day out, as their full time occupation. Back then I couldn't even conceive of this as a thing to do in this day and age! But I've done a full 360 degrees and realise it would be quite a neat life, this life of a shepherd. That's how far I've come, in terms of my growth in this country. How I've learned to relax and let life come to me, how I am much more aware and in the moment and how being in nature has become especially important to me, as opposed to my other life - charging through each day in order to get to the next. Oh - to be a shepherd - now there's a dream.

You don't discover the qualities of Italy by taking the place by storm
- No - A more subtle, quiet approach is the way to go.

Afterwards, we stopped at Guido's restaurant for a coffee. We were introduced to his family and friends. I had tried to book for lunch, but the restaurant, so busy on Sundays, was fully booked. We'll come sometime soon for lunch.

I pause to take in this unforgettable day, and to be thankful to experience these wonderful journeys and encounters we have.

Thursday 8th October 2009

'Galactica Phenomenon' is the name I've opted to call the piece for the Science to Art project I'm working on. All week I've been working on it and it's an interesting project and progressing well.

Working on Galactica

The weather for this time of year is settled and still quite warm, not at all like autumn. I spend most days on the top balcony doing handwork.

Monday 12th October 2009

I've machine stitched the top of the piece and have embroidered thousands of French knots along with other embellishments, added gold leaf as the final touch and pleased to say I've finally finished the art quilt, with the help of ABBA and other favourite music. The colourful, various hand-dyed silks, tulles and cotton fabrics provide an interesting array of textures. I'm happy with it. I photographed it and sent the form off to SAQA to enter the competition.

Starting the roof

Thursday 16th October 2009

Bruce has started to replace the old roof. This is a major job as the roofing material that's on there already is weird stuff and is breaking down. The new roof will be laid over the top without having to strip the old stuff off, which will add to the insulation. Just needs the finishing touches around the chimney. It looks really good, and from the Tower, you can't tell it is aluminium.

Just the finishing off around the chimney and our roof is beautiful.

I've started work on a collage art piece for Susan in France. Sorting and printing images onto fabric.

Sunday 19th October 2009

Someone left some delicious vintage bags on my doorstep today. Bruce reckons he has better cleaning rags than these. How can he be so brutal about these treasures? I still have work to do where he's concerned!

It's starting to get a little chilly in the evenings, so we've turned on the gas radiators last night and have had our first open fire. One of my favourite things is to cosy up before a roaring fire. I sorted my clothes and dug out my winter stuff.

Wednesday 21st October 2009

I'm struggling with this piece for Susan. I want to make something cool, but as usual, it is turning out to be a dog's breakfast. I tend to put too much stuff in and use too many techniques. I'll need to pare it down. I'll persevere today. Apart from that, it's been raining. Bruce is unable to work on the roof.

Thursday 29th October 2009

The week that was. I don't know where it went. Bruce has finished the roof. It is reassuring to have this new added insulation and security from the rain and snow and that he has finally finished. I'm quite nervous when he's working on roofs, as my Grandfather was killed when he fell from a roof he was working on. He was only 58 and it had a huge impact on our family. From then on it was I who was called on to keep my Nana company and to stay with her on nights when it all got too much for her.

I've finished the collaged piece for Susan and will get it in the post next week. It came together really well in the end and I'm happy with it. I've incorporated many of the things in her life and her familiar surroundings. The Calanque area where we hiked, her house is featured, her vineyard and apple orchard, plus other treasures I squirreled away while we were in the area, pastry serviettes, printed bags, New Zealand stamps etc. I've added three fold-out books, with images. So plenty of interest.

Susan's art piece

Carol and Ivan are back in town, so I decided to treat them to a delicious Provencal meal. I set a cosy ambiance in the lounge, lighting candles to create a warm atmosphere.

For our appetiser, we prepared bruschetta over the open fire, which added a rustic touch. As we savoured the food, we caught up on their experiences in the UK and shared stories of our recent travels. To round off the meal on a sweet note,

Bruce prepared a delectable apple crumble for dessert, which has now become his signature dish. It was a wonderful evening filled with good food and company.

A finished shot of the lounge.

Thursday 31st October 2009

Bruce leaves next week to go back to New Zealand, but he's decided to come back in December for my birthday and our twenty first wedding anniversary, both celebrated on 26th December, Boxing Day.

We've decided to celebrate both of those events in Paris. I've been trying to find a house exchange in Paris, but I haven't had any luck on that front so far. Overall, living in Italy gives us accessibility to exciting places, like Paris or London, which allows more convenient and frequent trips, compared to when travelling from New Zealand. It's a luxury that's not be as feasible when coming from Down Under.

Saturday 7th November 2009

I posted Susan's art piece to France the other day.

The past week flew by so quickly. The roof has been finished just in time, as the heavens opened with huge deluges these past couple of days. Yesterday we travelled up to Fiumicino Airport on the bus, then the express train from Termini to the airport. Such a hassle with two big bags.

Bruce flew back to New Zealand on Emirates at 2.30pm and I came home on my own to an empty house. It'll take a few days to get used to being on my own, especially now that we've fallen in love all over again.

One of the neat things about Bruce is the way he lights up the house. It was the first thing I loved, when we met. He would bowl into the house, loaded down with fruit and vegetables, as at that time he was helping out on his brother's vegetable run. Laughing and joking telling me all the funny things that had happened during the day. We had plenty of fruit and vegetables, so I'd make these huge lumberjack pies (my own version, with plenty of roughly chopped vegetables) full to the brim with the produce he'd bring home. He'd make delicious Rumtopf from the left over fruit. (You'll find recipes on Google.) Distance and time apart do that. We have a lot more respect for each other and he's such a clever guy who can put his hand to anything. You only need to see the size and the challenge of building the barn house, with just me as his hammer hand. He's a wonderful pianist and was studying music and he achieved high levels after we became a couple.

Though, this time his leaving isn't so bad, as he'll be back in seven weeks. Meanwhile, I have plenty to keep me busy, as tomorrow is Ringraziamento day here in Introdacqua. The annual craft day. I'm having an open day and need to document all the art pieces in the gallery.

Monday 9th November 2009

It was wet for the open day yesterday and went pretty much as predicted. There wasn't any interest in my art. They don't get it. Never mind, that isn't going to get me down. I'm much too motivated now that I belong to Studio Art Quilt Associates. Such an inspiring group.

I thought my Galleria looked pretty good as I organised the layout better.

The Brits, who have a house up by the tower, came to have a look. She has an air about her, which gives me the feeling she's looking down her nose at all and sundry. She was telling me all the things she thought were wrong with the Italians and how she really didn't like them. You have to wonder why they came here to live in the first place. Never a smile crosses her face, whinging and moaning the whole time she was here. She told me she watches British TV and reads magazines all day. He's OK though.

Now, this may seem harsh, but since their visit, it got me thinking and I've come to the conclusion that some women don't have a life! They do not have a life, period! They're more concerned with what other women are doing, what they're wearing or how they look! And of course, what they're driving. "For goodness sake," I want to shout, "stop stressing about unimportant stuff, and get a life. Find something you love to do, study it, research it, and become IT! Whatever IT is" Get on with IT, as you won't have this time again, you only have one shot at IT!

As Mary Oliver said:

"Tell me, what is IT you plan to do with your one wild and precious life?"

I'm thankful to live here so effortlessly. Foreign people who want to live in New Zealand have to jump through hoops to acquire a visa. Italy, in stark contrast, I just arrived, bought a house, became a resident, not to be confused with citizenship, bought a car, and can live here very easily. There are some things I don't like, barking dogs, dog poop in the streets, and bureaucracy, which are minor details in the grand scheme of things.

On the whole, I love it here in this lovely little village.

Chapter 36 - Always start at your end goal, then work your way back

Planning For Paris

"Tell me, what is IT you plan to do with your one wild and precious life"? Mary Oliver

Tuesday 10th November 2009

Bruce rang. He had a good flight back.

Cleaning, the house, from top to bottom. I find that when he leaves, I go through a cleaning ritual. It's wonderful therapy. Really it is.

Wednesday 11th November 2009

In the studio, I'm floundering – again. Not knowing what direction to take or where to start. Everything to this point has been done. The tracks are laid down. I need a major goal and a timetable to incorporate work, exercise, learning new techniques, etc. Though belonging to SAQA has given me some direction.

I'm gaining more confidence painting in acrylic

'Hydrangeas'

Becoming an accomplished artist in my field of textile and mixed media art. This is a list of what I need to do to get there. Even though it's a long list, it could be used as a goal for any type of artist.

Skills Development:

Continuously improve your skills in textile art techniques. Attend workshops, take online courses, and practice regularly.

Study and Research:

Study the works of renowned textile artists to understand their techniques and styles.

Research current trends and innovations.

Create a Portfolio:

Build a comprehensive portfolio showcasing your best work. Include a variety of styles and techniques.

Exhibit Your Work:

Look for local art galleries and exhibitions where you can showcase your art.

Consider participating in art fairs and craft shows.

Online Presence:

Create a website or online portfolio to display your work to a global audience.

Networking:

Attend art-related events, workshops, and conferences to connect with fellow artists, collectors, and gallery owners.

Artistic Statement:

Develop a clear and compelling artist statement that explains your style, inspiration, and artistic philosophy.

Marketing and Branding:

Create a brand identity for your art, including a logo and consistent branding across all platforms.

Develop marketing strategies to promote your work, such as email newsletters, blogs, or collaborations with other artists.

Exposure:

Submit your work to art competitions and publications.

Collaborate with local businesses to display your art.

Teaching and Workshops:

Consider teaching textile art workshops to share your knowledge and earn income.

Gallery Representation:

Seek representation by art galleries that specialise in textile art.

Time Management:

Dedicate regular time to your art practice, balancing creation, marketing, and professional development.

Persistence and Patience:

Understand that success in the art world often takes time. Stay persistent and maintain a positive attitude.

Document Your Work:

Keep records of your creations, including photos, descriptions, and sale details.

Stay Inspired:

Continuously seek inspiration from various sources, such as nature, culture, or personal experiences.

That's a big list, isn't it?

I've incorporated this list of ideas, as I thought it may help others who are starting out in their artistic journey. Another idea is to always start with the end in mind, and then work your way back with the steps necessary to get there.

Take photos and sketch. I'm not very good at sketching. Get started on my 'Introdacqua, Ancient Fragments' series. Doors, chimneys, buildings, stonewalls, poppies. It is all on my doorstep, so to speak.

Remember I'm here to create! There's a lot of self-talk going on!

Thursday 12th November 2009

Though the autumn colours are spectacular and my daily walks in the forest above my house are divine, the cold is starting to seep through the two-foot thick walls and into the house. A reminder winter is on its way.

Michele replaced the thermostat in the radiator heating system. What a difference it has made. The house is now at a constant temperature of around 22°. The new insulation and the old, very heavy quilts (but not quilts you could use, as they weigh a ton) which we put on the ceiling domes in the attic are helping to keep the heat in and save energy.

Monday 16th November 2009

I had notification today that my art piece *'Galactica Phenomenon'* was not chosen for the Science to Art exhibition. Oh, well, better luck next time.

I've been working on a collage for Lina and Salvatore. It includes images of them at the baptismo, Mt Vesuvius and the Bay of Naples. I wanted to thank them for their hospitality and for being wonderful hosts to us when we stayed with them.

Tuesday 17th November 2009

Posted Lina's art piece today. I've tidied the studio ready for a new project and it looks like it's going to be a collage interspersed with stonewalls and poppies. I'll head off for a walk and take photos and sketch some scenes and poppies.

Friday 20th November 2009

Susan wrote and thanked me for her piece of art. She said she was moved – and that moved me!

The evenings are growing longer, as darkness comes around 5:30ish. A good evening project is learning to weave. I've been teaching myself to weave on a small weaving frame. I thought in the future, I may be able to incorporate weaving into my art.

Tuesday 24th November 2009

Bruce rang. He's been asked by his cousin if he would help care for his wife. It's heartbreaking, as she has a terminal illness and recently had an accident and broke her leg. He will stay at their house, help with her meals and take her to Doctor's appointments. In between, there is quite a bit of building work to be done. The timing is perfect, as he'll be working there for a few months, apart from the six weeks he'll be back here.

Thursday 26th November 2009

Because our dial-up Internet is so slow, it has made planning for our Paris trip difficult. I'll give it another shot later.

Saturday 28th November 2009

I managed to book a flight on Ryanair to Paris and have found a hotel in the Latin Quarter, Paris, which I'm sure we'll be happy with and the price is quite reasonable.

Once upon a time when I was twelve, I would look through my Auntie's pattern books. She was a dressmaker and had these wonderful big thick pattern books by Simplicity. I would spend hours looking through them, always stopping at the page with the illustration of a girl in a houndstooth skirt and red jumper. So, here I am a hundred years later. I'd bought a woollen hounds-tooth remnant years ago, so now I know what to do with it. As it will be cold in Paris at Christmas time, I'll make myself a skirt.

I've booked our birthday dinner at the Eiffel Tower! It's a whole package—dinner at the Eiffel Tower, a cruise along the Seine, and wrapping up with a show at the Moulin Rouge. How amazing is that going to be?

Sunday 29th November 2009

This morning was spent making my skirt. It wasn't that difficult, really and I wondered why it's taken so long to make it.

Thoughts of the women and friends from over the years keep coming to mind, and for some reason, they just won't let go! It all started with an idea to create small abstract paintings, each carrying a simple, philosophical message. Not one of these people I know—or knew—seems truly happy.

They fret and hand-wring or they're bound up by old ideas, or they refuse to let go of the past and regurgitate old memories. I've made a list of simple messages. People may 'get' them or not. Things like "Don't Look Back" "U Be The Light" "Carpe Diem" "Take Action" or "Just Be'. I know it sounds corny, but it does help to be jolted out of downward spiraling thoughts. I found that if you want things to change, then you have to change! Period! I've managed to climb out of and through debilitating times in my life with other mantras like, "If it's going to be, then it's up to me".

When life throws me a curve ball, I find myself in the self-help or motivational department of a bookstore. I'll buy at least two books that speak to me and I'm always pleasantly surprised by the turn of events that occur when I take some of the suggestions on board.

A few years after we built our big red barn house in the country. Our bank manager, who had become our friend, retired and left our local branch. The next thing, out of the blue, our bank account was transferred to head office in Wellington and we had a demand to pay our overdraft within a few weeks or they were going to sell us up in a mortgagee sale! What! (Many other people around this time had the same experience!), it had even become quite a thing.

We'd had an Over Draught on our account while we were building and it had just continued on. It was around $30.000. No big deal, we were keeping up with payments and we'd been in discussions with our friendly manager about consolidating it with our current mortgage. Then the shit hit the fan and they demanded repayment, pronto.

We were really down with this turn of events and panic set it, as it does, and you're like a deer caught in the headlights. You can't do anything. You're paralysed with fear.

Eventually, I found myself in a bookstore in front of the self-help books and *'Rich Dad - Poor Dad'* jumped out at me.

I had just finished reading the book, when:

Well, long story short. An outgoing, vibrant couple from the city came to stay with us for their weekend break. They spent the evening telling us about their Nursing Home and how they were able to buy it with no deposit. That was enough for me and my newfound confidence from Robert T Kiyosaki. Plus, the Nursing Home industry is where I gained many years of experience working with the elderly in the past.

The next morning I made an appointment with a real estate agent in the city and we went looking at Nursing Homes to buy. At the end of the day, we'd put in an offer for a $1.3 million dollar Nursing Home. A large amount, back in the day!

Desperate times call for desperate measures!

The offer was accepted and we went back to our barn in the country to make plans on how we were going to finance it. I made appointments with every bank and finance company in the city, then went out to the shed, dug out my old briefcase, washed the bird shit off it and found some of my old office-type clothes hidden deep in my wardrobe. Then I made appointments to talk to these money magnates.

Over the course of the next few weeks, things happened. No, that first Nursing Home didn't work out, but I found another Home that was on its last legs and put in an offer. Yes, the offer was accepted. Back I went to the financiers with this new deal. I borrowed Bruce's cousin's flash Lexus car. We pulled up outside. I put the deal to them.

As the weeks progressed I had plenty of "no, not possible" phone calls, then came the one, "Yes, we can finance you into this Nursing Home and not only that, we will also take over the debt from the other bank on your lovely red barn house." Well, blow me down!

Within a month and now with a million dollar mortgage, we were ensconced in our spacious apartment, living above the nursing home. We still had our home in the country, which is now our weekend holiday home and a business that was able to cover both mortgage repayments.

Well, thank you Robert T Kiyosaki for giving me the courage to step out. This isn't the first time motivational books and self-help books have helped me. Reading about successful people always helps and can show you other ways of looking at things. I recommend taking the time to read some of these books if you are wanting to change direction in your life.

To this day Bruce still calls me 'Scarlet O'Hara.'

'Korobahn'

Chapter 37 – A Variety of Projects on the go.

PARIS ON MY MIND.

"Stay firmly in your path and dare. Be wild two hours a day"! Paul Gauguin

Tuesday 1st December 2009

Still working and trying to update my website, but it's difficult as we are only on dial-up Internet. Roll on ADSL!

Wednesday 2nd December 2009.

It's been over two weeks since I've been to Sulmona. I like that I can stay home and concentrate and not be distracted. It doesn't always relate to productivity. A lot of the time I study other artists, by reading about them and what they are doing.

Being warm in Paris has been top of mind lately. I was happy with the hound-stooth skirt it would go with my red Merino top and my lambs-wool legwarmers, topped off with my goose-down coat. Now what about a felted merino hat that would do Paris justice?

It's been two years since I exhibited at the Florence Biennale. Uphill and down dale, a couple of steps forward and a few back. That has been the way forward so far. It's taken longer than I expected to arrive at a place in my art journey where I can see a pathway to being where I want to be. I still have a way to go, but since I've joined Studio Art Quilts Association, I'm beginning to see where it can lead to.

Thursday 3rd December 2009

A couple of Aussies, Brian and Pat, have moved into Tom's casa and popped in for a vino and a chat. They're in Introdacqua for three months, and seem like kindred spirits and on the same wavelength as me at least, but I can see distractions looming. Of which, I am now aware!

Monday 7th December 2009

Bruce rang. He's happy in his new role as a carer for Gail. Each morning he makes her fresh juice and then works on their house when he isn't needed for caring duties or driving her to appointments.

Thursday 10th December 2009

An interesting few days. The Aussies took me to dinner at the new restaurant in Introdacqua. Brian's brother and his wife are visiting. It ended up being a very rowdy night! I haven't had so much fun in ages. Dick is a scream. Way too much to drink. The wine was flowing freely I can tell you. Dick disappeared and when he came back he had cigars for us all.

Fiorella, my lovely friend and waitress at the restaurant, relaxed the rules on no smoking in restaurants, turned up the expel air fans and let us smoke. There was no one else in the dining room. It was very late as we all staggered back to my place for one for the road...like we needed it! It took me two days to get over that night. And I swear I'll never smoke another cigar!

Brian and Pat are off to Barcelona, Spain for a week.

Friday 11th December 2009

I saved a couple of cute chairs from the garbage and have been busy recovering and upholstering them. What a great use for my African Faux animal fabrics. I knew there had to be a reason for me bringing them so far! The fabrics are soft types of velour and will be nice to sit on. Just what an art galleria needs.

One of two chairs saved from the garbage - pride of place in the Gallery.

Had an email today from Kate in Caloundra, Australia. She and her husband Lionel want to exchange houses for two months from September to the end of November next year. Yes. I'll be happy with that.

I've taken down the balcony tubs and flowers, as it's getting cold.

Saturday 12th December 2009

Spent the day laying out and felting a merino jacket. I used different coloured blue wool and silk tops. It looks great. Let's hope it turns out OK and is wearable.

Monday, December 14th 2009

It's only another week and we'll be in paris. The winters in Europe are miserable. Darkness arrives late afternoon.

Thursday 17th December 2009

It was such a big deal when my landline was finally hooked up and now the day has arrived where we are finally on ADSL.

Yay, no more dial-up. Only those who have experienced dial-up will understand what this means. My Internet will be faster now.

I felted another jacket and made a felted hat to wear as the long-range forecast for Paris is 4°.

I saw Myra at the market yesterday. She said she was heading to London from Fiumicino Airport on Monday. So it was agreed that I take her to the airport as I'm going on the same day. I feel better about driving to the airport now that I'll have company.

Friday 18th December 2009

It has been snowing this morning. I hope it has gone by Monday, as don't fancy driving in icy conditions to Fiumicino. Yikes! Driving to the airport is a big deal for me, as the van is a right-hand drive. But I'll be OK. I can picture Bruce now. I bet he's buzzing around trying to get all his jobs sorted before he leaves tomorrow.

It's not very Christmassy here in the village this year. The effects of the earthquake are still close to people's hearts, especially as so many people are living in tents around L'Aquila. There are no Christmas carols on the radio and very few houses with decorations. Otherwise, you wouldn't know Christmas at all. I've been busy packing. Tomorrow I'll be ready to go.

After I pick Bruce up from Fiumicino Airport we'll proceed to Ciampino Airport to catch our flight to Paris.

Monday 21st December 2009

Well, here it is the 21st. I'll be heading off to Fiumicino in an hour. The weather has cleared and there's no snow on the road. Brian and Pat popped in to wish me well. I've offered them the use of my house for their Christmas day to have with their guests, as the house they're staying in is a cold, mouldy dump and so depressing. Here in my casa, at least they can light the fire and have a comfortable warm day. They said yes, they will.

I'm picking Myra up from Il Borgo at 9.30. It's very cold and icy, but the autostrada is clear. An uneventful trip. We arrived at the airport around noon. I helped Myra upstairs with her bags then went back down to arrivals to wait for Bruce.

I have an hour to wait, which I spent it reminiscing and reliving the cherished memories we've had so far on this amazing journey.

Chapter 38 - Paris, the Perfect City to Celebrate

It's Christmas in Paris

"Colour is my day-long obsession, joy and torment". Claude Monet

Monday 21st Dec 2009

The Paris trip:

At Fiumicino, Bruce arrived on time from New Zealand. Big hugs and kisses and what was really unexpected was the way he looked at me. It was as if I was going to vanish before his eyes. We drove over to Ciampino Airport and parked the car at the 'park and go'. Our flight was delayed because of bad weather. Finally, we took off for Beauvais and arrived around 11pm. It was freezing and snowing lightly.

On arrival, there were no taxis, so we caught the bus and were dropped off at a street, the driver said if we go down there, turn right then turn left or something, we'd find ourselves at the Residence Hotel. Well, we must've made a mistake, because the next thing we were completely lost! 12.30 in the middle of the night and who knows where? It was now snowing heavily. We trundled along, suitcases in tow for what seemed like ages. I made contact with the Hotel, but the lady was hard to understand as her English wasn't very good. I had visions of us freezing to death on the street. By this time it was almost blizzard conditions and we were still no closer to getting to our bed!

What a predicament! Then lo and behold a car came by, slowed down and the girl asked "Where are you going?" I told her we were trying to find the Hotel. Thankfully she knew where it was. The car was so small, that once a couple of bags were in the car her boyfriend had to get out and walk behind the car along with Bruce. I got in beside her and she drove slowly to the B&B. We were overwhelmed by her kindness and thought of her as our Angel. I vowed to be more aware and to also offer help if I came across anyone in distress.

The owner of the Hotel was also very kind and I apologised for putting her to so much trouble.

The next morning, after a good night's sleep and a hearty breakfast, we caught the bus into Paris, which was further than we thought. About an hour and a half.

At Notre Dame Station, it was a short walk to our Hotel Abbatial, which looked totally lovely from the outside, but the room was small, though most probably normal for Paris. Anyway, here we were, and immediately we couldn't wait to get out and explore our area, St Germaine and The Latin Quarter. We browsed shops and the artist stalls along the Seine and in the evening found a delightful French restaurant. We started with a French Onion Soup. For the main dish, I chose Lamb Shank Navarin (lamb casserole), while Bruce had Boeuf Bourguignon, which is a traditional French dish of slow-cooked beef in a red wine sauce, with small onions, button mushrooms and bacon lardons.

It's traditionally named from the Burgundy region in France, where it origi-nated. It's cooked until the meat is falling apart, and the wine-rich gravy thickens slightly to coat the meat.

These dishes were very appropriate for the winter conditions outside. We chose a Pinot Noir wine from the Burgundy region, then another and we were quite tipsy as we walked back to our Hotel.

Wednesday 24th Dec 2009

The next day the cold seeped right into our bones even though we were rugged up. My felted hat was definitely well worth bringing. We caught the Metro to Arc De Triomphe and climbed to the top. There was Paris spread out before us, then the fog rolled in! With the weather the way it was, we made the decision to go on the Double Decker Tourist bus, as a way to see most of the city in comfort, then decide where to stop as we went. And so the day went, stopping to have lunch, coffee and just be Parisian. That night we discovered a friendly Greek restaurant. It was warm, cosy and the staff were more than welcoming, especially when we told them we were from New Zealand. The night was everything you'd want in a Greek party as we ended up dancing Zorba the Greek. Again, we sort of stumbled merrily home.

Christmas Day in Paris

The first stop of our day was at Notre Dame Cathedral, where we spent most of the morning. We were utterly captivated, as there was a service taking place, accompanied by a choir, featuring sopranos and accompanied by majestic organ music. This was an unforgettable and undoubtedly one of the highlights of our week. Following this, we came across a delightful, albeit tiny cafe for our lunch. Even though it was snug we enjoyed our meal. After returning to our hotel for a brief nap, we ventured to The Champs-Élysées. It was Christmas, and the scene before us resembled something from a postcard: a picturesque, festive specta cle. We strolled the entire length, from Place De La Concorde and back again. Parisians had poured onto the streets, elegantly dressed and in great numbers. We joined the throngs, experiencing the sheer wonder of Christmas in Paris: the resplendent lights, the festive decorations, and the enchanting Christmas market stalls. It was nothing short of magical.

Christmas in Paris

My Birthday and our 21st Wedding anniversary

Dec 26th 2009

Here I am at sixty, battling a cold and not feeling my best. However, we have a big night planned for tonight, and the beautiful weather outside is too tempting to pass up. Despite my sniffles, I'm determined not to let it ruin our day. Our decision for the day: head to the top of the Eiffel Tower.

As we stood under the Tower, waiting in the long queue, we couldn't help but marvel at the sheer size of the four massive buttresses supporting this iconic structure. It was unexpectedly colossal, making us feel quite small in comparison. Despite the cold breeze and the fact that it took us over two hours to reach the top, all discomfort was forgotten the moment we arrived. The views of the well-organised, pink and white city stretching out below us were nothing short of breathtaking. Afterwards, we strolled through the gardens around the Tower then crossed the Seine River to the Jardins du Trocadero for more amazing views of the Tower. We ended up walking back to our Hotel and were quite exhausted by the time we got back. But, there wasn't much time before we had to get ready and meet at our evening rendezvous point around the corner from our hotel.

Our evening was set to be an intimate affair with about six others joining us in the group. To kick off the celebrations, we headed to the Eiffel Tower restaurant for dinner. We shared a platter for our appetiser and for my main I chose Herb Crusted Rack Of Lamb, Roasted Turnips, Caraway, Garlic Flan and Bruce chose Rossini Style Filet Mignon, Foie Gras, and Truffle Sauce. For dessert, we shared Champagne Passion Fruit Meringue and Classic Creme Brulée. It was a wonderful birthday meal, and the waiter even brought a small cake to our table with a candle, while the entire restaurant joined in singing "Happy Birthday" to me. Being at this iconic Tower was already a treat, but that cake meant the world. Regrettably, our photos from the evening didn't turn out well, due to incorrect camera settings.

After dinner, we strolled across the road to embark on a river cruise. The twinkling lights on the water and the cruise turned out to be exceptionally romantic! Following the cruise, we were whisked away to the Moulin Rouge where we spent the next couple of hours utterly captivated by the stunning female dancers, who delighted us with a series of high kicks, splits, and cartwheels. The explosive, high-energy can-can dance was, of course, the grand finale of the evening.

It was a marvellous night, topped off by meeting Piero and his elderly parents. Piero had surprised them with this evening in Paris. They lived on a farm in the country a couple of hours from Paris and were staying the night. Piero spoke excellent English and was great company. But the strangest thing was the way both father and son treated Mother. It was like she wasn't there. At one stage when we were all crossing a very busy road to board the bus, Piero and Dad were engrossed in conversation and already on the bus, while Mother was left to her own devices to cross as best she could and how she didn't get hit by a car I'll never know. Another time, when we reached Moulin Rouge, they left the bus to join the queue, not even bothering to see where she was and she floundered around finally catching up with them. Bruce and I still discuss this and we're bemused by it, quite sure if she'd gone missing, they would've ended up back on the farm and said, "I wonder where Mama got to?"

I'm happy to be sixty, many people don't make it to this age.

Sunday 27th Dec 2009

Today we're going by train to the Palace of Versailles. We're a bit tired from last night and ended up on the wrong train! Once we realised, we backtracked and started again. Being a tourist can be quite exhausting. We arrived finally, along with hoards of other tourists, but the Palace was such an enormous space, at times you'd think you were the only ones there. It was sensational, especially the hall of mirrors. We wandered through the vast gardens and though it was clear and sunny, it was bitterly cold. But the vistas were immense and when you arrived at the fountain at the end and looked back to the grandiose scale of it all, you can understand why the peasants revolted! The money these monarchs squandered at the cost of people who were scratching around trying to keep warm and fed.

By the end of the day, we were pleased to be back in our room, we changed and went out for dinner in the Latin Quarter.

Monday 28th Dec, 2009

Well, here it is our last day today, we paid the hotel bill €630.00 which we thought was good value and would stay again, as it's so handy to everything.

We were going to go to the Louvre and to Musee D' Orsay, but, quite frankly, we are monumented out and are determined to come back to do these and other art galleries soon. For today, we strolled the Seine, and poked around old-world bookstores, tapestry shops and quaint little art galleries we came across. It was a truly delicious day. I bought some unusual old books to use for collages from Shakespeare's Bookshop. What a delight that was.

Shopping in Paris.

At the end of the day, we caught the bus back to Beauvais Airport to the same hotel where we stayed when we arrived and were welcomed like long lost friends. It was lovely and not at all like our previous experience.

Tuesday 29th Dec, 2009

Our taxi arrived first thing to take us to the Airport. We arrived in Rome around 11 am, picked up the car, after a bit of confusion. It was good to be back in Introdacqua.

Wednesday 30th Dec, 2009

We slept for most of the day. After lunch, it was all about reminiscing going over our photos and savouring our fabulous week in Paris, already excited about going back next year. Unfortunately, some photos have disappeared!

Tuesday 31st Dec 2009 New Year's Eve.

We decided to stay in and have a quiet evening. After going to Sulmona to replenish our food supplies and check in with Gianni, it was then back home. We lit the open fire, roasted a chicken in the oven, along with fennel, an eggplant dish and Bruce made an apple crumble. Candles were lit. I had a DVD of Mama Mia, which we watched again! Opened the bottle of Dom Perignon champers, which had been given to Bruce by a client! Yes, I know all a bit much, but 2010 was welcomed, in style.

The End of Book One.

This book has been about setting up house and my art studio and a few road trips.

Book Two, "Italy's Lasting Legacy" in contrast, it's about putting it all together and setting up our art school and tours.

www.averilstuartart.com

Here is an overview you can expect in Book Two:

Success with my art; as it is chosen to travel with three exhibitions in the USA.

Setting up a Creative Art School and customised tours.

We travel extensively to France; visiting the Châteaux of the Loire Valley and more

Australia's Sunshine Coast; via a two month home exchange.

A home exchange in Paris; discovering the Expressionist painters.